Neoliberal Transformations of the Italian State

Transforming Capitalism

Series Editors: Ian Bruff, University of Manchester, UK; Gemma Edwards, University of Manchester, UK; Simon Springer, University of Newcastle, Australia

This book series provides an open platform for the publication of path-breaking and interdisciplinary scholarship which seeks to understand and critique capitalism along four key lines: crisis, development, inequality, and resistance. At its core lies the assumption that the world is in various states of transformation, and that these transformations may build upon earlier paths of change and conflict while also potentially producing new forms of crisis, development, inequality, and resistance. Through this approach the series alerts us to how capitalism is always evolving and hints at how we could also transform capitalism itself through our own actions. It is rooted in the vibrant, broad and pluralistic debates spanning a range of approaches which are being practised in a number of fields and disciplines. As such, it will appeal to sociology, geography, cultural studies, international studies, development, social theory, politics, labour and welfare studies, economics, anthropology, law, and more.

Titles in the Series

The Radicalization of Pedagogy: Anarchism, Geography, and the Spirit of Revolt
Edited by Simon Springer, Marcelo de Souza and Richard J. White

Theories of Resistance: Anarchism, Geography, and the Spirit of Revolt
Edited by Marcelo Lopes de Souza, Richard J. White and Simon Springer

The Practice of Freedom: Anarchism, Geography, and the Spirit of Revolt
Edited by Richard J. White, Simon Springer and Marcelo Lopes de Souza

States of Discipline: Authoritarian Neoliberalism and the Contested Reproduction of Capitalist Order
Edited by Cemal Burak Tansel

The Limits to Capitalist Nature: Theorizing and Overcoming the Imperial Mode of Living
Ulrich Brand and Markus Wissen

Workers Movements and Strikes in the 21st Century
Edited by Jörg Nowak, Madhumita Dutta and Peter Birke

Rent and its Discontents: A Century of Housing Struggle
Edited by Neil Gray

Renewing Destruction: Wind Energy Development, Conflict and Resistance in a Latin American Context
Alexander Dunlap

Towards a Political Economy of Degrowth
Edited by Ekaterina Chertkovskaya, Alexander Paulsson and Stefania Barca

Producing and Contesting Urban Marginality: Interdisciplinary and Comparative Dialogues
Edited by Julie Cupples and Tom Slater

A Sense of Inequality
Wendy Bottero

Neoliberal Transformations of the Italian State: Understanding the Roots of the Crises
Adriano Cozzolino

Neoliberal Transformations of the Italian State

Understanding the Roots of the Crises

Adriano Cozzolino

ROWMAN & LITTLEFIELD
Lanham • Boulder • New York • London

Published by Rowman & Littlefield
An imprint of The Rowman & Littlefield Publishing Group, Inc.
4501 Forbes Boulevard, Suite 200, Lanham, Maryland 20706
www.rowman.com

6 Tinworth Street, London SE11 5AL, United Kingdom

British Library Cataloguing in Publication Data

A catalogue record for this book is available from the British Library

ISBN: HB 978-1-7866-1473-5

Library of Congress Control Number: 2020946823

Library of Congress Cataloging-in-Publication Data Is Available
ISBN 978-1-78661-473-5 (cloth)
ISBN 978-1-78661-475-9 (electronic)

Contents

Acknowledgements

This book, which is an improved and revised version of my PhD thesis completed in 2018, has benefited from the guidance, constructive criticism, and support from many people and communities over the years, within and beyond academia.

First of all, thanks to Ruth Hanau-Santini, my PhD supervisor at the Department of Human and Social Sciences at "L'Orientale" University, for her patience, guidance, and support throughout the doctorate and also after its completion—thanks for making me understand the importance of combining critical spirit and analytical rigor. Thanks to Ottorino Cappelli, Manuela Moschella, and Fortunato Musella, who teamed up for my viva and provided me with feedback and advice that, later on, helped me to focus on my post-doctoral research while also transforming the PhD thesis into this book. I have an intellectual debt to the pioneering works of Mauro Calise on presidentialization and democratic transformations. Before the start of my PhD, Massimo Fragola gave me the first opportunity to approach academia. Since the completion of the doctorate, Francesco Amoretti has believed in me and my research, showing his concrete support on many occasions. Sergio Marotta has accompanied me since the early stages of my PhD—and after —with support and enthusiasm. In Napoli, the Istituto Italiano per gli Studi Filosofici has been key for the intellectual growth of many generations of students, and I feel privileged to be among them. I also wish to thank the Department of Political Sciences of the University of Campania "Vanvitelli" for making me feel at home when I started my post as a post-doctoral researcher.

Away from Italy, I cannot thank enough Ian Bruff, who helped me to grow as a scholar in many ways: first, by welcoming me as a visiting PhD student at the University of Manchester; second, for providing me with "Gramscian" insights about the state and political institutions; third, for supporting this book as the editor of the *Transforming Capitalism* series while also carefully reading the manuscript. I am deeply grateful to Angela Wigger for accepting me at Radboud University during my second period as a visiting PhD student, and for all the discussions, suggestions, and constructive criticism revolving around the critique of international political economy. I am indebted to Laura Horn for taking the time to carefully read and comment on an earlier draft of the manuscript, helping me to significantly improve this work. Thanks to Adam David Morton and Andreas Bieler for the intellectual inspiration (even before I started my PhD) and for helping me, at various times and occasions, to refine my theoretical perspective. Thanks to the Critical Political Economy Research Network of the European Sociological Association for making me feel part of a community of like-minded critical scholars. I am particularly grateful to Rowman & Littlefield International for accepting my book proposal and assisting me throughout the production of this book. Thanks to the editorial team, the editorial board, and to Dhara Snowden, Rebecca Anastasi and Vignesh Vellaisamy for the assistance.

My friends supported me throughout this journey, and I cannot thank them enough for their love and care: thanks to Paolo, Francesco M., and Angela and their wonderful kids, Laura, Enzo, Alessandra, Michele, and all the people from the "Movimento di Giurisprudenza." Edoardo Baldaro and Irene Costantini gifted me with intellectual engagement and comradeship, within and beyond academia. Giulia Cimini has been the greatest PhD mate, and I am lucky to be her friend. L'Asilo and every single person in its community taught me the beauty of the collective dimension: this book owes to this experience something well beyond what words can describe. Giuseppe Micciarelli is a source of inspiration for his ability to combine grassroots activism and research. I want to thank also Clelia Romano: as a literature professor at my high school, she planted the seeds of the passion for politics that—throughout quite a long journey—have become this book. I owe a special thanks to Diego Giannone, a generous and passionate person who is also an example of the kind of academic I wish to become. Diego not only has been a mentor during all these years by providing me with advice, discussions, intellectual engagement and enthusiasm, but has also encouraged me when I felt distressed by academic precarity. Last but never least: thanks to Rosa, my love, for accompanying me throughout this beautiful and difficult journey. Her intelligence, generosity, strength and loving kindness are an example, a source of inspiration, a challenge for me to become a better version of myself.

Finally, my family supported me with generosity and love throughout my life. Words cannot describe how deeply grateful I am to them, to whom this book is dedicated.

Abbreviations

BI	Banca d'Italia (Bank of Italy)
CDA	Critical Discourse Analysis
CGIL	Confederazione Generale Italiana del Lavoro (Italian General Confederation of Labour)
CISL	Confederazione Italiana Sindacati Lavoratori (Italian Confederation of Workers' Unions)
DC	Democrazia Cristiana (Christian Democracy)
DEF	Documento di Economia e Finanza (Document of Economy and Finance)
DPEF	Documento di Programmazione Economico-Finanziaria (Economic and Financial Planning Document)
ECB	European Central Bank
EMU	Economic and Monetary Union
EP	European Parliament
EU	European Union
FDI	Foreign Direct Investment
FSM	Movimento 5 Stelle (Five Star Movement)
MEF	Ministero dell'Economia e delle Finanze (Ministry of Economy and Finance)
MSI	Movimento Sociale Italiano (Italian Social Movement)
NL	Northern League
OECD	Organisation for Economic Cooperation and Development
PCI	Partito Comunista Italiano (Italian Communist Party)
PD	Partito Democratico (Democratic Party)
PSI	Partito Socialista Italiano (Italian Socialist Party)
TNC	Transnational Corporation
UIL	Unione Italiana del Lavoro (Italian Labour Union)

List of Tables and Figures

TABLE

FIGURES

Chapter 1

Introduction

This book was being completed in the midst of the COVID-19 pandemic throwing Italy—and almost the entire world—into the worst social and economic crisis since World War II. While, as occurred after the great crisis of 2008, the state has been called upon to rescue capitalism from a generalized collapse once again, it is also likely that the pandemic will exacerbate some of the main tendencies that appeared in Italian society over the last several decades. To a name a few: persistently high unemployment, especially among women and young workforce; rising poverty levels and relentless growth of socioeconomic inequalities; long-standing stagnant growth of GDP; a large and growing socioeconomic gap between the North and the South, worsening further the historical territorial divide of the Peninsula. Italian politics has been part of this process. Especially after the global crisis of 2008, the political landscape of the country has been characterized by the rise of populist, eurosceptic and radical right-wing political actors, the crisis of centrist political forces on both the "left" and "right," and declining support for the European Union.

In specific relation to the changes at the macro-state level—the core question of this book—Italy can be conceived as a unique case of transition from democracy to democracy, namely from a regime based on the centrality of the parliament to one dominated by executive powers in which the legislature performs a marginal role (Fabbrini 2006; Musella 2019). Yet, so far the analyses of the Italian case have shied away from wider and comprehensive historical explorations of the transformations of the state in specific relation to neoliberal globalization. This book aims to shed light on two fundamental research questions: (1) What is the relation between the transformations of the state and the international turn linked to the rise of the neoliberal paradigm? (2) How can we conceptualize theoretically, and analyse empirically, the transformations of the state against the background of the historical unfolding—and contemporary crisis—of the neoliberal paradigm? In responding to these questions, this book is concerned with understanding the historical and political-economic roots of contemporary Italian crises through adopting a particular standpoint: the state. The state is not just a complex yet fascinating matter of study per se. The state is also a privileged perspective on society—a "viewpoint on viewpoints," as Pierre Bourdieu put it (2014, 28). By accepting the challenge of a non-reductionist theoretical approach to the "state question," the analysis of state transformations can help us to understand in-depth, complex, and multilayered social and political dynamics. From ideology and culture to political change, from the crisis of a social order to the relation between capitalism and democracy (namely the tension between "accumulation and legitimization"; see O'Connor 2002, 6), let alone the intertwining between the national dimension and the international sphere, the state is rooted in such processes while also remaining a crucial terrain for (contested) political agency in capitalist societies.

The goal of this book is threefold. The first two objectives concern, respectively, the theory of the state and the empirical analysis of state transformations. The third is related specifically to the Italian case. I will now consider each in turn, for the final, more concrete objective can be successfully arrived at only after having reflected on more "in principle" themes.

The first ambition is to provide for an innovative while systematic analytical framework to study the state comprising two main dimensions: (1) the relation between the state and society; (2) the complex and multilayered nature of the state. With respect to the first, this book challenges the conventional wisdom that, explicitly or (often) implicitly, separates ontologically the state from society. Drawing especially on the thinking of Antonio Gramsci, the point of departure of this book is the conceptualization of the state in relation to what I term the nexus of unity-distinction with society (Francioni 1984; Thomas 2009). As I argue in chapter 3, the state can be analytically distinguished from society while remaining always internally bound to it as a part of the same ontological unit. This allows us to study the state as a *relatively* autonomous terrain of political—ideological, discursive, oppositional, policymaking—agency and analyse empirically its transformations, while at the same time keeping in mind that the state is always part and parcel of broader societal processes (Poulantzas 1978). The second factor concerns the dual nature of the state. The state is an elusive essence, for it is not easy to identify the range of dimensions encompassed by the concept of state. In this book, I rely on a twofold conceptualization of the state as (i) a social construction constituted of specific ideas, symbols, and discourses, and thus possessing a distinct ideological power; and (ii) an institutional cluster (or "state-system") (Abrams 1988; Jessop 2016, Ch. 2; Hanau-Santini 2018, 5–6).

The second ambition of this book is to link this conceptualization to the empirical analysis of state transformations. In this regard, I distinguish analytically between transformations *of* the state, namely the overarching society-wide idea of the state or, better, "the construction of the state as an ideological power" (Abrams 1988, 78), and transformations *in* the state, which means those concerning the specific institutional cluster or state-system (more below). The aim is to deconstruct the neoliberal construction of the Italian state, hence unveiling its discursive and ideological underpinnings (chapter 5), while also exploring the—direct—relation between the strengthening of executive powers and neoliberal policy (chapter 6). By postulating a dual nature of the state, this work is concerned with the study of both these macro-changes at state level—the ideological-discursive and the institutional—for they are complementary to each other and constitute the fundamental dimension of the neoliberal reconfiguration of the state. In so doing and more generally, the book aspires to provide for an innovative theoretical-empirical framework to study the state and its historical transformations over time, and as such is applicable to different historical and geographical contexts.

The third ambition of this book is to rethink the Italian case in light of a critical understanding of the internal relation between neoliberalism and state transformations. By adopting a long-term historical perspective, the volume reconstructs the fundamental changes which occurred in the Italian state since World War II and zooms in on especially the 1990s, when the transition from the First to the Second Republic saw the consolidation of the joint process of the strengthening of executive powers and the introduction of neoliberal reforms (chapter 4). Also, and crucially, this allows us to comprehend in-depth contemporary Italian politics—among other things, the crisis of the consensus regarding European integration and the rise of populist and radical right forces—and the manifold crises of Italian democracy (chapter 7).

Intertwined with this threefold goal, the book adds a series of specific contributions to our understanding of Italy's neoliberal transition. The analysis, in particular, sheds light on:

- The transformations of the state as a political project and not as a sort of mechanical effect deriving from the changes in the global political economy or from European integration. To do so, I emphasize the role of political agency *in* the Italian state and ground its transformations in historical perspective, thus offering a detailed reconstruction of state reconfiguration as a political reaction—through and beyond the state—especially against mass democratic politics in the 1960s and 1970s (chapter 4).
- The critical role of technocrats and technocracy (i) as a peculiar form of political agency in the state (from the Bank of Italy to ministries and technocratic executives), and (ii) as a "collective intellectual" which has

provided the expertise and, above all, the legitimation for the neoliberal transition (chapters 4 and 5). Thus, the book provides for a systematic contextualization of technocracy within the neoliberalizing transformations of the state.

- The multifaceted aspects of the discursive construction of European integration, and how it constituted a source of legitimation of neoliberal restructuring since the late 1980s to the present. I also analyse the relation between the Italian "left" coalitions and the European Union, and conceptualize it as a form of *neoliberal-progressive Europeanism* (chapter 5). The resort to "Europe" to justify unpopular measures is key to understanding the crisis in the consensus regarding the European Union in Italy and, accordingly, of pro-European parties in particularly the post-2008 period (chapter 7).
- The forms and strategies of legitimation of permanent austerity ("*risanamento*") since the late 1980s, as a popular-cultural reform and thus as an attempt to change Italian society as a whole. I call the strategy to naturalize permanent austerity as *the political economy of sacrifice and promise* and analyse its manifold cultural integuments (chapter 5).
- While the presidentialization of Italian state has been extensively analysed (Calise 2005; Criscitiello 2004; Musella 2019), I discuss it from the perspective of critical international political economy, and show the great importance of the mobilization of executive apparatuses in the state for the implementation and imposition of neoliberal and austerity policies over time (chapter 6).
- Chapter 7 offers a critical analysis of contemporary Italian crises—especially after the global crisis of 2008—by grounding these into the structural contradictions of neoliberalism. Through the exploration of three axes of crises—*society, territory, and politics*—the analysis offers a detailed reconstruction of post-2008 politics, and specifically: (i) the crisis of neoliberal-progressive Europeanism and of the national consensus towards European integration; (ii) the rise of populist and eurosceptic forces, notably the Five Star Movement and The League, up until the formation of the first populist government in 2018.

Through the critique of the political economy of state transformations, this book provides for an anatomy of the neoliberal transition in Italy. Differently from mainstream scholarship, the approach I advocate enables us to understand Italian politics through a historically grounded and critical international political economy perspective, thus approaching dynamically politics *in* society and, also, the state as a dynamic terrain of political agency. In turn, the Italian case represents a unique perspective for those who want to understand the international political economy of neoliberalism and the fundamental role of state powers and practices. In other words, the key role of the state in the protection and reproduction of neoliberalism as a global regime of capital accumulation (Tansel 2017, 2). But the Italian case is also particularly relevant for understanding the transformations of the state and the (now) mature crisis of liberal democracy. Drawing on Giovanni Sartori's scheme (1982), it is possible to distinguish between three main typologies of democratic regimes: parliamentary regimes, presidential regimes, and semi-presidential regimes. Taxonomies can be misleading if they foster a static and reified picture of political and constitutional systems; by contrast, they have the potential to express a powerful heuristic relevance if serving as a cartography to trace processes of change and transition from one form to another. In this respect, the Italian transition towards a de facto—that is, in absence of a comprehensive reform of the constitution—presidential regime not only testifies, in general terms, that the state is a living terrain for political agency and that it changes over time, but also the critical importance of the mobilization and strengthening of executive and technocratic apparatuses for the imposition of neoliberal policy. This book, though devoted to the Italian case, aspires to be a critical voice in the debate concerning the structural tension between neoliberal capitalism and democracy (Giannone 2010, 2019; Streeck 2014) and the increasingly illiberal twist of contemporary democratic regimes (Bruff 2014; Tansel 2017; Koch 2018; Wigger 2019).

RETHINKING THE ITALIAN NEOLIBERAL TRANSITION, UNDERSTANDING THE ROOTS OF THE CRISES

The Italian political and institutional turning point in the 1990s represents a unique case of transition within a democracy (Fabbrini 2006; Almagisti et al. 2014). To a great extent, it is a case of rupture and transition from a type of political system based—thanks to the proportional electoral system—on the centrality of the legislature (and of political parties in the parliament) to a democracy in which the executive prevails, in this case also thanks to a majoritarian electoral system introduced in 1993. Thus, a regime in which the executive in particular started to take the upper hand in policymaking and agenda-setting (Calise 2005; Fabbrini and Donà 2003), with a parallel increasing marginalization of the parties ("the twilight of parties," in the words of Gianfranco Pasquino 1994) and of the parliament's policymaking role. Contemporary Italian politics has been thus described as increasingly led by leaders without party politics (namely the trend in the personalization of politics; see Calise 2018; Musella 2018, 65–94) or, from a different perspective, as a case of "government without a parliament" (Musella 2019; Criscitiello 2004).

Many authors, especially from a European studies/comparative politics perspective, saluted the 1990s changes as a much-awaited moment to improve governability thanks to the fundamental external help of the European Union. According to an influential thesis (Radaelli and Franchino 2004; see also Fabbrini and Donà 2003; Fabbrini 2006), while the changes in/of the Italian state during the 1980s were slow, the early 1990s represented a moment of intense dynamism. The main factor capable of explaining such a shift, according to this argument, is Europeanization. Radaelli and Franchino assert that "the Italian case shows how Europeanization has strengthened institutions and policies, and has increased domestic policy-making capabilities both in terms of efficiency and fairness" (2004, 944). The strengthening of the agenda setting and policymaking role of the prime minister is the main case in point of the domestic "effects" of European integration. In fact, "[t]he involvement of national governments in the EU has been a constant incentive for both the rationalisation of the decision-making process within the executive, and for the personalisation role of the head of government" (Fabbrini and Donà 2003, 37; Barbieri 2003). The academic titles of the time, on the other hand, partly reflect the optimism often linked to a progressive view of European integration. *Closing the Transition* (Ceccanti and Vassallo 2004), *Doomed to Success? Italy into an Integrated Europe* (Di Palma et al. 2002), *Rescued by Europe?*[1] (Ferrera and Gualmini 2004) are some of the main examples (see also Fabbrini 2003; Fabbrini and Piattoni 2007).

This scholarship, despite often achieving a very good level of empirical sophistication, suffers nonetheless from several shortcomings. In theoretical terms, the changes in the state are regarded as deriving, in rather mechanical terms, from the supranational dimension as "causal effects" of Europeanization. In other words, the changes at macro-state levels are conceived as deriving from the financial and macroeconomic convergence linked in particular to the Economic and Monetary Union (EMU) and the need to adjust the domestic economy. On the other hand, European integration is uncritically taken as a given external dimension without taking full account of the neoliberal nature of the European Union and its contradictions (van Apeldoorn et al. 2009; Streeck 2014; Giannone 2015); in addition, the specific *construction* of "Europe" in Italy as a form of legitimation of neoliberalization and permanent austerity is neglected (Cozzolino 2020). Thus, the historical process is not regarded as dialectical, conflictual, and open-ended but as a teleological parabola unfolding towards increased governability and democracy. As a consequence, the state is viewed as a thing rather than a terrain of political action, and the role of sociopolitical agency is dramatically overlooked, as are ideology, discourse, and other national cultural/cognitive factors that legitimate and naturalize change.

At the same time, many accounts often share a commonsensical adherence to the view of the "eccentric" and "not-normal" Southern Country versus the stability of Northern Europe (chapter 5). Let me clarify this with what I consider the starkest example of such discourse. The idea of Italian "fiscal profligacy" proved to be a powerful ideological and symbolic tool to favour the application of permanent austerity from the 1992 as a *necessary* cure to the Italian problems. Yet by adhering to the commonsensical image of "fiscal profligacy," many accounts not only neglect the fact that Italy has been, since the early 1990s, one of the most law-abiding countries in terms of fiscal rigour (chapter 4). But such perspectives also neglect that permanent fiscal restraint is a political option that reflects a constellation of—national and transnational—material class interests and relations, and therefore not a (depoliticized) technical necessity. As a further consequence, key factors—key also to explaining contemporary Italian and European crises—as permanent wage stagnation and socioeconomic class inequalities are removed from the analytical landscape, and thus the uneven social effects of austerity and neoliberalization—which actually account for an important part of the explanation of the contemporary Italian crises.

Thus, this book offers an alternative critical international political economy analysis of the Italian neoliberal transition through the "privileged" perspective of the transformations *of* and *in* the state, and does it through a critical approach to such transformations. Borrowing from Robert W. Cox, critical theory

> stands apart from the prevailing order of the world and asks how that order came about. Critical theory, unlike problem-solving theory, does not take institutions and social and power relations for granted but calls them into question by concerning itself with their origins and whether they might be in the process of changing [. . .] Critical theory is directed to the social and political complex as a whole rather than to separate parts [. . .] the critical approach leads towards the construction of a larger picture of the whole the initially contemplated part is just one component, and seeks to understand the process of change in which both parts and whole are involved. (1981, 129)

Let's try to apply this to the case of this book. First, my analysis reconstructs the *origins* of the transformations of the Italian state by taking into account the continuities and changes in the state especially in the 1980s and 1990s, in tandem with the rise and consolidation of the neoliberal paradigm. Taking the state as a terrain of action, some of the main changes in the 1980s—particularly revolving around key technocratic apparatuses such as the Bank of Italy—prepared the turning point in the 1990s. Drawing on Gramsci, I conceive the changes of the 1980s as a case of *war of position*, slow and incremental, while the transformations of the early 1990s as a case of *war of movement*, fast and dynamic, led in particular by technocrats in the state (chapter 4; see also Dyson and Featherstone 1996; Fabbrini and Donà 2003). In this respect, history and the historical process maintain a fundamental place in any evaluation of the processes of change within and outside the Italian state, taking full account of the multiform relevance of European integration to Italian transformations (Talani 2017). Chapter 4 is therefore entirely devoted to post-war Italian history. It aims to focus on the key historical moment of state transformations, namely the neoliberal shift. Let me dwell a bit further on the concept of neoliberalism to frame it better, and frame why it matters for the study of the state.

In general terms, neoliberalism can be conceived as a phase in contemporary history beginning with the prolonged crises of the 1970s (among which the fiscal crisis of the state: O'Connor 2002; see also Streeck 2014) and with the limits of the Keynesian mode of macroeconomic regulation to restore capital accumulation (Harvey 2005; Saad-Filho and Johnston 2006; Glyn 2006; Duménil and Lévy 2011). Neoliberalism emerged as a response to those crises—and to workers' struggles in the 1960s and 1970s—with the aim to re-establish inter/national class power through a twofold movement. On the one hand, by improving the income and wealth of the upper-class fractions, especially through empowering the financial sector (Harvey 2005); on the other, by centralizing power in the state and restricting the space for mass democratic politics and thus to alternatives (chapters 4, 5, and 6). Even if neoliberalism comprises a set of economic ideas that eventually constitute its "economic mythology" (Shaikh 2006), some have aptly framed it (in the North as well as in the Global South) as "a contingent response to the recurring crises of the capitalist mode of production" (Tansel 2017, 8; Harvey 2005) on a global scale. Thus, the adoption of neoliberal policies is directly linked to the preservation of capital accumulation before, during, and after capitalist crises (Bruff and Tansel 2019). The accent on the contingent/practical responses of the "actually existing neoliberalism" (Tansel 2017, 9; Cahill 2014) is particularly relevant in three main respects. First, it helps to link *internally* the transformations of the state to the global political economy. Second, it allows us to incorporate into our analytical framework the *structural* conditions (and contradictions) of global capitalism and the *agency* of policymakers in the state (more below), and thus to conceive the state as a living field of political action endowed with *relative* autonomy (Poulantzas 1978; see Chapter 3). Third, it enables us to capture the heterogeneous and context-based patterns of *neoliberalization*, namely processes that "assume place-specific forms within cities and city-regions [. . .] within a geo-regulatory context defined by systemic tendencies towards market-disciplinary institutional reform, the formation of transnational webs of market-oriented policy transfer [. . .] deepening patterns of crisis formation and accelerating cycles of crisis-driven policy experimentation" (Brenner et al. 2010, 329).

There are two further elements, revolving around the rise of neoliberal globalization. The first is the enhanced "structural power of capital" (Gill and Law 1993) against the background of processes of transnationalization of finance and production (Bieler and Morton 2018). Actually "the impact of increased capital mobility, and also of recessions, has worked to the advantage of large-scale transnational capital, relative to national capital" (Gill and Law 1993, 108). In light of the increasing centrality of transnational capitalist relations it is possible to avoid another frequent limitation of many accounts of the Italian transition, namely the separation between national and transnational dynamics and the view of the international/supranational dimension as external—ontologically separate—to the domestic plan. By contrast, the national dimension is deeply intertwined with global processes. In Gramsci's own words, "particular histories always exist within the frame of world history" (1971, 240). Anticipating a central point developed in chapter 3, there is a dialectical and internal relation between the national and the international. In other words, processes of *internationalization* of production imply a redefinition of national social (power) relations and, accordingly, an *internalization* of those processes at the domestic level (Bieler and Morton 2003, 2006a, 2006b, 2018).

The last element I wish to emphasize relates to the contemporary Italian crises, which are extensively discussed in chapter 7. In many accounts, the contemporary Italian context is not inserted organically into the historical unfolding of the neoliberal paradigm: crises are instead one-off, or unprecedented, occurrences that come in from the outside. Also, social relations, politics, and territory are often understood as separate dimensions only (at best) externally interacting with each other. This book reconsiders contemporary Italian crises by exploring the organic relation between society (and especially labour market reforms, inequalities, and rising poverty), territory (the increasing gap between the North and the South of Italy) and, last but not least, politics—which I consider three key axes of crises. In specific regard to politics, I explore the changes in the Italian political landscape after the global financial crisis of 2008. I conceive such changes within the broader evolution of Italian society over several decades, thus putting in their broader context both the crisis of European integration and traditional parties on the one hand, and the rise of populist and eurosceptic political forces (such as the Five Star Movement and The League) on the other. Therefore, crises in plural, but also crises in historical perspective: this book shows that the imperative of *governability*, the overarching principle that has oriented the political reaction against mass democracy (Hungtington et al. 1975) since the late 1970s, seems to have reached a dead end, turning into a phase of permanent instability and legitimacy crises (chapter 6). Once again, the state and the analysis of state transformations are a privileged analytical perspective through which light can be shed on the characteristics, failures, and contradictions of the neoliberal era.

INTRODUCING THE THEORETICAL PERSPECTIVE: THE POLITICAL ECONOMY OF STATE TRANSFORMATIONS

In theoretical terms, this book reconsiders the state and its transformations from a Gramscian perspective. Such a perspective implies the reassertion of the centrality of dialectics as the real unfolding—on the "concrete terrain of history," as Gramsci put it—of the internal relations and contradictions between different societal layers and, within each of these, between different structures and sociopolitical agency. Gramsci's radical ontology (Rupert 1993), creatively drawing on Marx's historical materialism, rejects the assumption of the existence of isolated and abstract individuals. Human experience blooms from the network of social relations and interactions in which it is inserted. Yet the social bond that ties humans together is not abstract (i.e., a "pure form") but mediated—in concrete everyday life and consciousness—by a number of intertwined semiotic and extra-semiotic factors: production relations, ideas and ideology, culture, symbolic forms, technologies, religions, and so on. Production retains a critical importance. Following Robert W. Cox, production constitutes the material basis of human existence and affects the ways in which human life is organized and shaped. Crucially, production is not only confined to the physical process of producing goods and services but "covers also the production and reproduction of knowledge and of the social relations, morals, and institutions that are prerequisites to the production of physical goods" (Cox 1989, 39). It thus engenders an array of national and transnational social relations which, on the one hand, "refer to everyday patterns of behaviour involved in the production and consumption of physical goods as well as the discursive institutional and cultural tactics established to ensure the hegemony of existing social relations" (Bieler and Morton 2018, 38).

On the other hand, social relations give rise to "social class forces as the key collective agents" (ibid.). Seen in this way, production embraces both material factors and ideational, discursive, and cognitive elements; hence, it is always relational in kind. The form-substance of social relations is thus rooted in historically specific modes of production—in our case, neoliberal capitalism. "Within capitalism"—Bieler and Morton suggest—"production is organised around the private ownership of the means of production and 'free' wage labour. It is this understanding that generates the key ontological properties of structure and agency" (ibid.). Capitalism, it is worth noting, is not just an organizational form of goods and services production. It is a (global) form of life and culture. Capitalism "shapes and gives content to the thoughts humans hold about the world" (Bruff 2008, 33), and is part and parcel of the society/nature complex (Moore 2015).

The relation between structure and agency in contemporary neoliberal capitalism is particularly important when it comes to understanding the state and its transformations. In general terms, and taking inspiration from Nicos Poulantzas, this book conceives structures as a "condensation" of specific patterns of social relations, hence possessing an intrinsic capability to persist over time and space. Each of the many existing societal structures gives rise, borrowing again from Poulantzas, to *relatively* autonomous spheres, processes, and moments. The institutionalization of political relations in the form of state, the condensation of gender relations into patriarchy, the crystallization of production relations into capitalism are examples of structured (and structuring) relations across time and space. Such relatively autonomous structures are also internally and dialectically related to one another so that none of them can be understood, theoretically and practically, in isolation. Humans are therefore socialized within those structured relations—material, ideological, cultural, symbolic, discursive—in which they find themselves in. Social existence is thus shaped by a set of highly complex, heterogeneous, and contradictory processes depending on a variety of factors: class, geography, gender, ethnicity, religion, culture, language, and so on. Yet structures also change over time. Organized social forces shape the network of relations in which they exist, reflecting social power relations and inequalities. In fact, it is worth noting that while possessing a relational, processual, and contradictory nature, structures also have a constraining (or enabling) power on social and political agency. In other words, structures do not determine agency automatically but "[t]hey may prevent, constrain or enable agency and they may be changed by collective agency" (Bieler and Morton 2018, 44).

The relation between structures and agency is particularly important for analysing the transformations of the state. Broadly speaking, scholarship on the state suffers from two intertwined limitations: the separation between state and society, and a structuralist and functionalist view of state transformations (see chapter 2). Beginning with the latter, often the dynamics of state transformations are (albeit implicitly) conceived in mechanical terms. In other words, changes in the state derive rather automatically and impersonally from changes in the global political economy or from European integration. This limit, I argue, derives from the ontological separation of state from society. Instead of seeing these plans as internally related, there is a widespread tendency to view the state as a thing discrete from societal relations, hence limiting the social bases of state powers while, on the other hand, overlooking the role of political agency *in* the state. Therefore, agency is dramatically downplayed and, accordingly, the role of politics. By contrast, "[t]aking agency seriously, and accepting the related assertion about the complex and open-ended nature of social reality, involves rejecting theories that purport to explain social phenomena by means of generally valid laws about social regularities" (Buch-Hansen and Wigger 2011, 11). With specific respect to the state, to explore "the transformation of the State implies to take into account the mechanisms, devices and processes that have provided (and still provide) a justification for changing, directing it towards a specific direction" (Giannone 2019, 12).

The intellectual legacy of Antonio Gramsci, from which I draw inspiration to conceptualize state transformations, is of paramount importance for developing a non-reductionist approach to the state and for taking due account of the state/society complex. To Gramsci, the state can never be reduced to the government or repressive functions. The state, Gramsci argues, is "the entire complex of practical and theoretical activities with which the ruling class not only justifies and maintains its dominance, but manages to win the active consent of those over whom it rule" (1975, 1765, Q15§10). The state is hence enlarged to comprehend the social bases of its powers and practices, and, accordingly, is the historical result of the dialectics between "political society" and "civil society," ultimately constituting a nexus of unity-distinction. The Gramscian approach to the state, as I discuss at length in chapter 3, enables us (i) to explore the state as a *terrain* of social–political–ideological interactions and (ii) to grasp the multilayered nature of the state as both an institutional cluster and ideological power. Hence, transformations of the state are not an automatic result of the changes in global capitalism or European integration as such, but the outcome of the dialectics between sociopolitical agency—within and outside the state—and the broader structure of global capitalism. As noted earlier, in this book I try to foster a *more political reading of the transformations of/in the state.* The naturalization of the supposed "necessary" nature of change is not the cause but the effect of hegemony and ideological practices in the neoliberal era.

METHODOLOGICAL THEMES AND ISSUES

Since this book is based on a holistic and dialectic understanding of the different spheres and layers of society, the methodological dimension of this research is part and parcel of this perspective. Following Jäger, Horn, and Becker (2016, 110), a critical methodological approach rejects positivist-oriented assumptions such as (among others) rational/individual actors, subject-object distinction, and causal inferences. In contrast, it is characterized by the following underpinnings. First, ontologically it regards social reality as complex and interdependent while also context-dependent; history is conceived as open-ended (i.e., the historical process is not directed towards any ultimate goals but unfolds according to societal power relations), and the focus is on social change. Second, in epistemological terms it is post-positivist, namely, knowledge is a historical and social product, and it is reflexive. Third, in terms of analytical strategies it relies on conceptualization and dialectics while, methodologically, it fosters the historical method, discursive analysis, and interpretation. Eventually, it is committed to human emancipation: theory is always *for* someone and *for* some purposes, as Robert W. Cox famously put it. This means, in concrete terms, that ontological issues (the property of being) and epistemology (knowledge and knowledge production) are conceived as internally related parts of the same unity and of its *real* knowableness. In turn, methodology and the use of specific research methods are also conceived as directly related to the "object" of our exploration since "methods should be appropriate to the nature of the object we study" (Sayer 2010, 3).

A Mixed Methods Approach to Studying the State

Let's enter, now, into the details of the research. Each of the empirical chapters is based on a different method. Chapters 4 and 7 rely on the method of the historical enquiry that has been sketched out above. They propose a holistic reconstruction of Italian post-war history up to the 1990s (chapter 4), and from 2008 to present times (chapter 7). On the other hand, chapters 5 and 6 are devoted to the specific analysis of state transformations. Methods, here, follow the object/process of enquiry. In a word, I conceptualize the state as a socio-ideological construction and as an institutional cluster (chapter 3). Thus, in relation to the first layer of the nature of the state, I use a specific qualitative method to deconstruct the socio-ideological construction of our "object": Critical Discourse Analysis (CDA). On the other hand, and in relation to the second layer of the state, I employ a quantitative method, namely descriptive statistics. The combination of these different methods provides for a holistic account of the neoliberal transformations of the state.

Starting with CDA, it is particularly well-suited for a critical analysis of the discursive construction of the state. In the words of Wodak and Fairclough:

> CDA sees discourse—language in speech and writing as a form of "social practice." Describing discourse as a social practice implies a dialectical relationship between a particular discursive event and the situation(s), institution(s) and social structure(s) which frame it. The discursive event is shaped by them,

> but it also shapes them. That is, discourse is socially constitutive as well as socially conditioned—it constitutes situations, objects of knowledge, and thus social identities of and relationships between people and groups of people. It is constitutive both in the sense that it helps to sustain and reproduce the social status-quo and in the sense that it contributes to transforming it. (Fairclough and Wodak 1997, 258)

Since language is a social process, "discourse has effects upon social structures and contributes to the achievement of social continuity and change" (Fairclough 2001, 30; 1992) inasmuch as "the relationship is dialectical, and every instance of language use makes its own contribution to reproducing or transforming culture and society, including power relations" (Fairclough and Wodak 1997, 273). Language, therefore, is co-determined by social structures and practices and in turn shapes social structures and practices. With specific respect to this research, I apply CDA to the official political economy/economic and financial planning documents[2] issued by the Italian governments from the late 1980s to the present.[3] In so doing, I deconstruct the discursive strategies through which change is legitimated, justified, and naturalized as "common sense." The actors taken into account are state representatives and policymakers. Indeed, the executive and economic ministries—those more involved in European negotiations and state politics—outline jointly (and with the respective offices) the documents analysed. Moreover, since the study explores the discursive strategies across the entire party system it also sheds light on the cross-party extension of neoliberal culture and common sense. Especially common sense, as Ian Bruff notes, "can be most clearly observed and analysed at the state level, because elites are a rarefied embodiment of their society's culture" (2008, 11).

Let's turn, now, to descriptive statistics and explain how it is employed in the research process. The aim of this segment of the research is to understand how specific institutions in the state evolve over time, and how this is related to processes of neoliberal restructuring and fiscal consolidation. To do so, I gathered and analysed the entire legislation issued from 1976 to 2015 to understand the changes in the Italian institutional complex over a period of forty years. More specifically, the research process is based on a three-stage codification of all the laws issued in Italy in the mentioned period for a total of 3,130 observations. The laws have been classified according to the nature of the law, the political economy policy domain and, to refine the accuracy of the research, the political economy policy sub-domain.[4] This data are now part of my *Political Economy Legislation Dataset* (Cozzolino 2018c). For reasons of space in this book, I only provide part of the findings of my research by zooming in on two key aspects. First, I present data concerning the general evolution of legislation (parliamentary law, decrees, and so on) to retain sight of the broader picture of state transformations. Second, I present and analyse the data specific to the political economy and look at key policy domains such as structural reforms, public finance, regional and local finance, labour law, and EU-sponsored legislation. Chapter 6 shows in full length the results of the research and discusses in greater detail the relation between the strengthening of executive powers and the making of neoliberalism.

OUTLINE OF THE BOOK

Through the in-depth analysis of the Italian case, this book offers a theoretical reflection on the nature of the state, the broader societal conditions for its transformations, and the empirical analysis of the changes. All of these are tied to one another. More specifically, the book is structured as follows. Chapter 2 offers an overview of some of the main theoretical approaches developed after World War II with respect to the state and to the transformations of the state. Several approaches are considered: I take into account especially neo-Weberian theory since it has proved to be highly influential in these debates—whether the influence is acknowledged explicitly or not—and I develop an alternative/critical view of the state in relation to it. Hence, chapter 3, by extensively drawing on Gramsci's theory of the state, offers an alternative approach to the state and state transformations, while also conceptualizing the multilayered nature of the state. From chapter 4, we leave the shores of theory and enter into the empirical analysis of the Italian case. Chapter 4 reconstructs Italian Republican history and zooms in on the characteristics of the neoliberal transition in Italian society and of/in the state. The chapter reads Italian history within broader Western and European dynamics. In chapter 5, I analyse—that is, deconstruct—the discursive construction of the neoliberal state or, more specifically, the Italian version of the neoliberal "semiotic order." Chapter 6 deals with the hallmark element of the neoliberalization process: the centralization of power in the state in the form of the enforcement of executive powers, with the parallel marginalization of the national parliament. Chapter 7 analyses the post-2008 Italian context by looking at society, territory, and political relations. It zooms in on the crisis of European integration in Italy and the rise of populist and eurosceptic political forces. Finally, in the concluding chapter of the book, I reconsider the post-democratic evolution of the neoliberal state in Italy and beyond. Moreover, drawing on Gramsci's commentaries on the crisis of the twentieth century and with the advent of fascism in Italy, the chapter—though without establishing automatic parallels—seeks to make sense of some key characteristics of the contemporary organic crisis of the international neoliberal order.

Chapter 2

The State and Its Transformations

An Unfolding Debate

The state is the main political institution of the modern era. Born in Europe and spread (almost) over the entire globe, the ongoing relevance of the "state question" is one of the main themes in political science and theory, political sociology, international relations, comparative and international political economy. In this chapter I take into account, in the guise of a bird's eye view, some of the main theories of the state developed after World War II, and especially those accounts influenced by the thinking of Max Weber, who—besides analysing some key characteristics of the modern state as administrative and legal order, both subjected to the rule of law—famously framed the state as "the claim to monopolize the use of force,"—a claim considered legitimate only insofar as it is either permitted or prescribed by the state (1978, 56). My (alternative) approach to the theory and transformations of the state is developed—dialectically—after discussing some limitations of especially neo-Weberian accounts (see chapter 3). After the overview of the main theories of the state, I take into account the scholarship developed since the 1990s and related to the question of *transformations* of the state. In so doing, I aim to show how scholars from different theoretical perspectives and empirical foci explored and conceptualized the transformations of the state in the epoch of neoliberal globalization. The following section, in addition, reviews the "competition state" literature and more recent contributions regarding the relation between the state and capitalism after the crisis of 2008. In the chapter's conclusions, I outline some of the main limits of current approaches to state theory and transformations, thus setting the stage for an alternative theory of the state and, accordingly, of its transformations.

THE STUDY OF THE STATE AFTER WORLD WAR II

The study of the state in the aftermath of World War II has been characterized by multiple lines of enquiry. While some approaches—especially in U.S. political science—leaned towards a critique of the relevance of the category of state *as such* for the understanding of politics, others, as a response, have tried to "bring the state back in" to the analysis to explain processes of social and political change. Let's try to unfold the main elements of the debate.

In the 1950s and 1960s, the ascendancy of behaviourism and neo-positivism in the social sciences discarded the state as a viable category for the study of politics (for a reconstruction of the origins of behaviourism in political science, see Barrow 2008). As noted by Philip Abrams, the analytical effort became "not to explain the state at all but to explain it away" (1988, 67; see also Mitchell 1991, 78–81). David Easton, one of the main proponents of the new positivist approach in political science, wrote that "it is difficult to understand how [the state] could ever prove to be fruitful for empirical work," so that "asking 'what is the nature of the state?' [. . .] is at best to mistake a part for the whole" (1953, 110–115; see also Easton's later rejoinder 1981). Easton's "whole" is the political system. This was conceived as a system of interacting units (parties, interest groups) and functions that, within an environment characterized by a series of political pressures from social groups, determine a flow of inputs (social demands) and outputs (responses, policies) that give structure to the system (Easton 1953; also Almond and Powell 1966). As such, the political system is deemed to be composed of observable, measurable, testable, quantifiable elements analysed through quantitative methodologies drawn from the "hard" sciences (such as physics).

But there is another reason for a decline in the attention to the state question, in a way more relevant for the immediate conditions in which this new approach started to develop. As argued by Timothy Mitchell, also important was the role of U.S. political science in the overall U.S. system as a rising imperialist superpower, so that "[p]olitical science had to expand its boundaries to match the growth of postwar US power, whose ambitions it would offer to serve" (2006, 171). In this phase of Copernican revolution in the study of politics, the centrality of the concept of the state was therefore set aside due to its supposed ideological nature. Thus, the state was no longer the centre of such a system but, at best, an element among others. Most importantly indeed, neo-positivist approaches reduced the nature of the state to the government and bureaucratic apparatuses, while the concept of the political system ascended to analytical primacy. Moving away from the state as the hierarchical apex of the society, the political system was imagined in terms of a neutral and horizontal battleground among competing social and political groups[1]. In this regard, Dunleavy and O'Leary (1987, 43–28) listed three main images of the state that were developed within such approaches: (1) The state as "weathervane," namely as a cypher-coding machine which processes the inputs received by the strongest pressure groups. (2) The state as neutral site, namely a mediator and harmonizer among different interests. (3) The broker state, whereby public policy is conceived as the outcome of the interests of pressure groups somehow filtered by state apparatuses and bureaucratic agencies. The consequence of this "was to abandon the state as a concept too vague and too narrow to the basis of a general science of politics, replacing it most frequently with the concept of political system" (Mitchell 1991, 78).

Farewell to the state? Actually, the effort to develop a response to behaviourism eventually poured fresh water into the theory of the state especially during the late 1970s and 1980s, when behaviouralist theory lost appeal and new, "meso-theoretical"[2] perspectives on politics emerged. The aim of this new wave of (neo-Weberian) state studies was to "bring the state back in," following the title of an influential collection of essays devoted to the subject (Skocpol et al. 1985; see also Tilly 1975; Waltz 1979; Krasner 1978; Nordlinger 1981, 1988; Mann 1984). Generally, neo-Weberian scholarship has produced important studies concerning the history of the formation of modern states in Europe (Tilly 1975; Poggi 1978; Mann 1986, 1993). The modern state, in this approach, is framed as

> a complex set of institutional arrangements for rule operating through the continuous and regulated activities of individuals acting as occupant of offices. The state, as the sum of such offices, reserves to itself the business of rule over a territorially bounded society; it monopolises, in law and as far as possible in fact, all faculties and facilities pertaining to that business. (Poggi 1978, 1)

The state is therefore regarded as the outcome of a process of authority centralization over a certain territory, which progressively marginalized rival authority claimants (Tilly 1975). A central element is also the growth of the infrastructural power of the state, that Michael Mann identifies in terms of ideological, economic, and military power. In its turn, this allows the state to make a distinctive contribution in terms of social impact and transformation, as "[t]he growth of the infrastructural power of the state is one in the logistics of political control" (Mann 1984, 192).

If the post-war analytical focus shifted from the vertical centrality of the state to the political system as a whole, the "new" scholarship moved back again to the specific analytical relevance of the state to understand—often by adopting a comparative method of analysis—processes of social and political change (Skocpol 1985, 4). Moreover, while pluralist theory conceived the government as a "horizontal" environment in which political units constantly interact, by contrast the state-centric perspective aimed to lay emphasis on the role and functions of the state as an *autonomous*, independent, and unitary actor (with its own preferences, see Krasner 1976) capable of triggering patterns of social change. In the words of Michael Mann, "the state elite's resources radiate authoritatively outwards from a centre but stop at defined territorial boundaries" (1984, 198). Such authority "provides the state with a potentially independent basis of power mobilization being necessary to social development and uniquely in the possession of the state itself" (ibid., 200). The state is therefore conceived as endowed with its own proper political agency and will. Thus, statist approaches—as Mitchell contends—"to political explanation present the state as an autonomous entity whose actions are not reducible to or determined by forces in society. To present the state in this way requires not so much a shift in focus, from society back to the state, *but some way of establishing a clear boundary between the two*" (1991, 82; emphasis added). Hence, while explicitly avoiding "to offer any general theory of the state and social structure" (Skocpol 1985, 8), statist approaches, in analytical terms, aimed to zoom in on state structures and capacities to explore how states, as autonomous actors and organizations, shape politics and society (Evans et al. 1985).

Continuing with the neo-Weberian approach to the state, one of the most recent strands of scholarship is the "limited statehood" perspective (Risse 2011; Risse and Borzel 2014; Risse and Krasner 2014). This is founded on the Weberian notion of statehood as the monopoly of the means of violence and ability to make and enforce central decisions, and maintains that such definitional conditions are not met in most existing states (Risse 2011). In such cases, we have governance without a state, namely non-hierarchical forms of steering that involves both public and private actors. This approach, despite some commendable efforts to promote a non-Western-centric perspective on the state and its transformations, and rightly framing the state as a Western and signally European historical product, nevertheless remains quite a remarkable example of the simplification of the nature, functions, effects, conceptual layers, symbolic power, and complexity of the state-system.

In the final conclusions, I will return to some of the above themes. However, prior to exploring the possibility of developing an alternative approach, it is necessary to review first of all the literature on the *transformations* of the state.

APPROACHES TO STATE TRANSFORMATIONS IN THE AGE OF GLOBALIZATION

Prior to the paramount historical changes in the geography of global capitalism over the last few decades, the state was usually regarded as a rather static entity. In fact, the idea that the state changes over time emerged especially across the late 1980s and the early 1990s, when a series of national and transnational processes of—social, economic, political, technological—change paved the way to the idea that "even" the state would actually transform. Thus, many scholars started to question the role of the state in light of new dynamics such as the liberalization and integration of financial markets, the rise of networks based on the transnational flow of goods, technologies, services, and capitals (the global value chains), and the strengthening of actors such as transnational corporations (TNCs) and credit rating agencies. In other words, neoliberal globalization. For its part, the concept of globalization represents not only a complex, multilinear, and contradictory set of socioeconomic, cultural, and political processes but also an *epistemic* rupture with the previous bodies of scholarship in state affairs, mainly circumscribed to the borders of the nation-state (for a comprehensive and critical assessment of globalization debates, see Bruff 2005).

The conundrum that still occupies many students of the state is if nation-states are actually constrained by processes of political-economic globalization and accordingly "hollowed out" in terms of political authority, or, by contrast, if states not only remain relevant in the global political economy but are also eventually even empowered by it. Globalization has therefore pushed many scholars (*both* "post-statist" and "state-centric") to seriously question the relation between changes in the global political economy and the state. In general terms, the literature on transformations of the state vis-à-vis the global political economy is usually divided into two broad categories: the "state decline" (or "post-statism") approach and "state-centric" (or "statist") perspectives (Sørensen 2004, 1–7; Genschel and Zangl 2014, 340–347). It is worth noting, though, that rigid schematizations in clean-cut fields do not pay justice either to the *internal* nuances of the different approaches taken into account, which vary significantly within the same theoretical perspective, or to the complexity of the arguments at stake. In reconstructing the debate, rather than attempting to foster rigid categorizations I will present some of the main arguments developed over the last three decades from different theoretical approaches by letting the authors speak. Methodologically, this is a necessary step to emphasize limitations and shortcomings of many current analyses of state transformations and subsequently to offer an alternative approach.

The "State Decline" Approach

The influential *The Retreat of the State* (1996) by Susan Strange is a case in point of analyses of the "hollowing out" of state authority. Questioning the primacy of the state as the key actor of the international system (cf. Waltz 1979), Strange's approach revolves around the international political economy of market integration and, accordingly, the strengthening of market actors, prominently TNCs and financial firms. Her argument posits that the state-market balance of power shifted towards the second since the national economies were gradually merging into one single global market, determining thus a decline of the authority of all governments (1996, 13–14; see also Cable 1995). Strange contends that "the domain of state authority in society and economy is shrinking" (1996, 82) and new loci and sources of authority appear, bringing about a diffusion of power and authority within the global political economy (e.g., in the form of private-public partnerships). An even more radical perspective than Strange's is what Sørensen (2004, 3) calls the "Endist" approach, which posits the increasing obsolescence of the nation-state. A prominent case is *The End of Nation State* by Kenichi Ohmae (1996). According to Ohmae, the transformations and global integrations in information technology, investments flows and industry were rendering increasingly obsolete the national dimension of the state, in favour of the emergence of "regional states" more suitable to the new global political economy (see also, for similar perspectives, Guehenno 1995; Naisbitt 1995).

The rethinking of political institutions and processes since the 1990s also involved the category of "government." In fact, (i) the emergence of new actors such as TNCs and credit rating agencies, (ii) the strengthening of the global reach of International Organizations (IOs) such as the International Monetary Fund and the World Bank, and (iii) the European integration process, led some to put under scrutiny not only the steering capacity but also the *heuristic* relevance of the (national) government for understanding post-national politics. The emergence of the category of *governance* is a case in point. In this respect, James Rosenau et al. (1993) maintained that processes occurring at global and sub-national levels were undermining the steering capacity of national governments and creating new shifts in the loci of authority (1992, 3–4, 2007). The analytical proposal of Rosenau et al. aimed to shift the analytical attention from government to governance, "a more encompassing phenomenon than government" (1993, 4) conceived as a set of governmental as well as informal and non-governmental mechanisms, more suitable for understanding the transformations of contemporary authority beyond the formal authority of the state (see also Sørenesen 2004; Held and McGrew 2002).

From a more radical perspective, a well-known case of the "decline" thesis is represented by Michael Hardt's and Tony Negri's *Empire: The New Order of Globalization* (2001). The authors' perspective begins with the paradigm change of the postmodern era. The key argument of *Empire* is that postmodern market ideology is, in essence, anti-foundationalist and militates against strong national/local identities. Since their condition of possibility is the free circulation of goods, mobility, and diversities of all sorts (2001, 148–149), markets constantly struggle to overcome national boundaries and give value to differences (gender, ethnicity, sexual orientations) to include as many social groups as possible in the mechanisms of global capital accumulation. At the same time, the expansion of capitalism also parallels the changes in the nature of imperialism and U.S. power, which after the end of the Cold War became the guarantor of the liberal global order. In this view, the Empire is conceived as a global "flat" space of markets and flexible capital accumulation spanning all over the world; *pace* world-system theory approaches (Wallerstein 1979), the Empire has no centre and no centre-periphery divisions but is crossed by multiple lines of fragmentation and conflicts (2001, 311). In this fashion, the "in" and the "out" of the national and the international gets increasingly blurred, and the function of *mediation* of national politics becomes obsolete if not impossible (2001, 179).

Among other important elements, *Empire* emphasized the sociological dimension of globalization. In this respect, however, the thesis of the rise of a global political and cultural framework that superimposes on that of nation-states was not new to students of globalization and of the "global age" (Beck 2002; Castells 1996). Martin Albrow, for example, theorized the emergence of a "global state" as a new reality emerging from the pressures exerted by citizens on global and national institutions to deal with global issues (1994, 178). "The new global state"—Albrow writes—"is coming into existence [. . .] through the activities of all those who have responded to globality by making the globe the criterion for their active engagement in common purposes" (1994, 179). A global state seems to be firstly a sociocultural phenomenon, rather than a full-blown hierarchical and global institutional system, emerging along with the formation of a shared consciousness—the rise of something like a global civil society—about crucial global issues such as military interventions, gender issues, or the environmental question. For example, Martin Shaw (1997) contends that globalization has actually undermined nation-state autonomy, but this occurred for *military* purposes and not due to economic globalization (at least as a "first mover"). In the West, military integration of nation-states has led to the emergence of a conglomerate of states into one "western state" with no "borders of violence" within it. The global state is seen as "a more or less coherent raft of state institutions which possesses, to some degree, global reach and legitimacy, and which function as a state in regulating economy, society and politics on a global level" (1997, 504). Moreover, and not too dissimilarly from Hardt and Negri, Shaw stresses the "global projection of power" (1997, 502) of Western states' military interventions.

The State/Space Debate

Especially geographers and critical sociologists have introduced the question of *state/space* into the analysis of the re-articulation of the *territorial* dimension of the nation-state form, exploring in particular the rise of global cities (Tokyo, New York, Paris, Frankfurt, etc.)—these latter understood as organizing and critical nodes of global capitalism and "intensive sites" of capital accumulation (Brenner 1999; Sassen 1996; Jessop 2003, ch. 5; Rossi 2017)—and then taking into account how the shifting geography of global capitalism has impacted on state territory and powers (Harvey 2001). For instance, Neil Brenner emphasized the new *scalar* organization of capitalism since the 1970s, arguing that "state territorial power is not being eroded, but rearticulated and re-territorialized in relation to both sub- and supra-national scales" (1999, 3, see also Brenner, Peck and Theodore 2010). Importantly, Brenner adds that "current transformations may indeed herald the partial erosion of central state regulatory control over global flows of capital, commodities and labour power, but *the state remains a central institutional matrix of political power*" (1999, 9, emphasis added; see also Brenner et al. 2003). Saskia Sassen (1996, 2008), on the other hand, while aptly rejecting the zero-sum game logic that usually opposes the global dimension versus the nation-state, developed a more nuanced vision of how the state participates in the global political economy and changes within such processes. Resorting to the image of the "frontier zone," Sassen conceptualizes it as a space of "political and economic interactions that produce new institutional forms and alter the old ones" (1999, 410). In addition, Sassen notes that globalization strengthens *specific* components *in* the state. While much of state scholarship has focused on the homogenizing effects of global dynamics on the state as unitary actor, Sassen captures "the *internal* shifts of power within the state brought about by globalization" (2008, 169, emphasis added), and especially the strengthening of executive powers and economic ministries (see chapters 4 and 6).

The Resilience of (National) State Powers

So far, this bird's eye view on the transformations of the state has taken into account especially those visions of decline/reconfiguration/re-territorialization of the nation-state. However, there has been a consistent body of scholarship that has frequently reasserted the centrality and resilience of the national state. The scholars working in this tradition have tried to demonstrate, often in light of a historically grounded perspective (H. Thompson 1999; Shaw 1997; Mann 1997), not only the ongoing centrality of nation-states (Weiss 1998, 2003; Gritsch 2005; Lake 2008) but also, given specific conditions, the strengthening of national governments (Evans 1997, 67–69). Michael Mann, for instance, in light of the "survival of the nation-state as wielder of some economic, national, military and political resources" (1997, 474; Shaw 1997), zoomed in on the relevance of national institutions, which *differ* and *matter* from nation-state to nation-state and therefore determine variations in the patterns of transformations. In similar fashion, Weiss (1998) detailed empirically the relevance of national institutions in the "global" era. By questioning the view of the state as "passive victim" of external forces, and adopting the neo-Weberian category of state capacities[3] (Skocpol 1985), in *The Myth of the Powerless State* Weiss emphasizes the concepts of *adaptation* and *coordination* of state powers, grounded in both the institutional framework's capacity and in the agency of policymakers to pursue domestic adjustment strategies (1998, 5–6). In a later work, Weiss contends that, first, states generally have more room for manoeuvre than the "state decline" approach concedes, especially in those areas such as social protection, wealth creation, and even industrial policy; second, globalization may also enable domestic economic governance in the form of the "expansion of governing capacities through the transformation of both public–private sector relations and the growth of new policy networks" (2003, 315); third, the character of domestic institutions is decisive for explaining national variations. Weiss concludes that "*the main institutional impact of global markets is a tendency to weaken statist forms of rule and to encourage, domestically, the growth of various forms of 'governed interdependence*'" (2003, 313; emphasis in the original).

From a different perspective and through a more eclectic theoretical framework, Maria Gritsch (2005) has focused on the agency of states and the political-democratic implications regarding the implementation of economic globalization. Gritsch emphasizes that by expanding transnationally the infrastructure of capital accumulation, states and capitalists have reduced their dependence on national factors and markets. In so doing, states disempower subordinate groups in civil society, gain further autonomy in agenda-setting and neutralize possible sources of contestation. "By implementing globalization"—Gritsch writes—"states [. . .] establish conditions allowing them to call into question traditional states functions" (2005, 17), prominently welfare provisions, with negative implications for democratic systems and political participation (see also, for a structurationist treatment of the state as both "made and maker" by/of globalization, Hobson and Ramesh 2002). Therefore, either from a more orthodox or from a more critical view of the relation between the state and global capitalism, the instinctive response of these scholars has been to emphasize the role of the state in the making of the global political economy.

While the first wave of studies aimed to counteract the "state decline" approach, from the mid-2000s especially new studies have tried to "unpack" the state and conceptualize state transformations in greater detail, especially through extensive empirical research. For instance, by exploring state transformations in discrete spheres—democracy, rule of law, taxation, welfare—Hurrelman et al. (2007; see also Leibfried and Zürn 2005), noted that the authority of the state is being "de-monopolized" in favour of a diffusion (rather than an outright shift) of responsibilities towards IOs and other nonstate actors, and conceptualized state transformations as *self-transformation.* States can act as *initiators*, *promoters* or *managers* of change, variously retaining key regulatory functions (2007, 12–13). Genshel and Zangl, similarly stressing that the state remains the basic unity of authority in OECD countries *because* of the spread of nonstate actors authority, frame contemporary transformations in terms of the changing role of "the state from vital monopolist of authority to a key manager of partly private and international political authority" (2014, 338; also Schneider and Rothgang 2015; Levy 2015). Yet, one of the most extensive explorations of the subject of state transformations is the *Oxford Handbook of The Transformation of the State* (Huber et al. 2015), including forty-four chapters that explore determinants, dimensions, and intensity/extent of state transformations in OECD and non-OECD economies. In their conclusions, the editors of the volume emphasize that the state is *not* in a process of obsolescence but, at the same time, they also add that halting or reversing global economic integration is not plausible. They offer two main reasons. First, private actors such as TNCs and financial institutions "control more resources than many states" (2015, 835). Second, "governments in the most powerful countries still believe in the benefits of at least large parts of globalization" (ibid.). Therefore, in this scenario "a more likely trajectory than de jure delegation of decision-making powers by the national state upwards, to supra- and international bodies, is a de facto diminution of state capacities to regulate and tax corporate actors even within the state's own territory" (ibid., 837).

FROM THE COMPETITION STATE TO THE RETURN OF STATE CAPITALISM

Along with the debate on the extent, determinants, and implications of state transformations in the epoch of globalization, some have also tried to conceptualize the changes in statehood and/or in the overall scope of the state. More recently, the global financial crisis of 2008 (with widespread interventions of states to rescue banks and private firms) and the rise of new political-economic powers as China, India, and Russia, have proposed again the question of the relation between the state and capitalism. Let's consider this strand of state debates.

The Competition State: Exploring the Shift in Contemporary Statehood

The "regulatory state" (Majone 1994), the "competition state" (Cerny 1997, 2010), and the "Schumpeterian competition state" (Jessop 2002, 1990) represent different but related efforts to conceptualize the major shifts occurring in contemporary statehood.

Majone argues that privatization and deregulation do not imply a return to laissez-faire or the end of regulation but, on the contrary, these have determined an increasing burden of regulation of newly privatized and liberalized economic activities. Thus, the shift from "dirigisme" (i.e., the direct management of economic activities) to *regulative* tasks marks the key change in European statehood in the 1980s and 1990s, at national and especially EU level. A significant step in the rise of the "regulatory state" is the creation, at the national level, of an array of independent agencies (telecommunication, services, energy, etc.) which provide state bureaucracies with the necessary technocratic expertise and independence. For Majone, while the strengthening of non-majoritarian institutions raises the problem of the political accountability of EU regulators, "who are neither elected nor directly responsible to elected officials" (1994, 94), at the same time policymaking would benefit, in terms of efficacy and rationality, from the insulation of EU regulators from short-run political considerations. In this respect, Majone makes the case for the strengthening of the policymaking role of courts (prominently the Court of Justice of the European Union) and the increasing importance of judicial reviews, which also "shows that the triad of government powers is no longer considered an inviolable principle" (1994, 93).

Philip Cerny's approach, on the other hand, places greater emphasis on international market integration and competition because such pressures have significantly impacted on the overall *scope* of the state, whose powers are now mainly mobilized to improve the competitive position of the domestic economy within global markets. More specifically, the transition from the welfare state to the *competition* state entails four main changes: (i) a shift from macroeconomic fine-tuning to microeconomic interventionism; (ii) a focus on the supply-side rather than on domestic demand; (iii) the prioritization of inflation targeting (instead of jobs creation); (iv) the promotion of enterprise, innovation, and profitability rather than citizens' welfare (full employment, redistribution, social services) (1997, 260). Moreover, while the welfare state's aim was to "decommodify" certain activities (e.g., health, education), the competition state continuously expands markets and commodification as its "increasingly crucial overarching goal is maintaining and promoting competitiveness in a world marketplace and multi-level political system" (Cerny 2010, 6); accordingly, it is "key promoter of globalisation and therefore of global competition" (ibid., 8; see also Soederberg et al. 2005).

In *The Future of the Capitalist State* (2002), Bob Jessop provides a more compelling and articulated picture. Jessop's analysis starts by zooming in on the mode of production and regulation (see also Boyer 1990). The transition from Fordism to post-Fordism constitutes the framework in which he tracks the rise of what he calls the "Schumpeterian competition state." Fordism is conceptualized as a social formation in which a number of elements (contingently and in light of specific national variations) coexist: (i) a mode of regulation (norms, institutions, organizational forms, social networks); (ii) a regime of capital accumulation based on mass production, mass consumption, and rising wages; (iii) a type of labour process and division of labour, based in particular on semi-skilled and mass workers and in which public sector employment plays an important role; (iv) a process of "societalization" (i.e., social integration of subaltern classes) founded upon determined patterns of institutional and social cohesion (de facto securing the dominance of industrial capital accumulation) (2002, 55–58). The Keynesian Welfare National State (KWNS) was the historical political-institutional and territorial form of the Fordist epoch. In its turn, it was based on a distinctive set of economic policies (full employment, demand management, provision of infrastructure for mass production) and social measures (in the form of welfare provision and collective bargaining), a *national* territorial scale of development and relatively closed national economies, and a *dirigist* role for the state in the form of a "mixed economy" (i.e., direct provision by the state of public goods and services) coupled with trial-and-error attempts to govern and stabilize the cycle of capital accumulation and compensations for market failures (ibid., 58–61, 71–80). In the 1970s, due to structural and conjunctural conditions, the KWNS—and the Fordist patterns of accumulation—entered a prolonged set of economic, fiscal, social, and political crises, which seriously undermined the state's management-crisis capacities (ibid., 80–92; see also Offe 1984). While I will return to the crisis of KWNS with a more detailed account when describing the Italian case (chapter 4), in general terms the crisis of Fordism and the emergence of post-Fordism[4] as a mode of capital accumulation and regulation led to the emergence of the "Schumpterian competition state," conceived as the

> state that aims to secure economic growth within its borders and/or to secure competitive advantages for capitals bases in its borders, even when they operate abroad, by promoting the economic and extra-economic conditions that are currently deemed vital for success in competition with economic actors and spaces located in other states [. . .] Although the competition state's strategies may be

targeted on specific places [. . .] they are always mediated through the operations of the world market as a whole. (2002, 96)

The "competition state" thesis seems to portray a state that *accompanies,* with economic and extra-economic features, the accumulation of capitals in the world market through policies such as privatization, liberalization, fiscal consolidation, wage moderation, and inflation targeting. In other words, a neoliberal configuration of the state that gives up its mediating role between labour and capital and re-orients its regulatory role and scope of intervention towards ongoing market-making policies, competition enhancement, and global capital accumulation. The crisis of 2008, however, significantly disrupted the image of a mere "watchdog" state which is only in charge of market supervision and the enhancement of competitiveness. In fact, capitalism—the elephant in the room (Bruff 2011a; Bruff and Horn 2012)—has returned to the analysis.

The Return of the Capitalist State?

While in the wake of neoliberal globalization the state *appeared* to be relegated "only" to the function of regulation and supervision of markets, the global financial crisis of 2008, paired with the sovereign debt crisis in Southern Europe in 2010–2011, led some to rethink (*again*) the role of the state, because "in the crisis-ridden core of the global economy, a full-blown depression was averted by the state taking over the reins from capital" (van Apeldoorn et al. 2012, 472). Moreover, while the previous waves of state debate mainly targeted Western states and neoliberal global capitalism, post-2008 scholarship has enlarged the geographical spectrum to include non-Western cases such as China, Russia, Brazil, India, Taiwan, South Korea, and so on, to the extent that, as we shall see, state capitalism is actually mainly associated with such consolidating economies.[5] Clearly, this reflects the fact that "the supremacy of the West, established in the fourteenth to sixteenth centuries, appears to be waning with the declining of US hegemony and the rise of Asia as a rival centre of capital accumulation" (ibid., 471; see also McNally 2013; Nölke 2014).

Hence, an important strand of recent state scholarship is increasingly characterized by the resurgence of "state capitalism." The "new" state capitalism is usually associated, in the Global South, with state-owned enterprises, sovereign wealth funds, a limited scope of markets, and the fostering of national industrial champions—more broadly, with a state-led development model. In the Global North, on the other hand, it is associated especially with the range of public interventions aimed at rescuing large firms and banks, which are then left again to markets after the refurbishment operations of the state

(Bremmer 2011). Whether in light of new state interventions in the West or state-led development in consolidating economies, scholars from different theoretical views and empirical foci started to speak of the "return of the state" (Bremmer 2010), "rebound of the state" (van Apeldoorn et al. 2012), "refurbished capitalism" (McNally 2013), "reinventing state capitalism" (Musacchio and Lazzarini 2014), "state capitalism 3.0" (Nölke 2014), "stabilizing state through the use of state capitalism" (Carney 2015), "return of statism" (Kurlantzik 2016). According to Ian Bremmer, state capitalism is "a form of bureaucratically engineered capitalism particular to each government that practices it. It's a system in which the state dominates markets primarily for political gains" (2010, 5). For Musacchio and Lazzarini, it is the "widespread influence of the government in the economy, either by owning majority or minority equity positions in companies or by providing subsidized credit and/or other privileges to private companies" (2014, 2). Stressing that every state intervenes in the economy, Kurlantzick opts for a more quantitative definition of state capitalism, as "countries whose government has a ownership stake in or significant influence over more than one-third of the five hundred largest companies [. . .] Generally, in these state-capitalist countries the government sees itself as having a direct role to play in managing the economy and guiding the corporate sector" (2016, 9). Below this threshold, Kurlantzick notes, it is the market the guides the economy.

From a critical international political economy standpoint, van Apeldoorn et al. (2012) have developed a compelling account of state–capital nexus and of the "return of the state." They raise several important points. First, the state has never retreated as the relation between capital and the state is *internal*, that is, "state power cannot be abstracted from the private power of capital" (2012, 472). Thus, after the 2008 crash, states rescued banks and large private firms through stimulus programmes, bank bailouts, and even nationalizations to restore the conditions for capital accumulation—as is also happening with the current Covid-19 crisis. Second, the "rebound of the state" as territorial entities *combines* with processes of ongoing capitalist transnationalization and globalization. Third, the authors distinguish between the reconfiguration of the state–capital nexus *within* the West and *outside* the Western capitalist core, the latter being characterized by state-owned enterprises. However, in both cases "state strategies seem to be geared towards deepening commodification of labour and nature rather than towards decommodification" (ibid., 473).

To conclude this brief and final overview, while the "competition state" approach has sought to identify some of the main changes in the scope of state action, the post-2008 debate on state capitalism—despite some conceptual overstretching and under-theorization of the state—has nonetheless put forth again the relevance of the category of state and state transformations to understand the paradigm changes in contemporary global societies. This scholarship has made a significant contribution in pushing us to rethink the relation between the state and capitalism, yet this relation is often conceived as external and sporadic (e.g., the state returns to visibility only after crises), and ultimately fails to conceptualize the internal relation between the state (and its manifold transformations) and global capitalism as a form of life.

CONCLUSION: LIMITATIONS OF CURRENT APPROACHES AND ALTERNATIVE AVENUES

Clearly, it is no easy task to outline a compelling critique of the rich and variegated scholarship concerning the transformations of the state during the period of neoliberal globalization. In what follows, I identify three intertwined problematic foci in how the state and its transformations are theorized. The first is the relation between state and society. The second is the reification of the state and, accordingly, a widespread reductionism with regard to the state's ontological properties. The third concerns the empirical analysis of the internal transformations of the state.

On state and society, albeit often implicitly, the state is mostly regarded as an autonomous actor capable of triggering processes of transformation according to its own will and material capacities. In other words, states are regarded as unitary actors "trying to realize policy goals" (Skocpol 1985, 8) with respect to their peculiar society or as actors in the international system (Waltz 1979). Yet, without a proper theory of the state *and* without taking into account the social bases of state power, the analysis can at best describe the external shell of the state but not *understand* its complex and multiform nature or *explain* why the state takes certain forms when transforming. In so doing, the state-as-actor is necessarily reified as an autonomous agent with its own will and plans. At the same time, "[c]onstructed as a machine of intensions—usually termed 'rule making,' 'decision making,' or 'policy making'—the state becomes essentially a subjective realm of plans, programs, or ideas" (Mitchell 1991, 82). It becomes, in other words, an individual agent abstracted from broader societal relations. In addition, the international states system—as argued by Bieler and Morton—"is here abstracted from history, leading to a failure to account for the social bases of state power or the historically specific ideologies and material that have constituted and sustained state identities across different orders" (2018, 8).

The second problem in mainstream approaches to the state is reductionism. In other words, states are regarded as a conglomerate of material capabilities and resources (furthermore, circumscribed to the perimeter of the state and not as derived from the state-society nexus) and/or as a set of institutional structures. Along with the under-theorization of the social roots of state powers, the view of the state as a set of material capacities and cluster of institutions actually overlooks a fundamental dimension of the *social construction* of the state. A fundamental strand of state theory has indeed called attention towards the nature of the state as an ideological power or, to quote Philip Abrams, "an exercise in legitimation" (1988, more in chapter 3). In other words, when the state appears as the "disinterested servant of the common interest" (Jessop 2015, 18)—detached from society and autonomous—at stake there is a process of reification, namely the state *appears* to be a thing (with its own will) and not a human construct. By contrast, it is important to emphasize that the state is a sociocultural construction that possesses an intrinsic ideological power which, in turn, veils the many lines of fracture of society. Not by chance did Marx and Engels define the state as an "illusory community" (1975, 22–24, chapter 3), a definition that resounds with Benedict Anderson's definition of nationalism as an "imagined community" (2006)—and again not by chance has every nation aimed to create its own state. Behind both of these social constructs there is an immense ideological and symbolic power. Therefore and crucially, the task of critical theory is not to accept the state-as-actor at face value but to *deconstruct* the state-as-construction and link it to specific material and ideological/discursive factors. In this respect, chapter 5 is devoted to deconstructing the construction of the neoliberal Italian state in state representatives' discourse from the late 1980s to the present.

In conclusion, let me briefly emphasize some key points to move forward to the theory of the state and the analysis of its transformations. First, to theorize the state is a necessary step to avoid the trap of the separation between the state and society. This is also necessary to explore the social roots of state powers and, at the same time, to locate in the dialectical relation between structural factors and socialpolitical agency (in and through the state) the engine of state transformations (Bruff and Horn 2012). Second, it is also necessary to conceptualize the different layers of the nature of the state and thus avoid reducing it to a unitary conglomerate of material factors or to the government. Actually, the state is a terrain of multiple struggles occurring within its framework, through its powers, beyond its boundaries; but it is also an ideological force and a kaleidoscope of ideological struggles concerning the image of state and, accordingly, of society. The next chapter is devoted to theorizing and conceptualizing the state. I draw especially on the thought of Antonio Gramsci and Gramscian-inspired critical international political economy.

Chapter 3

The Integral State and Its Transformations in the Global Political Economy

An Alternative Approach

IN SEARCH OF A THEORY OF THE STATE AND STATE TRANSFORMATIONS

As argued in the previous chapter, in many scholarly works the state is often under-theorized. This has negative effects, especially when it comes to the analysis of transformations of the state, when only rarely these are conceptually defined and, accordingly, the specific *dimensions* of the transformations are identified. In turn, this determines further limitations—and often confusion—in the overall analytical landscape and prevents the development of a broader and more complex picture of the changes of/in the state. By drawing in particular on Gramsci's theory of the *integral* state and related Gramscian-inspired scholarship, in this chapter I develop an alternative theoretical framework for conceptualizing the "state problem" in contemporary societies. This is a necessary step because the analysis of the transformations of the state necessarily implies, in the guise of a epistemological and ontological *a priori*, to conceptualize *what is the state*; hence, first of all to engage critically with the nature of the state in capitalist societies and, along with this, with the relation between state and society.

HEGEMONY, CIVIL SOCIETY, AND INTEGRAL STATE: IN THE GRAMSCIAN WORKSHOP

Before and especially during the years of his detention under the fascist regime (from 1926 until his death in 1937), Gramsci attempted to sketch a conceptualization of the state as a theoretical problem within the growing "thick structure of modern democracies, both as state organization and complex articulation of associations in civil life" (1975, 1567; Q13§7). Gramsci's critique was in fact addressed against "the impoverished concept of state" (1975, 1765; Q13§10), which had the state limited to the sphere of government or to the functions of violence and coercion. The backbone and strength of Gramsci's conceptual workshop lies in his non-reductionist approach to the political sphere and to the state, which is neither scaled down to the government or legal system nor separated from society or class relations (Cox 1993, 53).

While in the pre-prison years Gramsci devoted much attention to the manifestations of the political crisis of the liberal state before the advent of the fascist regime in Italy (see Gramsci 1974; Chapter 8), it is especially in the *Prison Notebooks* that he rethinks the "state problem" and the relation between the state, civil society and the construction of political hegemony. As we shall see, it is impossible to understand Gramsci's theory of the *integral* state without relating this to factors such as hegemony and civil society. It is in fact an *internal* and *dialectical* relation that characterizes this "triadic nexus" (state–hegemony–civil society) and constitutes the key to conceptualizing the transformations of the state.

Prior to beginning our conceptual exploration, it is worth advancing a preliminary remark on the structure of the *Prison Notebooks* and Gramsci's "rhythm of thought." As is widely known, the *Notebooks* are an ensemble of notes written by Gramsci during his detention and over a period of six years (1929–1935). The notes do not follow a specific or predefined research programme but constitute a fragmentary set of "open lines of research, right up until the moment of their (contingently determined, temporally necessary) incompletion" (Thomas 2009, 136). As Christine Buci-Glucksmann put it (1980, 8), Gramsci's work involves "a kind of dialectization of different realms of knowledge which definitely breaks with all distinctions into isolated activities, instances that are labelled 'economic,' 'political,' 'literary,' 'cultural,' etc.". Thus, every key concept in the *Notebooks* (hegemony, integral state, intellectuals, civil society, common sense, passive revolution, etc.) is dialectically interrelated to all the others, so that none of these can be understood as standalone ideas.[1] As Gramsci himself wrote about his own research into Marxist philosophy (the "philosophy of praxis"), "the search for *leit-motiv,* of the rhythm of thought, [is] more important that single affirmations in isolation" (1975, 41; Q4§1). The dialectic of internal relations is therefore central (see also Bieler and Morton 2018). It not only characterizes, ontologically, dimensions such as civil society and political society or force and consensus but also marks the relation between theory and praxis and the development of knowledge.

The Ground of the Integral State: Hegemony, Ideology, and Intellectuals

The concept of hegemony occupies a central position in Gramsci's prison reflections and is key to understanding his theory of the *integral* state. While a philological exploration of this concept as developed in the *Notebooks* goes beyond the scope of this study,[2] in what follows I concentrate my attention on three fundamental dimensions of Gramsci's distinctive conceptualization of hegemony. First, hegemony as the intersection of two intertwined dialectical poles: consensus and force, and political society and civil society. Second, the relation between hegemony and ideology, and the role of intellectuals. Third, the question of the crisis of hegemony (or organic crisis), particularly relevant for interpreting the contemporary crisis of the state and, more broadly, democratic crisis in Italy (chapter 8).

Let's begin with hegemony as a set of dialectical intersection*s*. The concept of hegemony already appeared in the pre-prison writings,[3] but it is only in the *Notebooks* that Gramsci develops and "amplifies" it (Francioni 1984, 161)[4] within his network of concepts. In his critique of Gramsci, P. Anderson (1976; see also Eagleton 1991, 113–114) wrote that hegemony seems to characterize in particular the element of consent *as opposed* to coercion, and to belong to civil society *rather than* to the state. This reading of Gramsci's hegemony, though, misses the already-mentioned foundational element of Gramsci's "rhythm of thought" and of hegemony more specifically: dialectics. Also, it neglects how hegemony is actually and concretely related to specific social formations as their "glue."

From the very first *Notebook*, meaningfully titled *Political class leadership before and after assuming government*, Gramsci writes that

> a class is dominant in two ways: it is "leading" [*dirigente*] and "dominant" [*dominante*]. It is leading of allied classes and dominant over adversarial classes. Therefore, even before attaining power a class can (and must) lead; when it is in power it becomes dominant, but continues to lead as well [. . .] there can and must be a "political hegemony" even before going to government, and one should count not just on the power and material force which such a position gives in order to exercise political leadership or hegemony.[5] (1975, 41, Q1§44; cf. Q19§24)

This first appearance of the concept of hegemony already contains three key factors. First, hegemony is grounded in class relations as the force of leadership (*political direction*) by a hegemonic social class, and cannot be abstracted from the *historical bloc* in which it is exercised. A historical bloc is a "complex, politically contestable and dynamic ensemble of social relations [. . .] grounded in historically specific conditions and production relations"

(Rupert 1993, 81), which, borrowing from Robert Cox, involves the "juxtaposition and *reciprocal* relationships of the political, ethical and ideological spheres of activity" (1993, 56; emphasis added). At the same time, the leadership-domination nexus (within a historical bloc) is not "antinomial" but dialectical and strategic because "hegemony is the form of political power exercised over those classes in close proximity to the leading group, while domination is exerted over those opposing it" (Thomas 2009, 163). In other words, hegemony designs the form and strategies that allow a leading social group to exercise its hegemony over society *as a whole*. Hence, the "core" of Gramsci's conception of hegemony emerges as a balance between the dimensions of consensus and force, therefore as the capacity of *both* leadership (over allied) and domination (over enemies).

Importantly, Gramsci "tests" a concept in concrete historical situations (Cox 1993, 50). In this respect, the concept of hegemony as a balance of force and consensus finds a historically mature achievement with the Jacobins in revolutionary France, especially in the *active* phase of the Revolution through the establishment of the legal-constitutional ("*giuridico-costitutzionale*") regime (see Buci-Glucksmann 1980, 54–56). Gramsci writes that, in such a case, "the 'normal' exercise of hegemony on the terrain of the parliamentary regime is characterised by the combination of force and consent variously balanced [*che si equilibrano variamente*]," making "the force appear as grounded in the consensus of the majority expressed through the so called organs of the public opinion" (1975, 1638; Q13§37).[6] Read through historical lenses, hegemony seems to define political relations in the modern era, namely the key historical stage in the development of civil society (Burgio 2014, ch. 7). At the same time, it also emerges within the long process of the secularization of power—namely when God starts to be substituted by the state—and in the light of the separation of powers within the state. Thus, civil society and the state/political society are organically and dialectically related "moments" in the exercising of hegemony (Bieler and Morton 2018, 69–70). But hegemony is also, and crucially, a combination of *material factors* and *ideas/ideology*. Speaking about the relation between the economic-corporative moment and the political sphere, Gramsci writes that

> the fact of the hegemony undoubtedly presupposes that the interests of those groups upon which hegemony is exercised must be taken into account, that a certain compromise is established, that is, that the leading group [*gruppo dirigente*] makes economic-corporative sacrifices because if hegemony is ethico-political, it is also economic, and find its foundation in the decisive function that the leading group exercises in the decisive nucleus of economic activity. (1975, 1591, Q13§18; cf. Q4,§38)

The dialectical combination of force and consensus is therefore further dialecticized by "opening" it to the historical-concrete terrain and the modalities in which *the sphere of production relations interacts with the forms, strategies, and processes of political power and ideology*. In other words, "Gramsci leaves no doubt that the exercise of hegemony, elaborated within civil society, also impacts upon that other superstructural 'level' of the integral state, 'political society or State'" (Thomas 2009, 194). As effectively put by Terry Eagleton,

> A ruling group or class may secure consent to its power by ideological means; but it may also do so by, say, altering the tax system in ways favourable to those groups whose support it needs, or creating a layer of relatively affluent, and thus somewhat politically quiescent, workers. Or hegemony may take political rather than economic forms: the parliamentary system in Western democracies is a crucial aspect of such power, since it fosters the illusion of self-government on the part of the populace. (1991, 112)

This "amplification" of the concept of hegemony contains both strategic and dialectical elements, and allows to ground the consensus/force nexus into the historical-concrete evolution of class relations and political struggles. While domination is exercised over adversary/excluded (subaltern) classes, *active* consent is obtained by a *selective integration* of those social groups in proximity to the leading group through "socioeconomic" concessions, the strategic function of which is to *extend over time* the political hegemony/domination of the leading group thanks to the mediation of political forces in the state—therefore relatively autonomous from the specific social class forces (more below; Poulantzas 1978). Put in other words, "[c]ompromises and concessions to subordinate groups with which the class is seeking to ally can be offered successfully once it is able to transcend its core economic interests and develop a *national–popular* dimension to its hegemonic project" (Bruff 2008, 58). As such, hegemony revolves around a fourfold dialectical combination between the *horizontal* dimension of "force–consensus" and the *vertical* dimension of "political society–civil society". It is the "glue" of a *modern* social formation (figure 3.1).

The second point of our discussion regarding hegemony revolves around the relation between hegemony and ideology, and the role of intellectuals. As noted again by Terry Eagleton, "hegemony is a broader category than ideology. It *includes* ideology, but is not reducible to it" (1991, 112). While hegemony is made of socioeconomic, cultural, and discursive elements, ideology is a fundamental "instrument" to achieve societal hegemony. "It is with Gramsci that the crucial transition is effected from ideology as 'system of ideas' to ideologies as lived, habitual social practices" (ibid., 115), encompassing social

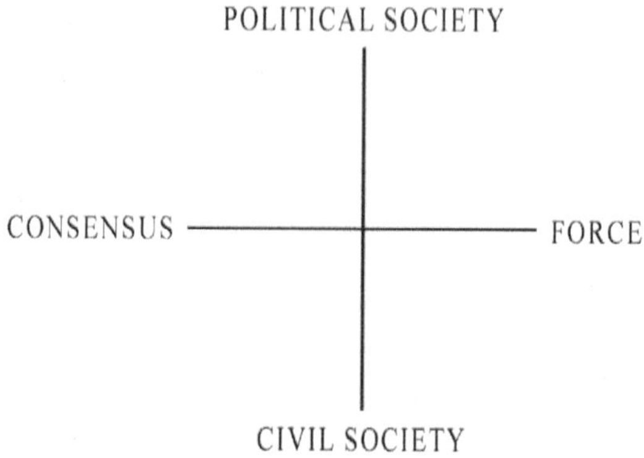

Figure 3.1 A Configuration of Gramsci's Hegemony.

experiences and formal institutions in both conscious and unconscious ways—that is in this last case, in those "implicit aspects as materialized in the practices and cultural norms that are accepted or experienced" (Buci-Glucksmann 1980, 59). Hence, following the Marx of the Preface of the *Critique of the Political Economy*, Gramsci conceives ideologies as the terrain in which "men [*sic*] become conscious of their social position and of their tasks" (1975, 1321; Q10§41). More importantly, ideologies are portrayed as "practical constructions, instruments of political direction" (1975, 436; Q4§15) through which the political battle is discursively articulated. They even "organize human masses, shape [*formano*] the terrain in which men [*sic*] move, acquire consciousness of their position, struggle, etc." (1975, 869; Q7§19).

Contra idealistic conceptions of ideologies and ideas as causal powers in their own right, in "Gramsci's historical materialism [. . .] ideas and material conditions are always bound together, mutually influencing one another, and not reducible to one another" (Cox 1993, 56). So changes in politics and ideology are not "an immediate expression of the structure" since this would be, to Gramsci, a theoretical "primitive infantilism" (1975, 871; Q7§24). Instead, between ideologies and structures there is a "necessary and vital nexus," as such not teleological or deterministic but dialectical. If "hegemony is a particular practice of consolidating social forces and condensing them into political power on a mass basis" (Thomas 2009, 194), at the same time "the fight for hegemony is a struggle of ideologies" (Liguori 2006, 143). Ideas—as organically related to production relations—are *material* forces that become an "independent force when maintained in dialectical connectivity, or internally related, *with the social relations of production*" (Bieler and Morton 2018, 70; emphasis added).

Ideology, as hegemony, embraces both civil society and political society: "ideology cements civil society and therefore the State" (Gramsci 1975,

1036; Q10§41). Yet ideologies do not arise "automatically" from the social structure but are crafted and produced by social and political agents with a specific intellectual function. In the light of production and "transmission" of ideology and hegemony, Gramsci redefines the concept and role of intellectuals. He notes that every social group born out of production relations creates, organically, its own rank of intellectuals, the function of which is to confer *homogeneity* and *awareness* not only at the level of production but also at the social and political level. The "new" intellectuals are, to Gramsci, organic to capitalist/industrial production relations: they are, for instance, capitalist entrepreneurs and industry technicians, the "scientists" of political economy, legal scholars, organizers of culture, and so on (1975, 1514; Q12§1). Yet this does not imply that every single person also performs "public" ideological functions. Gramsci writes that every "man [*sic*] is an intellectual but not every man [*sic*] has intellectual functions in society" (1976, 1514; Q12§1). In fact, "specialized" categories of intellectuals—journalists, academics, public intellectuals, even judges—arise in connection to every social group but especially leading forces, and render a group's ideology "common sense," that is, naturalize the worldview of the dominant (Bruff 2008). For example, in my analysis of the Italian neoliberal transformation, I focus on the top officials of the Bank of Italy as a "technocratic collective intellectual" decisive for the development of neoliberal hegemony within and beyond the Italian state (chapter 4). The function of such groups is, for Gramsci, to connect and organize the intellectual and even pedagogical practices through the "hegemonic apparatuses"[7] of the *integral* state, hence securing the hegemony of leading groups across civil society and political society:

> intellectuals have a function in the "hegemony" that ruling groups exercise in society as a whole and in the "dominancy" over society embodied in the state, and this function is precisely "organizational" and connective: intellectuals have the function of organizing the social hegemony of a group and its state dominancy, that is, consent that comes from the prestige attached to the function in the world of production and the apparatus of coercion for those who do not "consent" either actively or passively or for those moments of crisis of command and leadership when spontaneous consent undergoes a crisis. (1975, 476; Q4§49)

Before coming to the analysis of the integral state, the third and last element worth mentioning is the question of the *crisis of hegemony* (chapters 7 and 8). Gramsci has been aptly defined as a "paramount theorist of capillary power" (Bieler and Morton 2018, 69; Morton 2007), for his attention to the manifold ways in which hegemonic power is achieved and exercised in society as a whole. Hegemony implies the *selective* integration—by means of socioeconomic concessions and ideological practices—of fractions of allied/subaltern groups to win their *active consent*, thus achieving a reasonable degree of legitimation and stability. However, Gramsci's theory of hegemony is, as noted earlier, dialectical and strategic, not functional and/or structuralist. For this reason, as aptly noted by Buci-Glucksmann, "any use of a model of integration requires a model of *disintegration* [. . .] No theory of hegemony, in other words, without a theory of the crisis of hegemony (or organic crisis)" (1980, 59; emphasis added). If hegemony is the "glue" of a social formation, a crisis of hegemony cannot but imply a phase of disintegration of the hegemonic apparatuses and corresponding increasing difficulties of the exercise of "normal" functions (see Q1§48) by ruling social groups. A crisis of hegemony, Gramsci notes, is one in which traditional parties are no more recognized as *representing* those classes and/or class fractions they were previously related to. The hegemony of ruling classes is then transmitted from the existing parties to the state as a whole, in the form of the crisis of "the principle of political authority" (see Q13§23). In chapter 8, I return to Gramsci's commentaries on the hegemonic crisis of the liberal order and the advent of fascism in Italy in the early 1920s, while also discussing the category of organic crisis to understand the contemporary crisis of the neoliberal order in the capitalist West.

The Integral State

The above discussion already shows the paramount importance of hegemony, ideology, and civil society in Gramsci's political theory of the state. As with the concept of hegemony, the word "state" pops up many times throughout the *Notebooks*. Yet the decisive insight of Gramsci and his "novel contribution to Marxist political theory" (Thomas 2009, 137) lies in the concept of *integral* state, which is broadly conceivable as an attempt to reconsider the state question by taking full account of the social, political, and institutional complexity of capitalist societies in the West (Francioni 1984, 195). The concept of integral state represents a theoretical alternative to mainstream theories that reduce the state to the government or material capabilities. As we shall see, it also enables us to avoid an organic separation of the state from society and the market. In addition, "by rejecting any kind of instrumental model of the state"—Buci-Glucksmann notes—"as a weapon of the ruling class endowed with consciousness and will, Gramsci [. . .] also escapes the problematic of the state as violence" (1980, 13), thus also definitively departing from Marxian-oriented instrumentalist theories of the state as apparatuses of coercion on behalf of the dominant classes.

Gramsci gradually arrives at the concept of integral state by examining the historical development of parliamentary regimes in continental Europe and particularly in France—which he regarded as the most advanced example of bourgeois hegemony (see Thomas 2009, 140)—since the late eighteenth century. In this way, Gramsci compares Western European society to Eastern and develops the concepts of *war of position* and *war of movement*, two important categories for understanding contemporary politics. Western modernity, Gramsci notes, is characterized by the development of civil society and thus by a complex relation between the state and social forces in civil society; by contrast, in Russia "the state was everything [*and*] civil society was primordial and gelatinous" (1971, 53). This has important consequences on the political level. In the first type of society, organized social forces and groups operate and concur to the creation of consensus around specific conceptions of the world. Gramsci describes this type of (civil) society as a powerful system of "fortresses and earthworks" to argue that ideological production is not confined only to state apparatuses and to political parties but emerges also within a complex set of "private" apparatuses (media, associations, foundations, the church, grassroots movements, and so on). In this type of society a slow and incremental ideological, political, and social (namely at the level of production relations) struggle is needed to achieve hegemony in civil society *and* the state. This is the war of position. By contrast, whereby the state is "everything" and civil society lacks the complexity of the powerful system of "fortresses and earthworks," a war of movement (a sort of blitzkrieg) can attempt to lay siege to the state and seize political power—Gramsci, of course, had the Bolshevik revolution in mind.

In this fashion, we can understand that the historical development of the modern European state (for instance, through the separations of powers and the establishment of new institutional and constitutional clusters) is the other side of the *birth of modern civil society*, which now appears as constituting the societal texture of the "thick structure of modern democracies, both as state organization and complex articulation of associations in civil life" (1975, 1567; Q13§7). This passage is crucial for understanding the notion of the integral state. Rather than disappearing from the "spectrum" of the state, civil society is actually comprehended *organically* within its historical and political form. In his critique of economism, for instance, Gramsci remarks that the separation between civil society and political society is methodological and not natural, because "in concrete historical life civil society and political society are the same thing" (1975, 460, Q4§38). This does not imply, as noted by Liguori (2006, 212), a complete identification between civil society and political society but only that these are linked, *organically*, by a *dialectical* nexus of unity-distinction, which "produces an enlarged concept of state in which the two poles of this unity are encompassed" (Francioni 1984, 196; Bieler and Morton 2018, 14). In other important notes, Gramsci defines the state as "political society + civil society, hegemony armoured by coercion"

(1975, 764; Q6§88) and remarks that "the State must be conceived not only as government apparatus but also as the 'private' apparatus of hegemony or civil society" (1975, 801; Q6§137), later also adding that "in political affairs the error occurs due to a wrong conceptualisation of what is the State (*in its integral meaning: dictatorship + hegemony*)" (1975, 811; Q6§155; emphasis added). Gramsci thus rejects the idea of a supposed realm of the "economy" as an autonomous and self-governed sphere separated from the state. In relation to the market, for instance, he writes that "laissez-faire must be enacted by the law through the intervention of political power. It is a *matter of will* and not the spontaneous expression of the economy" (1975, 460; Q4, §38; emphasis added). And the sources of this political power are necessarily *social*, that is, rooted in the realm of social relations of production.

The integral state is a fundamental "moment" in the achievement of hegemony within a historical bloc. As Adam Morton notes, "an 'integral' concept of the state is central to understanding the moment of hegemony involving leadership and the development of active consent through the social relations of state–civil society" (2007, 90). Coming once again to the concrete terrain of history, Gramsci wrote that during the French Revolution, the bourgeoisie "could appear as an integral 'State,' with all the necessary and sufficient intellectual and moral forces to organise a complete and perfect society" (1975, 691; Q6§10). I will return to the question of the "foundation" of the integral state and its ideological and symbolic power. For now, it is worth citing what is perhaps the definition of the state that bears the most far-reaching implications. In the *Notebook 15*, Gramsci defines the state as

> the entire complex of practical and theoretical activities with which the ruling class not only justifies and maintains its dominance, but manages to win the active consent of those over whom it rules. (1975, 1765, Q15, §10)

This definition is, in my view, of paramount relevance as it involves several key implications for both the theory and the empirical analysis of the state. First of all, the state as *complex of activities* opens the full possibility to develop a *dynamic vision* (and analysis) of the state as the *terrain* of sociopolitical interactions and conflicts. In fact, "the state's institutional terrain"—as Ian Bruff notes—"gives ample opportunity for a historical bloc to remain hegemonic for an extended period of time, stabilizing its inherent dynamism and giving the state's social content a path-dependence which can be observed and analysed" (2008, 60). Opposite to a reified and static vision of the state as a material unit/structure, Gramsci's conceptualization grasps the reality of the integral state as a *terrain of activities* embedded in national/transnational social relations. Second, state activities are "*theoretical*" and "*practical*." What does this mean? Assuming the risk of overstretching

Gramsci's concepts, I think that it is possible—given the importance that Gramsci assigns to hegemony and ideology—to associate the "theoretical" dimension of state activities with the sphere of ideological practices and ideas. Ideological practices are not only developed in/on the terrain of the integral state, *they are also inscribed in the very idea* of the state as "illusory community", that is, "through the illusory 'general' interest in the form of the State", as Marx and Engels put it in *The German Ideology* (1974, 54; also 83, 88) (I shall go in greater detail below). On the other hand, in the "practical" sphere of state activities I would locate especially the dimension of policy-making, bureaucratic activities, the judiciary, and the coercive functions (the police). These sets of practices (i.e., theoretical-ideological and practical-governmental) are clearly part of the same process, and are expressions of a contingent historical bloc: the attention to "practices" reinforces the view of the state as terrain of "activities" and as a key strategic dimension within a hegemonic order. This enables us to arrive at the third element, namely that ruling social groups need to *win* the *active* consent of allied social groups (extending the hegemony over time) and to dominate the subaltern classes (e.g., the contemporary proletarian migrant working class). Once again, the state is integrally embedded into the national and transnational configuration of social relations of production, and is part and parcel of the strategic interactions and conflict between classes and class politics.

A MULTILAYERED CONCEPTUALIZATION OF THE STATE AND STATE TRANSFORMATIONS

If the integral state is a moment of the hegemony of a certain historical bloc, in its turn the state has a special complexity. In this section, I discuss two fundamental themes: (i) the state-society nexus; (ii) the multilayered nature of the state. This is, as I remarked earlier, a necessary step towards conceptualizing the *transformations* of the state in the neoliberal epoch.

The State-Society Nexus: Analytical Implications and Political Consequences

The section zooms in on the question of political agency (and struggles) *in* the state and explores the concept of relative autonomy. Drawing on Nicos Poulantzas, "the political field of the state (as well as the sphere of ideology) has always, in different forms, been present in the constitution and reproduction of the relations of production" (1978, 17), and so "class struggle, and especially political struggle and domination, are inscribed in the institutional structure of the State" (ibid., 125). The state emerges as a condensation of past social relations but especially as a dynamic *terrain* of—in Gramsci's words—"theoretical" and "practical" activities among competing forces, aimed at securing the reproduction of a specific hegemonic order vis-à-vis its own contradictions and political contestations.

The state is a field of both interactions and conflicts among different political forces and projects and also of mediation among different coalitions of material interests and values. In general terms, it is important to note that the conditions for conflict in the state (and outside) to occur and for mediation among material interests to be fulfilled always depend on the overall characteristics of a historical context, and on the relative societal power relations. Nevertheless, the field of the state and political forces within it enjoy a *relative* autonomy from the broader social class structure, namely a degree of autonomy in managing the conflicts and the potentials for consensus through an array of weapons, from economic and fiscal policy to ideology and police repression. This autonomy, however, should be always read against the structural conditions of global capitalism (and the social relations of production that it engenders), and thus within the primary aim of securing the reproduction of capital accumulation (Tansel 2017; Bieler and Morton 2018; Bruff and Tansel 2019). The mobilization of the state during capitalist crises (see chapter 2) is a case in point: public powers intervene through fiscal expansionary policies or welfare measures (for the unemployed) to avoid the possibility of a *political* crisis of capitalism. This is to say that the content and the forms of the relative autonomy of the "state field" are always historical and societally rooted. Hence, the historical characteristics of relative autonomy actually and ultimately depend on the concrete forms, processes, and conditions of social power relations at national and transnational levels, and on the specific characteristics of the existing institutional framework which constrains or enables sociopolitical agency. State powers, given such underlying social relations, can be more autonomous from specific social classes (e.g., national labour) and, at the same time, less autonomous from other social forces (e.g., transnational capital). Let's sketch two scenarios to clarify the question.

In society A, conceivable as a rough ideal-type of a post–World War II social-democratic configuration, the relation between the forces of capital and labour with regard to production and ideology may result in a relative balance within civil society (unions, associations, foundations, and so on) and within the party system. Thus, social forces are tied to political parties that represent them in the state (e.g., in the parliament) with a reasonable degree of homogeneity of material interests and values. In such a scenario, two interlinked consequences may occur: the hegemonic group may have to accept, willingly or not, the need to make socioeconomic concessions not only to allied classes (white collars, landowners, professionals) but also to fractions of subaltern classes—for example, in the form of welfare provisions or higher wages—to secure political hegemony in the long run. Some of the parties in power can act as mediators or even "stabilizers" of the system through these socioeconomic concessions, forms of economic planning, ideological practices—especially in moments of intense sociopolitical conflict in and beyond the state (such a case is the Italian political context in the 1960s and 1970s, as I show in the next chapter).

In society B, conceivable as a rough approximation of an abstract neoliberal society, the "structural power of capital" (Gill and Law 1993)—thanks to a number of restructuring dynamics such as the transnationalization of production, commodification, and privatization, financialization, increased competition, and so on—expresses a higher influence in society as a whole, managing also to exert a stronger grip over the party system (and party cadres) and, at the same time, over political-ideological relations in and outside the state. In such a case, there are several implications. First, some apparatuses of the state—executive power, economic ministries, or technocratic agencies—can be used/empowered *strategically* by certain forces in the state to change the institutional balance of power (e.g., through centralizing decision-making power) and through this to rewrite the "economic constitution" of society—perhaps advocating, ideologically, the improvement of "governability" (chapters 4 and 6). In specific relation to society, this can reflect a minor inclination towards socioeconomic compromises that can materialize (on the part of labour) as wage moderation policies in exchange for job retention, cuts in welfare state and public expenditures in the name of employability, high unemployment accompanied by the stigmatization of the unemployed, anti-progressive taxation as a form of "equal opportunity," privatization of public services as a means of (allegedly) achieving a higher quality of service, and so on.

Also, there can be a declining trend in the mechanism of political representation within the state, and a gradual but steady detachment of *some* traditional parties from their historical social class basis (Streeck 2013; Mair 2013). Crucially, processes of centralization of power in the state, the decline in political representation, and increasing impossibility to mediate *in* the state among broad material interests rooted in society *may cause in the long run a decline of the consensus towards established political groups* and also towards state authority, especially if the material conditions of significant portions of the population decline. I document this scenario in chapter 7, when I discuss the decline in the consensus towards mainstream centrist parties on the left and right. Gramsci locates the roots of an organic crisis in the deterioration of the representative mechanism: "[d]etachment of civil society from political society: a problem of hegemony has arisen, that is, the historical basis of the State has shifted. There is a new extreme form of political society: either to fight against the new or to preserve the shaky existing order by strengthening it through coercive means" (1975, 876; Q7§28).

These two cases are descriptively and abstractly sketched, but this enables us to relate concretely the theoretical discussion with empirical cases. Above all, it is now possible to tackle and frame the fundamental question of *state transformations*. The dialectical relation between civil society and political society and their space–scale–time configurations allows us *to identify and comprehend the social roots of state transformations*, hence avoiding an agentless or reified account of changes *of* (and *in*) the state.

In the previous chapter, I argued that shortcomings in many current theories of state transformations are rooted in their descriptive nature. In other words, they can (at best) frame, empirically, *if* and *how* states transform, *not why*. By treating the state as a unit/thing, elements such as hegemony and ideology, the evolution of capitalist relations, and even changes within the apparatuses of the state, are dramatically neglected. Above all, transformations of the state are read through technocratic and teleological lenses, dramatically overlooking the role of politics and political agency at national and international levels. This limit is the result of the ontological separation between the state and society, which leads us to locate in the state (as "self-transformation") or outside the state (e.g., European integration) the "prime mover" of change. By contrast, I argue that transformations of the state are part and parcel of the dialectical relations between the situated political *agency* in the state and broader *structural* processes of change in society at national and international levels.

The Dual Nature of the State: As Social Construction and as Institutional System

So far, the analysis has sought to dissect the relation between the state and society. Yet the state as such is composed of further, distinctive dimensions that can be analysed as specific *layers* of the nature of the state. In other words, while the state-society nexus captures the reality of the state as an ever-changing *terrain* of hegemonic struggles, at the same time we can "open up" further the state and explore its multilayered nature. In what follows, I deal with two dimensions of the stratified ontology of the state: the state as *sociocultural construct* and *the state as system*—both conceived as two aspects of the same entity/process (Mitchell 1991). Importantly, this will also allow us to definitively break with instrumentalist, functionalist and structuralist conceptions of the state.

Let's start by saying that, most often, current theories of the state, and especially the accounts of state transformations, take the state as a given and *a priori* entity. In so doing, while "states are seen as being devoid of culture" (Sharma and Gupta 2006, 7), at the same time "[n]either the profoundly cultural content of state institutions and activities nor the nature and extent of state regulation of cultural forms are adequately addressed in much of the literature" (Corrigan and Sayer 1985, 2). In contrast, I argue that the dimension of culture—along with ideology—is fundamental for understanding not only the historical evolution of modern and contemporary states but also the contemporary transformations of the state as situated within the rise of the neoliberal paradigm. Following Stuart Hall, who aptly links cultural practices to social groups and classes, culture can be conceived as something encompassing "both the meanings and values which arise amongst distinctive social groups and classes [. . .] [*and*] the lived traditions and practices through which those 'understandings' are expressed and in which they are embodied" (cited in Steinmetz 1999, 7). In the words of Ian Bruff, culture "cannot be conflated with institutional norms, bracketed off as a variable or viewed as a vague umbrella term: it traverses all parts of the social world—*including state and society*" (2008, 10; emphasis added). The rise and evolution of modern states would not be understandable without having these firmly rooted *within* the cultural revolution of the bourgeoisie and of the capitalistic ethos (Corrigan and Sayer 1985). Broadly speaking, the state is a social and cultural construct—endowed with ideological power—of a particular historical epoch and not just an institutional cluster or unit with specific material capacities.

Within specific cultures, the state unfolds its ideological power. As noted earlier, ideological practices—arising from classes and social groups—become hegemonic when they are able to transcend the boundaries of specific social groups and classes and acquire a national-popular dimension, even a universalistic aim. The *idea* of the state as "tutelary deity" of the community—detached and above society—and "disinterested servant of the common interest" (Jessop 2015, 18) is, in fact, an *intrinsic ideological power* which needs to be taken into account in its own right. As Philip Abrams wrote in his seminal article *Notes on the Difficulty of Studying the State*, "[t]he state is first and foremost an exercise in legitimation—and what is legitimated is, we may assume, something which if seen directly and as itself would be illegitimate, an unacceptable domination" (1988, 79; see also Mitchell 1991, 2006; Hay 2014, 461–462). Thus, the *idea* of the state becomes, as such, a "'significant political reality' and the state itself an 'ideological thing [. . .] the device in terms of which subjugation is legitimated'" (1988, 68). On the other hand, the *appearance* of the state as autonomous entity separated from society and its social and political fractures (a "phantom of the intellect," to use the words of Gramsci) is the outcome of a process of reification. As Berger and Luckmann put it in their classic *The Social Construction of Reality*, reification is

> the apprehension of human phenomena as if they were things, that is, in non-human or possibly suprahuman terms. Another way of saying this is that reification is the apprehension of the products of human activity as if they were

> something other than human products—such as facts of nature, results of cosmic laws, or manifestations of divine will. (1966, 106)

As seen in the previous chapter, reification is not only a mode of apprehension of the existence of the state by the population at large but also *implicit* in those approaches to the state that conceive it as a mere infrastructure or as a thing with its own will. The popular reification of the state as an "illusory community" implies, as Marx noted in *The Jewish Question* (2019, 48–49; see also *The German Ideology*, 1974, 53–54), that "the state" *masks*, through the abstraction of formal equality before the law, the *real* differences of birth, education, occupation, condition—and class, and gender, and race. Yet the state is not a static or inert reification: it is actually a set of *historical-concrete* ideological, discursive, and symbolic practices, namely the already-discussed "theoretical practices" detected by Gramsci. Singing the national anthem, celebrating the establishment of the state, military parades, raising the flag, institutionalized hierarchies, and so on, are social practices aimed at strengthening the idea of state as an *imagined* national community (B. Anderson 2006); plus at enhancing the legitimation of a hegemonic order (Corrigan and Sayer 1985, 6–8) through the accumulation of a certain symbolic and ideological power (in fact, Pierre Bourdieu (2015, 2) defined the state as the "monopoly of symbolic power"). The state, hence, is itself constituted by ideas and discourses and, at the same time, such discourses are articulated, amplified and diffused by "organic" intellectuals in and through the hegemonic apparatuses of the state and civil society. Moreover, and as a result, we should recognize the "cogency of the idea of state as an ideological power and treat it as a *compelling object of analysis*" (Abrams 1988, 79; emphasis added), and so *demystifying* "the state, to unmask it radically, to prove that *the state as a substantial, unitary entity does not 'always already' exist*" (Jessop 2015, 18; emphasis in the original). This implies the need to deconstruct the state (and allied discourses) as an ideological construct and to show how this is related to specific conceptions of the world, hegemonic orders, and/or processes of economic restructuring. In chapter 5, for instance, I will analyse the neoliberal construction of the state in Italy.

In light of the above discussion, we can conceive the state as a social and cultural construction provided with an intrinsic ideological power. This can be conceived as the first nature of the state—and yet, the state as a social and ideological construct clearly does not exhaust all the dimensions of the state. Along with the ideas, discourses, and symbols, the state is also made of an institutional cluster conceivable as the "state system" (Abrams 1988; Mitchell 1991, 2006), which operates in a given territory and on a population settled on that territory. The state system is composed of various branches and apparatuses that comprise its institutional cluster: public administration and bureaucracy, the government, the elected assemblies, police and armed force, secret services, the judiciary system, local governments (see Milliband 1969).[8] Between the various branches of the state there can be conflicts, contradictions, specific internal interests and overlapping functions. Drawing once again on Poulantzas (1978, 134), the internal configuration of the state can be characterized by, among others things, (i) a contradictory movement of decisions and "non-decisions" (lack of state action) derived from the intrinsic contradictions in the state; (ii) a differentiated determination of priorities within each of the branches of the state, network or level and hence in contradiction with each other (e.g., the department of education may have different interests and even worldviews with respect to the military branch or the economic ministries); (iii) a system of branches and apparatuses that filter the measures proposed by other branches and select them for practical execution (for instance, a specific segment of public administration that filters the measures adopted by the parliament for practical execution); (iv) a set of conjunctural, conflictual, and compensatory measures responding to particular periods of crises and dislocations. "The policy of the State—Poulantzas adds—is thus established through a real process of intra-state contradictions" (ibid.). In chapter 6, I zoom in on a segment of the state system (the government-parliament relation) and analyse the question of the consolidation of executive powers as key to understanding the overall neoliberal transformation of the Italian state. The final step in this chapter is to explore the relation between the state and global capitalism.

THE INTERNATIONAL DIMENSION: STATE TRANSFORMATIONS AND GLOBAL CAPITALISM

The theoretical discussion revolving around the state and its transformations needs to be expanded to include the transnational/global level, because this is necessary for understanding the transformations of the state in the neoliberal era (Saad-Filho and Johnston 2005; Harvey 2005), and thus avoid sealing the dynamics of change only to the national level. In what follows, I tackle the question of global capitalism by drawing on some strands of Gramscian IR/IPE scholarship that have sought to develop a dialectical view of the relation between the national (and *intra*national) dimension and the international (Bieler and Morton 2003, 2018; Morton 2007; Bruff 2008, 2011a; Bieler et al. 2015) without overlooking the importance of both of these. In fact, even if his analytical starting point was the national dimension, Gramsci "was a fastidious student of 'the international,' the world circumstances of hegemony, and argued that [. . .] capitalism was a world-historical phenomenon within conditions of uneven development" (Bieler and Morton 2018, 124). In more general terms, Gramsci maintained that transformations at the level of international relations are always preceded by changes in the composition of (territorialized) social relations of production, which modify "organically absolute and relative relations in the international field" (1971, 176). The territorial dimension matters because, historically, the national state form emerged (in Europe) from a *pre*-capitalist formation, that is, Western feudalism (Wood 2002, 168). Hence, industrial capitalism primarily developed within the territoriality of the national state and within its "environmental" conditions (social, political, cultural, territorial, institutional) (see Lacher 2006, 109; Morton 2007) to express thereafter a constant tendency to overcome the territorial boundaries of the state. At the same time, the uneven territorial conditions of the Italian state—that is, the division between the North and the South—led Gramsci to understand states as "the product of *inter*national relations combining with *intra*national relations. This intertwining of 'global' and 'local' developments and factors renders each 'national' state unique" (Bieler et al. 2015, 140). This will be clearer when I analyse the territorial dimension of the contemporary crisis in Italy (chapter 7).

This specified, it is now necessary to explore two further intertwined questions. The first is the question of power relations at the international level. The second is to frame the *current* phase of the transnational form of capitalism, and how this is related to the state and state transformations. In the classic scheme of Cox (1981, 1993), three main levels interact with each other so as to constitute an international hegemonic configuration: *social relations of production*, encompassing material, institutional, and discursive forms that engender particular social forces; *forms of state*, comprising specific state-society complexes, and *world orders* under the hegemony of particular states or conglomerates of states (see also Bieler and Morton 2006a, 11–12). Accordingly, not all state-society complexes have equal powers, capacities, and resources to influence other states-societies and the international system as a whole. Gramsci, for instance, developed his account of international relations from a place-specific perspective, the Italian (a case of *passive* revolution; see Morton 2007, 2010), which was historically influenced by foreign powers. Robert Cox has aptly noted that

> [a]t an ever deeper level, those states which are powerful are precisely those which have undergone a social and economic revolution and have most fully worked out the consequences of this revolution in the form of state and of social relations [. . .] These were all nation-based developments which spilled over national boundaries to become internationally expansive phenomena. Other countries have received the impact of these developments in a more passive way. (1993, 59)

State-centric international relations scholarship, especially neorealist (Waltz 1979), regards the international structure as composed by states-as-units that interact *externally* with each other and are endowed with material capacities (economy, military power) that make particular states able to influence international relations. In other words, the "default approach is to consider state, society and economy as predefined, separate entities with their own intrinsic properties. By obscuring the complex, interconnected and always-evolving character of these entities such scholarship prevents us from enquiring fully into the capitalist society or societies being studied" (Bieler et al. 2015, 148). The Gramscian perspective, by contrast, always begins with the state-society complex to understand how this influences not a generic "external" projection of the state but how specific state-society complexes change according to the development of transnational capitalist relations. Borrowing again from Cox, a "world hegemony is thus in its beginnings an outward expansion of the internal (national) hegemony established by a dominant social class. The economic and social institutions, the culture, the technology associated with this national hegemony become patterns for emulation abroad" (1993, 61; Bieler and Morton 2006a). Thus, Cox's conceptualization of hegemony has allowed us "to broaden the domain of hegemony from merely coercive dominance to encompass systems of power shaped by different patterns of production relations and the ideas and institutions which permeate international relations as well," while at the same time "it also enabled [. . .] to discuss the changing nature of US hegemony after the 1970s, where a globalizing world economy shifted the centers of power toward transnational corporations, global finance and international institutions without challenging an American leadership which had evolved to promote and thus guide these developments" (Bieler et al. 2015, 138–139).

The question, now, is to understand more closely the relation between the national dimension and the international within a specific phase of the history of capitalism: neoliberal globalization. Globalization, in brief, represents a new phase in the history of capitalism expressed in particular through a transnational integration of productive structures (e.g., the dramatic increase in FDI) across a range of developed and developing countries (Bieler and Morton 2018, 116) and, at the same time, of international financial integration, which has significantly empowered international finance and financial corporations (Cozzolino 2019b). Furthermore, the transnationalization of capital relations led to a "double movement" of centralization of control over the production process (for instance, in the form of interlocking directorates of multinational corporations) on the one hand, and spatial decentralization and fragmentation of production on the other (Bieler and Morton 2018, 116–117; see also Robinson 2004). The transnationalization of capital always interacts with previous *historical* national social formations and territorial conditions, hence producing forms of uneven and combined development as a result of "specific class struggles within forms of state through which the restructuring of capital and socio-spatial relations are produced" (Bieler and Morton 2018, 119) and reproduced. Andreas Bieler and Adam Morton, by drawing on Cox (1981), Poulantzas (1974) and Gramsci's theory of integral state, have coupled the concepts of *internationalization* and *internalization* to frame the relation between transnational capitalism and the national state level (2006a, 2006b, 2006c, 2018; see also Bruff 2008, 65–70). "In short, capital is not simply represented as an autonomous force beyond the power of the state but is embodied by classes or fractions of classes *within* the very constitution of the state. There are contradictory and heterogeneous relations internal to the state" (Bieler and Morton 2018, 127; emphasis added).

For this reason, the movement towards the transnationalization of production networks implies a parallel "*internalization*" process in terms of changes in the social relations of production. The relation between the transnational and the national does not belong to the order of necessity but, as already noted, is *dialectical* and bears important political consequences. Therefore, from a neo-Gramscian perspective, we can hold that (i) the transnationalization of production always begins within the boundaries of the state according to a number of intertwined conditions (production relations, technology, military complex, political system, ideology, etc.), in turn bounded with international factors; (ii) the development and/or impact of transnationalization always interacts with the overall conditions located in the territory of the state (hence determining the multi-scalar nature of capitalism), so that at stake there is a dialectical movement going from the national to the transnational and back; (iii) the state field, relatively autonomous from class and class fractions (see below), mediates not only between these at domestic level but also between the transnational and national dimension because "class struggle does not take place only between capital and labour at the national level but also between national and transnational class fractions" (ibid., 116). In relation to this last point, is worth remarking that transformations of the state are not an automatic/necessary outcome of transnationalization/globalization. At stake is always a relation between the structural changes in—national and transnational—production *and* the situated sociopolitical agency in (and outside) the state system, thus in light of multiple spatial and temporal dialectics. As Gramsci reminds us, "particular histories always exist within the frame of world history" (1971, 240).

CONCLUSION: TRANSFORMATIONS *OF* THE STATE, TRANSFORMATIONS *IN* THE STATE

This chapter aimed to develop a theory of the state and of state transformations. The political intervention of the state is ever-present in the constitution and reproduction of the social relations of production. Thus, between civil society and the state there is a dialectical relation of unity *and* distinction. While the dimension of unity points (ultimately) to the social constitution of the state, the distinction implies especially the relative autonomy of the state as a peculiar terrain of political, ideological and institutional action and mediation.

In the remaining chapters, I dovetail the question of the transformations of the Italian state by adopting a historical perspective (chapter 4) and thus looking into the "concrete terrain of history," as Gramsci put it. This is important to find some of the long- and middle-term "commonsensical" sedimentations (Bruff 2008) that can help us to explain the Italian neoliberal transition. Then, in chapters 5 and 6, I provide a comprehensive analysis of the transformations of the Italian state. I look at the transformations *of* the state and transformations *in* the state. As noted in the Introduction, the transformations *of* the state revolve around the fundamental redefinition of the idea of state within the rise and historical unfolding of the neoliberal paradigm. On the other hand, the transformations *in* the state revolve around the changes in the state system. I analyse in particular the processes of concentration of power in the state in the form of executive strengthening. By looking at the transformations *of* and *in* the state, the book provides for a distinctive framework for the analysis of the state, Italian or otherwise. In chapter 7, finally, I return to the contemporary Italian political and institutional context and its manifold crises, while chapter 8 reflects on the organic crisis of the neoliberal order.

Chapter 4

A Difficult Republic

Italy from the "Economic Miracle" to the Neoliberal Order

This chapter deals with the social and political history of the Italian Republic from 1946 to the transition to the Second Republic in the 1990s, thus setting the scene for the following chapters, which analyse more specific aspects of state transformations. In general terms, the history of the Italian Republic represents an extraordinary case of state transformations in the neoliberal era. For instance, Italy in the initial post-war period can be conceived as an earlier form of neoliberalism, in the sense that the "economic miracle" was possible (among other factors) due to low wages and to the overexploitation of the abundant labour force that emigrated from the South of Italy to the factories of the North. Importantly, the transition towards what is conventionally called the "Keynesian compromise" occurred via an unprecedented process of mobilization by the working classes that lasted for twenty years, from the early 1960s to the early 1980s. Thus, in Italy, the post-war compromise between capital and labour would be best described as a "conflictual Keynesianism," in which labour conflicts led salaries to grow and new labour rights to be achieved. The third element of great interest is the reaction to conflictual Keynesianism since the 1980s. As I show in this and in later chapters, the mobilization of state apparatuses proved to be a critical factor that accompanied the processes of neoliberalization and permanent austerity. In particular, the Bank of Italy (BI) proved in many respects to be a fundamental player in the transition, thanks to its technocratic expertise and legitimation, in tandem with a parallel process of centralization of decision-making power in the state (more below). Such processes are key elements in the transition from the First to the Second Republic in the early 1990s.

The analysis tries to pay equal attention to social forces and political agency, as well as to production relations and ideas, identities, collective memory, and ideology. At the same time, I read contemporary Italian history in constant dialogue with international and supranational/European factors. As Marx (1993, 408) reminds us in the *Grundrisse*, "the tendency to create the world market is directly given in the concept of capital itself." As we shall see, the Italian capitalist system was immediately inserted, in the post-war era, into European and (to a lesser extent) international markets; contextually, the Peninsula entered into the U.S. sphere of influence. The chapter begins with a long-term perspective and frames the fragile bases of the Italian state. At the same time, the chapter adopts also a medium-term perspective by taking into account the post-war period. This will help to put the neoliberal response (especially through the state) in its context and in light of the social conflicts that characterized the country in the 1960s and 1970s. In the conclusion to this chapter, I provide for an alternative interpretation of the Italian transition in the 1980s and 1990s, and of the European integration of the Peninsula as a process of normalization through the disciplinary force of markets and austerity.

A STATE WITH CLAY FEET: A *LONGUE DURÉE* VIEW OF ITALIAN HISTORY AND COLLECTIVE IDENTITY

The fragile bases of Italian identity and its problematic—yet fascinating—history have ancient roots. As noted by Andrea Giardina (1997, 35), the main reason why Italian identity has remained largely undefined can be dated to the days of the Roman Empire. The process of formation of a sort of prototypical "national" Italian identity did not reach a sufficient level of territorial cohesion *before* the constitution of the Roman imperial system. The "governance" system of the Roman Empire was, in fact, characterized by a flexible system of social, cultural, and ethnic integration, where local customs and worships were not only allowed but, above all, assimilated into Rome's customs and institutions. Thus, a mix of universalistic and cosmopolitan aims intertwined with a "spurious assimilation" of local sub-systems constituted the texture of the Empire of Rome from the shores of North Africa to Spain, from Western Europe to the Middle East. This intrinsically fragmented constitution of the Italian Peninsula was enhanced by the impact of the long crisis and fall of the Western Roman Empire in the fifth century, mostly under the Lombard and Byzantine influence spanning both the North and the South, and thus preventing a process of national and territorial unification.

The precarious balance of power between the Sacred Roman Empire (successor to the Western Roman Empire) and the pope furthered the fragmentation of Italian territory and led, between the ninth and fifteenth centuries, to the formation of several city-states, the so-called *Signorie*. While the papacy resisted any project of territorial unification (P. Anderson 1974, 143) to exert a greater control over the divided and perpetually conflicting territorial political units, the historical period known as *Rinascimento* (from fourteenth to XVI century) represented a moment of development of the arts, trade, finance and "proto-state" forms. Particularly the northern city-states of Florence, Venice, Genoa, and Milan can be conceived as prototypes of capitalist states which gave rise to an interstate system of trade and finance (see in particular Arrighi 1994, 37–41). On the other hand, the South and Sicily were governed by an interweaving combination of Mediterranean and North European civilizations (Langobardic, Byzantines, Arabs, French, Spanish, etc.) based on strong centralization of government and a feudal system, which remained largely so even after Italian unification in 1861 (Barbagallo 2002). However, the crisis of *Rinascimento* triggered a period of decline of the Peninsula and of its urban civilization over several centuries (Chabod 1967). The dynamism of merchant-bankers turned into a rentier-like system (Barbagallo 2002, 41), and the Counter-Reformation, a de facto regressive response to the rise and spread of Protestantism in Northern Europe, favoured "the weakening of the principle of individual and collective responsibility" (Barbagallo 2002, 41) while strengthening the control of the papacy over the public and cultural life of the Peninsula.

Crucially, from the Lombard invasions in 568 to 1860 Italy was an aggregation of many different territorial units. Moreover, Italian national unification was not only a late unification (compared to France, Spain, or the UK), which indeed occurred only in 1861, but also a case of *institutional engineering from above* with very little grassroots, nation-wide mobilization. In fact, "it is possible to speak of a multinational character of Italian pre-unitary history, and also of a strongly regional dimension of its socio-political history" (ibid.). In other words, unification occurred in the absence of *national* social forces. Gramsci's famous interpretation of Italian unification in this respect, that it was a *passive revolution*, highlighted that it was a compromise between northern industrialists and southern landowners within the continuity of monarchic political structures. Italy therefore lacked a proper *autonomous* national revolutionary class such as the bourgeoisie (as in the French case). In fact, the Italian bourgeoisie did not manage to overcome the economic-corporative phase to acquire a *political* identity and role, and therefore did not "create an autonomous State" (1975, 658; Q5§127; Martin 2015). Gramsci also noted that Italian "cosmopolitanism" (found especially among intellectuals and deriving from the lack of *national* cohesion) coexisted with a "frenetic chauvinism"—clearly, he had fascism in mind—which idealistically, and fancifully, linked itself to the legacy of the Roman Empire. Only the memory of the war of national liberation from Nazism and fascism and the strengthening of mass parties after World War II actually encouraged the birth of a national identity. The anti-fascist pact, however, proved to be precarious and short-lived. In the last decades in particular, territorial divisions and centrifugal/authoritarian forces have emerged again, putting at stake the social and national cohesion and the democratic form of the Italian state.

THE BIRTH OF THE REPUBLIC, THE INTERNATIONAL, AND THE DOMESTIC POLITICAL ECONOMY

The collapse of the fascist regime (1943) and the following anti-fascist war of national liberation (1943–1945) led to the establishment of a liberal-democratic Republic (1946) and to the enactment of the Constitution (1948), which sanctioned the principle of popular sovereignty in the very first article. To mark the rupture with the fascist regime, the new Republic was centred on parties and party system, and on a sort of constitutionalized network of mutual guarantees between different political forces (Sartori 1982). At the time of the Constituent Assembly (1946–1948), parties could be grouped into three main political cultures: socialist-communist, liberal, and catholic (Farnetti 1976, 65; Giovagnoli 2019). The institutional and political structure of the new state was based on a polycentric framework characterized by the centrality of the legislative assemblies (Cotta 1987); it was also further strengthened thanks to the proportional electoral system that aimed to guarantee a broad sociopolitical representation within the parliament (Barbagallo 2002, 119). Accordingly, the legislative assemblies, during the First Republic (1946–1993), gained a structural function of negotiation by fostering the establishment of consensus, mediation, and integration of conflicting socio-economic and political instances (Sartori 1963; De Micheli 2016). Such relevant changes, however, should not downplay the continuities between fascism and the Republic within the structures of the state. The transition was, in fact, marked by continuity in the bureaucratic apparatuses and state police, while the civil and criminal codes were maintained with only a few changes. At the social level, "the restoration of traditional hierarchies within corporate property (from factories to newspapers) emblematically confirmed, after 1945, the capacity of powerful groups that emerged during the years of Fascism to preserve themselves [in the new regime]" (Castronovo 1976, 5).

In general terms, the post-war order after 1948 was both influenced and structurally characterized by three key interrelated elements, respectively concerning the international dimension, national political and social relations, and political economy developments.

The first element to take into account concerns the domestic effects of the Cold War, which divided Italian society and its political system along the lines of the international fracture between liberal capitalism and the Soviet regime (Di Nolfo 2016). Immediately after World War II, Italy entered into the sphere of influence of the United States. This implied, first of all, the liberalization of trade and the primacy of private property relations. In 1946, Italy adhered (seven years before Germany and Japan) to Bretton Woods arrangements (liberalization of trade, market integration, fixed exchange rates), while the Marshall Plan—an array of financial aids aimed at favouring post-war reconstruction and economic recovery, especially in the 1948–1952 years—sought to foster Italy's insertion into Western and especially European markets through a swift reconstruction of the industrial system (Ginsborg 1990, 157–160; Crescenzi and Dente 2007, 10). Membership in the NATO military alliance (1949), in the European Organization for Economic Cooperation (1948), and, in 1951, in the European Coal and Steel Community were emblematic of this shift (for a detailed and critical account of post-war Western hegemony, see van der Pijl 2012, 138–166).

Hence, national configurations and processes were strongly influenced by international dynamics. "After 1948"—Giovagnoli writes—"the conflict between communism and anti-communism largely shaped, in Italy, not only the political dynamics but also the social, economic and cultural life" (2016, 35). The main national political effect of the international post-war division was (up until the crisis of the First Republic in the early 1990s) the exclusion of the main workers' party—the Italian Communist Party (PCI)—from the government by means of "political engineering." Indeed, the Christian Democratic Party (DC) remained in power for forty-nine years, through a network of shifting coalitions with a number of orbiting parties from both the left and the liberal/conservative right. For forty-three years the Italian prime minister was a DC member (Ginsborg 1990, especially ch. 5; see also Sartori 1982; La Palombara 1987). However, it is also worth noting that, *given the centrality of parliament as a chamber of negotiation and political mediation*, the PCI was regularly involved in the decision-making and legislative processes, especially during the 1970s (see De Micheli 2016).

The post-war historical bloc, the political pivot of which was the DC, comprised ideological elements and a strong inter-class aptitude. Ideologically, rather than a proper liberal ideology the bloc relied on a combination of anti-communism and "collateral confessionalism" (Castronovo 1976, 8). The Italian capitalist class, on the other hand, did not exercise an autonomous intellectual and ideological function. "Bourgeois liberal ideology"—as Grant Amyot maintains—"was a poor third to Catholicism and Marxism in terms of mass influence [. . .] Therefore, the DC had to perform the function of legitimating the state and its policies" (2004, 19; see also Martin 2015). With respect to social forces, the DC managed to represent a heterogeneous array of social groups: some sectors of public employment, white-collar middle-class (lawyers, doctors), commercial bourgeoisie, landowners. However, the main social supporters of the DC were large private industry and, especially during the 1970s, the "state bourgeoisie" (Castronovo 2013, 350); that is, the management layers of the public industrial sector. While solidarity (*solidarismo*), the duty to protect the family and a generally inter-classist aptitude, "officially" characterized the DC worldview, on the other hand, as noted by Paul Ginsborg (1990, 153–154), "the liberty of the individual and of the firm, the unfettered development of technology and consumer capitalism, the free play of market forces" were espoused by the majority of the party.

An "Early Neoliberal" Post-War Model and the "Economic Miracle"

World War II caused heavy damage to the Italian productive structure and infrastructure, which was coupled with rampant inflation, indebtedness, rising poverty, and unemployment. While political relations soon stabilized around the DC with the parallel marginalization of communists and socialists, the first years of the Republic were dominated by an "early neoliberal" growth model (Zamagni 1993; Crescenzi and Dente 2007, 17), which prevailed over the left alternative based on economic planning and nationalization of big industries (Castronovo 2013, 267–269; Graziani 1998). Most importantly, neoliberal technocrats, mainly coming from academic positions, played an important role in providing the necessary expertise and authority during the years of the reconstruction—just like this "collective intellectual" did in the 1980s and 1990s (more below). Laissez-faire theories, in fact, after a period of marginalization under fascism and corporative arrangements, gained momentum from the second half of the 1940s and throughout the 1950s (Vicarelli 1981, 19–25; Masini 2019) thanks to personalities such as Luigi Einaudi (Budget minister and then governor of the BI) and Gustavo Del Vecchio (Treasury minister). Thus, soon after the war, the BI opted for a policy mix of cuts in public spending, a credit squeeze, and fiscal consolidation (Crescenzi and Dente 2007, 18) to tackle inflation, in so doing diverting the cash flow from the public to the private sector (Graziani 1998, 40). If the credit crunch managed to reduce inflation and stabilize the Lira (Fratianni and Spinelli 1997, 171–175), on the other hand, it also produced several years of economic depression (notwithstanding the impact of the Marshall Plan, which in fact provoked the concerns of the U.S. officials), stagnant internal demand, and rising unemployment. In the meantime, in 1953, the abolition of tariffs favoured the complete liberalization of trade (raw materials, industrial and agricultural products, semi-finished products).

The years after the war, however, are conventionally known as the "economic miracle." This term means a phase of unprecedented growth of wealth, industrial production, and productivity especially between 1958 and 1963, and is usually associated to the industrial modernization of the country. The level of industrial investments in manufacturing industry grew from 4.5 percent in the mid-1950s to 6.3 percent in 1963 (Castronovo 2013, 305), while the average annual growth of domestic product was around 6.3 percent (Ginsborg 1990, 214). Exports played a major role in this phase of capital accumulation, increasing between 1959 and 1963 by 16.1 percent every year (Castronovo 2013, 301–302; Graziani 1998, 59), and especially the share destined to the European markets that improved from 23 percent in 1955 to 29.8 in 1965 (Ginsborg 1990, 214). And yet, the main—usually hidden—element of the miracle was labour. In fact, the dominance of the "liberal orthodoxy" (Crescenzi and Dente 2007, 19) in the initial post-war years should lead us to rethink the narrative of the "miracle." First of all, the industrial boom and rapid capital accumulation was actually possible thanks to low real salaries, strict discipline and control of workers at the firm level (especially trade union members), and the weakness of union action due to internal divisions. As a consequence, the increase of the salary level between 1953 and 1961 amounted to 46.9 percent, while the average rate of increase in productivity was 84 percent (Castronovo 2013, 302), thus determining "an increasing volume of profits and a redistribution of income towards corporations and at the expense of workers" (Graziani 1998, 68) and their working conditions (Foa 1976, 255). At the same time, industrialization occurred mainly in the North of the country (the "triangle" of Genoa, Turin, and Milan) and thanks to mass emigration from the South, which provided for a cheap and abundant workforce. Between 1951 and 1976, four million people left southern regions for northern Italy and elsewhere in Europe (Barbagallo 2002, 73), thus reproducing in new forms the endemic territorial division of Italian society.

THE *GOLDEN HORDE*[1]: CLASS STRUGGLES, INSTITUTIONAL AGENCY, AND THE POLITICAL SYSTEM FROM THE 1960S TO THE 1980S

The Cycle of Class Struggles in Italy: Characteristics and Sociopolitical Effects

While the 1950s can be considered a phase of *relative* pacification, from 1960 social and political conflict erupted, henceforth deeply marking—and changing—the Italian society for the following decades. The year 1960 is particularly crucial. In June, an anti-fascist mass protest took place in Genoa against the national congress announced by the Italian Social Movement (MSI), a neo-fascist organization. The main Italian trade union, the CGIL, proclaimed a general strike, which gained massive support and brought fresh political cohesion to the working class (Foa 1976, 259–267), something which was enhanced by conditions of near-full employment (the unemployment rate was around 2 percent). The first wave of strikes occurred between 1960 and 1963, when the number of industrial conflicts tripled compared to the previous period and the lost working hours increased by three and a half times (Graziani 1998, 83). This cycle of workers' struggles had an immediate impact on income distribution by "overturning a seemingly established tendency just in favour of profits" (ibid.) and of capital accumulation (also Bellofiore 2001, 91). The level of real salaries from 1957 to 1970 doubled (Sylos Labyni 1974, 186), and squeezed profits.

While the intensity of conflict and politicization of the working class after 1963 remained high, the second massive wave of struggles took place between 1968 and 1969, "the second *Biennio Rosso*" (Trentin and Liguori 1999), and lasted until 1973 (Davanzati et al. 2019). The lost hours in manufacturing industries grew to more than 200 million (Graziani 1998, 90). Also, the grassroots struggles of the working class increasingly acquired a broader and stronger ideological, political, and cultural fabric (Farneti 1976, 88). The class struggles in Italy both anticipated and outlasted those of other countries due to the peculiarity of the Italian case. In fact, the country's industrial relations system was not inserted into a structured framework of negotiation; at the same time, this condition was paralleled by the already-mentioned permanent exclusion of the working class' party from the government, hence blocking more "institutional" channels of political bargaining. This occurrence partly explains the strong extra-parliamentary nature of the conflict and its radicalization, and the decisive "from-the-outside" pressures on parliamentary forces for social reforms.[2]

In terms of governing coalitions, the wave of struggles in the early 1960s favoured the formation of the first centre-left government in Italy (1962), composed by the left-wing branch of the DC with the support of the Italian Socialist Party (PSI), at a time when Keynesian theory gained momentum among domestic policymakers (Ginsborg 1990, 258–260, 267–268). With respect to policymaking, in 1963 the electricity production industry (ENEL) was nationalized, while a coupon tax on dividends was introduced. Furthermore, the government created the *national commission for economic planning* and launched the first five-year National Economic Programme (1966–1970), with the aim to govern the economic cycle through an array of new policy instruments and public interventions/investments in schools, health, housing, social security, professional training, and transportation. Many are the documents enacted in these years,[3] and the public commissions created for macroeconomic planning purposes.[4] While a numerous planning interventions were not actually implemented, the analysis of planning efforts and models is useful for understanding the political environment of the time—and the role of public interventions—before the market-oriented turn in the 1980s.

Clearly, working-class agency provoked fierce reactions from other social and institutional actors, prominently big industry and the BI. In fact, especially large industries developed several strategies to tackle the intensification of struggles in the 1960s. First of all, the tax on stock dividends provoked a flight of capital abroad due to the weak control exerted by domestic institutions (Graziani 1998, 88). The second answer to social conflicts occurred through the increase in price levels (Balducci and Marconi 1981, 84). The third and main action taken by industries to confront workers' struggles was the restructuring of production process through (i) increases in working hours, (ii) resorts to overtime, (iii) a greater focus on individual incentives. This managed to improve productivity and, at the same time, reduce employment (Graziani 1998, 89). In fact, hourly productivity in the manufacturing industry had grown at an annual rate of 6.4 percent over the five years since 1963, while investment had fallen sharply. Meanwhile, industrial production had increased by 58 percent overall between 1961 and 1966, compared with employment growth of just over 1.5 percent (Castronovo 2013, 355). That is, a case of "capital accumulation without investments," as Riccardo Bellofiore put it (2001, 86). This strategy of productive restructuring even intensified after 1969, with the decentralization of segments of production outside of the main industrial plants to reduce labour costs through subcontracts, piecework, and greater flexibility. Importantly, this strategy managed to fragment and weaken unions (Foa 1976, 275), favouring also the formation of small and medium enterprises (Graziani 1998, 95; more below).

The BI played a very important role in this period. The role of the Bank is particularly interesting because, as we shall see in greater detail below, it proved to be at the forefront of monetarist and neoliberal restructuring since the 1980s, often supplying—in terms of political legitimation and authority, but also of "personnel" in key government positions—to national parties on various occasions (Quaglia 2005; I shall go in greater detail below). In the specific events of the 1960s, the BI implemented a mix of deflationary and expansionary monetary policy every time the salary dynamic would potentially harm capital accumulation and the competitiveness of the industrial system. In 1963–1964, Guido Carli (governor of the BI, later appointed president of Confindustria, namely the employers' association, in 1975 and minister of the Treasury between 1989 and 1992) opted for a harsh credit crunch by cutting off the monetary base. As Fratianni and Spinelli report (1997, 209), "the monetary base decelerated by a ratio of five to one before and after September 1963 [. . .] Industrial output had four consecutive quarters of negative growth [. . .] Inflation slowed from 7.8 percent in the third quarter of 1963 to 5.8 in the last quarter of 1964." The deflationary policy led to a reduction of investments and, for the first time in the post-war era, a crisis after twelve years of ongoing expansion, along with a fall in the employment rate. As some noted

(Balducci and Marconi 1981, 90; Nardozzi 1981, 115–116), the bank aimed to revamp the export-led and low-wage model of post-war era; above all, it fostered its own vision of income distribution by entering into the distributive conflict (see also Paggi and D'Angelillo 1986, 62–63). The agency of the BI, as Graziani remarks, "seemed to be aimed at expanding the depression instead of having it stopped" (1998, 87). Incidentally, this would confirm Kalecki's thesis (*Political Aspects of Full Employment*, 1990) that the capitalist class as a whole prefers, for the sake of its own preservation, a short-term profit squeeze and (at least a temporary) economic depression to full employment, a condition that greatly improves workers' contractual—and therefore political—force.

From 1970s Upheaval to 1980s Restoration

Struggles and conflicts erupted in the 1960s continued throughout the 1970s, increasing the sclerosis of the Italian political system. On the one hand, conflicts and contestations expanded to new segments of society: urban proletariat (the key social actor of the protests of 1977), students, women's and feminist movements, school teachers (see Ginsborg 1990, 358–370). On the other hand, by the mid-1970s a parallel process of *normalization* of unions and of the PCI through the discourse of "national solidarity" had taken place. Crucially, while the tensions of the 1960s occurred in a phase of expanding international markets, in the 1970s intra-capitalist conflicts increased (Bellofore 2001, 97). The first oil shock in 1973 (the second occurring in 1979), the Nixon's administration decision to suspend the convertibility of dollar to gold (1971), the new system of free-floating interest and exchange rates, the rise of new industrial powers such as West Germany and Japan (later followed by Eastern powers such as Hong Kong, Taiwan, Singapore) were some of the main factors that changed the post-war geography of global capitalism, constituting the premises of the era of global finance as it evolved in the following decades.

The deterioration of the international context prompted a tightening of the external constraint on the Italian productive system, which was heavily dependent on foreign markets. Faced with increasing global competitive pressures, the president of Confindustria (and of FIAT industries) Giovanni Agnelli proposed an "alliance of producers" to the unions, calling for a common struggle between industrial capital and labour against parasitic elements of national economy, such as large parts of the state bureaucracy plus state-owned enterprises (Amyot 2004, 24). Thus, in 1975, Confindustria and the unions achieved an agreement, the so-called *scala mobile*, regarding the complete indexation of salaries to inflation, which actually started to rise from the early 1970s due to international factors (oil shocks, prominently) and internal devaluations of the currency. In return, unions agreed to a policy of moderation in the name of national responsibility in times of "economic emergency" (especially due to the worsening of the balance of payments).

In the meantime the PCI, after several victories in the local elections in the mid-1970s, granted its external support to the DC government, allowing the party to form an executive (with the PSI) of "national solidarity" in 1977. "Austerity, collective values and cooperation" (Ginsborg 1990, 356) were the keywords through which the PCI became keen to show its *responsibility* vis-à-vis the country and international actors. "Austerity"—Ginsborg adds—"became the antechamber of salvation. Berlinguer [the leader of the PCI] called on the working people of Italy to make sacrifices, and he promised them that it would be not in vain" (ibid.). The "national solidarity" experiment, however, was short-lived. Italian accession to the European Monetary System in 1979 was immediately opposed by the PCI and, already in 1979, industrialists started in their turn to oppose the *scala mobile*, in a context characterized by an upsurge of political violence by both the extreme left and the extreme right. The second half of the 1970s was the swansong of the rising cycle of working-class struggles and, accordingly, the beginning of a process of the downsizing of unions and of grassroots mobilization. The historians Paggi and D'Angelillo aptly noted that the political insertion (and normalization) of the communists into government corresponded with a socioeconomic penalization of the PCI's electoral base (1986, 60), a scheme that was reproduced by the centre-left governments in the 1990s and beyond (chapter 5).

If the cycle of class struggles was catalysed by a specific event—the anti-fascist protest against the Tambroni government in 1960—exactly twenty years later another strike marked symbolically the beginning of a new epoch. In 1980, a confrontation between unions and industrial capital took place at FIAT. Workers went on strike but, in this case, the answer came not from the top management of the enterprise but from white-collar workers, who marched to ask for the strike to end (the so-called "rally of the forty thousand"). "FIAT's victory of October 1980"—as Ginsborg writes—"had been a watershed of national significance. The balance of power between capital and labour had swung back decisively to the employers" (1990, 407). Soon afterwards, the political economy model, due to changes in social power relations and in production, started to shift to more (neoliberal) orthodox avenues. Wages were *the* target. This cycle of industrial restructuring (1981–1985), also due to the non-accommodating monetary policy enacted by the BI, was mainly geared towards squeezing the salary level (Simonazzi 1999, 76) to increase the country's competitiveness, while others have also emphasized the beginning of the financialization of Italian firms during these years (Davanzati et al. 2019). Most importantly, between 1983 and 1984, the

Italian government fostered wage moderation by revising the *scala mobile* indexation mechanism. Internal divisions between unions, on the other hand, led to a split between the CGIL, which opposed the wage moderation policy, and the more moderate unions CISL and UIL, thus weakening the overall industrial action capacity (Accornero 1992, 151). Moreover, the strengthening of the tertiary sector and the growth of industrial restructuring saw a decline in the number of industrial workers, which decreased by 4 percent between 1980 and 1985, gradually depriving the unions of its most militant base. Actually, by 1988, the hours lost to industrial action decreased from 50 million (1979) to 8 million (Castronovo 2013, 382). The reduction of the strength of blue-collar workers and the emergence of autonomous workers, professionals, financiers, and managers (Simonazzi 1999, 71) favoured the spread of the "new spirit of capitalism" (Boltanski and Chiapello 2005) and its emphasis on competitiveness, self-entrepreneurship, profit-orientation, and enterprise culture.

THE ROOTS OF CHANGE: POLITICAL ECONOMY AND STATE TRANSFORMATIONS IN THE 1980S

The BI and the Growth of Public Debt

The above changes should be seen as directly related to the patterns of transformations *in* the state which emerged during the 1980s. Generally, the state is a terrain of political agency, but such terrain is *uneven*. While, in fact, some segments of the apparatus of the state are more exposed to societal pressures and conflicts (think of parliamentary forces), others, particularly technocratic institutions, such as central banks, retain a greater space for autonomous action. In Italy (and elsewhere), the 1980s should be understood as the roots of the changes consolidated during the 1990s. In my analysis, I place particular emphasis on the BI and its function as a "technocratic collective intellectual," namely a group which played a fundamental role in Italian neoliberalization. Indeed, it provided for neoliberal expertise to guide the process of capitalist restructuring and the legitimation of such a process thanks to the "symbolic capital" (in Bourdieu's words) of technocratic expertise. Also, "[t]he appointment of men [*sic*] from universities and the Bank of Italy to decision-making positions within the executive was accompanied by a strengthening of the technical staff of the ministers" (Fabbrini and Donà 2003, 37). Comprehending the agency of key bank members is particularly important for understanding the concrete internal functioning of the state and, more specifically, the characteristics of the political economy changes in Italy.

A study by Lucia Quaglia (2005) is especially worth mentioning in this respect. Quaglia notes, first of all, that the research department of the BI (*Servizio Studi*) had a "near monopoly of specialized economic knowledge" for "it has been by far the most important think thank and research center in the economic field in Italy" (2005, 549). At the same time, Quaglia reports that the bank's top personnel were trained in U.S. and UK universities (especially at PhD level), thus developing key *transnational* linkages as a "technocratic collective intellectual." "The monopoly of expertise"—Quaglia adds—"and the reputation of the Bank were such that foreign authorities and international organizations often regarded this institution as their best or only resource in Italy for economic data and analysis of economic policy" (ibid., 550). Moreover, "the Bank has been very keen to promote its image of a *professional* and *depoliticized bureaucracy*" (ibid.). Given this framework, the early 1980s saw tremendous changes in the Italian "monetary constitution." Prior to the separation in 1981 of the Treasury and BI (more on this below), the Bank used to purchase all the Treasury bonds that were not subscribed by private investors (i.e., a process of monetary base creation). The Treasury could rely on a permanent credit account towards the Bank of 14 percent of budgetary expenditures, so that "[w]hen the Bank bought bonds, it was in essence financing a part of the government deficit by printing money" (Amyot 2004, 130). In 1981, the "divorce" between the BI and the Treasury[5] produced a sea change in the monetary policy regime. As the former governor of the European Central Bank Mario Draghi remarked, the new *political* objectives of the regime change were: (i) pursuing the independence of monetary regulation from political authorities; (ii) the harmonization of public spending with the target of balanced budget; (iii) keeping wages in line with low inflation and price stability (2011, 35–36). In political economy terms, there were two consequences. The first was the aforementioned strengthening of a *non-accommodating* policy towards wage earners—indirectly confirming that, as aptly noted by Alfredo Saad-Filho, monetary regimes

> are irreducibly political. They do not simply offer alternative approaches to macroeconomic management; policy regimes also discipline nation states and social actors in different ways. For example, they constrain the choice of economic policy priorities and the use of available policy tools, influence inter-capitalist relations within and between countries, and limit the demands of the working class. (Saad-Filho 2010, 89)

Second, the "divorce" had a paramount influence on the evolution of public debt. Once the expansion of the monetary base and the increase of taxation levels had exhausted themselves as policy options, the Treasury resorted to private investors to finance budgetary deficits, which grew during the 1970s due to the expenditures in areas such as pensions, health and social insurance but were not matched by a corresponding rise of revenues. The resort to financial markets to finance the budgetary deficit led to the rise of interest rates, and therefore increased the *cost* of debt. Consider, for instance, that the debt-GDP ratio from 1970 to 1980 rose from 34.2 percent to 54.8 (20.6 percentage points), while from 1981 to 1991 the ratio skyrocketed from 57.7 percent to 101.9 percent (44.2 percentage points) (Amyot 2004, 145), notwithstanding the fact that already by mid-1980s the growth of the budget deficit was actually halted (Palombarini 2002, 62). Thus, "already from the early 1980s, most of the public debt was due to the accumulation of passive interests, while current government deficit was quickly decreasing" (Graziani 1998, 176; Cozzolino 2020, 2019b). At the same time and crucially, the influence (and expectations) of financial creditors dramatically constrained the national political economy, with *systemic* and *structural* consequences that I analyse in the next chapter.

Pentapartito, Reverse Distribution and the Centralization of Budgetary Procedures

One of the main arguments of this book is that neoliberal transformations of the state entail a process of *concentration* of power especially in "decision-making" institutions and, accordingly, a gradual but steady insulation from democratic processes. The case of budget procedures and the unification of economic ministries is another important element in this process. But before tackling this, let us first dwell on the question of public finance, reverse distribution and the so-called *pentapartito*. *Pentapartito* means the political alliance between the DC and the PSI[6] (plus several other minor parties such as the Republican Party) in the government from 1981 to 1991, a period of great distress for Italian public finance. On the one hand, expenditures grew due to the social reforms in the mid-1970s (particularly health and pensions) and also because of the 1970s international economic crises. On the other, new expenditures accompanied the processes of restructuring of enterprises, for example, fiscalization of social security, redundancy funds, early retirements. As aptly noted by Simonazzi, "the new costs linked to the management of conflict added up to the old interests linked to the management of consensus" (Simonazzi 1999, 76). The "consensus machine" of *pentapartito* actually worsened the stability of public finances in the 1980s (Palombarini 2002). As this political alliance did not want to raise taxes on wealthier households for redistributive purposes and thus to cover the increasing government deficit, it preferred to finance the expenditures by borrowing from financial markets, this also being a way to foster the deeper international financial integration of the Italian economy. Thus, once again, the *real* determinants of Italian high debt were not public spending for welfare provisions but the accumulation of passive interests—a dangerous method for crafting political consensus. In fact, while especially upper classes in the North benefited from high interest rates, the real costs of debt were (and are) paid by taxpayers, especially through indirect taxation: a case of "reverse distribution," since this mechanism implies a redistributive pattern from lower to upper incomes (Simonazzi 1999, 76; Barba 2011).

The cumbersome public debt, passive interests, and unbalanced public finance showed their negative effects towards the end of the decade in terms of a decline of competitiveness for both small and medium enterprises and large firms (Palombarini 2002, 81–85). The decline of investment, which fell from 24.5 percent in 1980 to 19.7 percent in 1987 (Ferrera and Gualmini 2004, 61), was an important aspect of the problem. On the other hand, the state of the public finances led to the perceived necessity to begin a permanent process of fiscal adjustment—which, incidentally, would dominate Italian politics and political economy from the early 1990s to the present (see the next chapter). Such adjustment followed a process of reconfiguration/centralization of budgetary procedures and ended up strengthening further the "core" executive. Particularly from the mid-1980s,[7] budget decisions gradually started to fall into the domain of executive powers and economic ministries, with a parallel marginalization of parliament. The main innovation of the budgetary procedure was launched in 1986 with the introduction of the *Documento di Programmazione Economico Finanziaria* (DPEF—Economic and Financial Planning Document), through which the executive and the economic ministries strengthened their control over the cycle of financial planning/public spending and the implementation of budget and fiscal policy (for an overview of all the changes related to budget procedures see Ferrera and Gualmini 2004, 61–65). The centralization of macroeconomic decision-making found another decisive moment with the creation of what Lucia Quaglia has called the "super-ministry for the economy" (2007, 139). Before the organizational changes that occurred in the 1990s, Italy had three economic ministries: (a) Treasury, (b) Budget and Economic Planning, and (c) Finance, plus a number of planning committees[8]. In 1997, the ministries of Budget and Treasury were merged into one body, while in 2001 the Ministry of Finance was incorporated into the single structure of the Ministry for the Economy and Finance, whose tasks were (i) to manage the political economy in compliance with the convergence and stability obligations of the EU and (ii) to assist the executive with expertise and operational support regarding fiscal and macroeconomic policy. "Over the 1990s"—Quaglia notes—"the increasing prominence of the Treasury in macro-economic policy making has been due to an upgrading of its *institutional capacity* and an *empowerment* prompted by EMU"[9] (2005, 552; emphasis in the original). The last main segment of state reconfiguration concerns the strengthening of executive powers (see Crisitiello 2004, 2019; Della Sala 1997). I take into account this fundamental dimension of state transformations in chapter 6 with specific respect to the political economy, the backbone of the neoliberal state transformation.

THE SECOND REPUBLIC AND THE ITALIAN NEOLIBERAL TRANSITION

The contradictory processes of state transformations in the 1980s convey the sense of the state as a dynamic *terrain* of intersections of different power networks and hegemonic projects. The technocratic apparatus, a "largely autonomous state bureaucracy" (Quaglia 2006, 558)—yet relatively autonomous (see chapter 3)—played a fundamental role in spreading monetarist and neoliberal ideas, often in open contrast with other political factions in the government and in the apparatuses of the state. More broadly, if the 1980s can be conceived as a period of *war of position* within the apparatuses of the state, the early 1990s saw instead a *war of movement* through which, in a few months, the conditions for the consolidation of neoliberalism were implemented *in* and *through* the state, transforming further the state in the process.

The Crises of the Early 1990s: Neoliberalism Makes Its Way, Again

The early 1990s, especially the years 1992 and 1993, saw an unprecedented rupture in the Italian political system, conventionally framed as the moment of transition from the First to the Second Republic. In relation to the political economy, some of the structural contradictions and imbalances accumulated in the previous decade came to the fore. The growth of public debt and unbalanced public finances were causing serious difficulties for the productive system as a whole (Palombarini 2002). In the meantime, international and European pressures were becoming increasingly strong. In Europe, the creation of a single market had been agreed in 1986, thus revamping the supranational process through a strict market-oriented integration. In 1990, the movement of financial capital was eventually liberalized with the aim to foster the financial integration of European economies. The global political economy was likewise undergoing important changes, with the transition to post-Fordist modes of accumulation (Jessop 2002), the expansion of financial capital and transnational networks of production (Bieler and Morton 2018).

More conjuncturally, the combination of two contingent developments allowed, within a few months, for the introduction of important changes in the Italian political system and the implementation of neoliberal and austerity reforms: the corruption scandal of *Tangentopoli* ("bribesville") in 1992, and the speculative attack on the Lira in that same year. The word *Tangentopoli* refers to the network of payoffs and corrupting practices which involved especially two of the main parties of the time, the DC and PSI (Amyot 2004, 106). The scandal, importantly, had a deep symbolic impact on the Italian population as it discredited the existing party system as a whole and, more broadly, politics as such, to the extent that this moment is the precursor of the discourse against the "political caste" exploited recently by the Five Star Movement and The League. In the window of opportunity opened by the political crisis, Giuliano Amato, law professor and PSI member[10], became prime minister of a technocratic government in 1992, soon followed by the "full technocratic"[11] executive of Carlo A. Ciampi in 1993: since then, "technocrats and university professors began to fill the more relevant positions within the cabinet" (Fabbrini and Donà 2003, 33). Interestingly, in a 1997 World Bank publication, we read that "[economic] reforms have political implications but do not require the overhaul of institutions. They can be undertaken quickly, *often through decree*, by a small group of competent technocrats" (1997, 13; emphasis added). This is actually what happened in the Italian case.

Generally, the technocratic nature of the new governments made it possible for a series of measures to be passed that, through the usual institutional channels, would have met with widespread dissent and been extremely costly in political terms. In a context of unprecedented weakness of parties, technocrats managed to strengthen the powers of the executive branch, especially by resorting to decrees (see chapter 6). In a few months, such governments implemented an impressive series of reforms concerning privatization, the pension system, the labour market, industrial relations, and budget consolidation (more below). The second contingent cause that favoured the acceptance of permanent austerity programs was the speculative attack on the Italian Lira in 1992, triggered by the downgrading of Italy's rating by the rating agency Moody's. The speculation led to a devaluation of Lira and to the upsurge in the rate of interest and therefore of public debt, which skyrocketed from 102 to 121 percent of GDP between 1991 and 1994. As I document in next chapter, the call for *risanamento* (that is, permanent adjustment) of state finance—in the wake of the emergency—favoured the acceptance of massive cuts in state budget and the introduction of a permanent wage moderation policy (chapter 5).

The strengthening of executive powers thus accompanies the imposition of neoliberal restructuring. The 1990s are a phase of intense reform activity revolving around three main policy tools: wage moderation and reform of the labour market, privatization, and fiscal consolidation. Starting with wage policy, in 1993 Ciampi government abolished the *scala mobile*, "finally demolishing the little guarantees remaining under the already substantially reformed Scala Mobile with the Accord of 31 July 1992" (Talani 2017, 265). Wage moderation turned into an ordinary instrument of political economy (see Biraschi and Crescenzi 2007, 302). We read indeed in a government document (DPEF 1995–97, 10) that "it is necessary that salary moderation continues to provide for a condition of stability to economic operators and reduce inflation." In fact, "between 1992 and 2002, according to the OECD, real wages in Italy decreased by 5 percent, marking the third worst performance within all OECD countries [. . .] *real* wage compression experienced by the salaried class in the 1990s is without precedent in the post-war history of the country and also in comparison to other European countries" (Ghiani and Binotti 2011, 172, quoted in Bradanini 2012, 400). Wage moderation became the chief policy tool to improve the competitiveness of Italian enterprises, actually reproducing the core of the growth model in the initial post-war period (see chapter 7 for the analysis of the long-term *political* consequences of this policy).

For reasons of space, I can only mention here other important reforms such as that of the pension system—enacted by the governments led by Amato (1992) and Dini (1995) and seeking to raise the retirement age and decrease expenditures—and, only a few years later, the reform of labour market regulations enacted by the centre-left government of Romano Prodi ("Treu reform" 1997), which introduced an array of temporary employment possibilities to improve "flexibility." Privatization is another key dimension of state intervention. The Amato and Ciampi[12] governments started an ambitious programme of privatization that continued with the governments of the centre-left and centre-right thereafter. Technocrats resorted to an impressive amount of executive decrees through which some of the main public-owned industries[13] were transformed into joint-stock companies in just a few months (chapter 6), attracting also foreign capital (Graziani 1998, 202–203). Additionally, throughout the 1990s, there was a series of cuts in public expenditures. In the wake of the fiscal emergency in 1992, the Amato government passed an overall financial adjustment measure of 93,000 billion liras made up of 52,000 billion liras of cuts, 34,000 billion liras of new revenues, and 7,000 billion liras coming from privatizations, to which a further 12,500 billion of cuts (as "corrective measure") were added during the year 1993 by the Ciampi government, which then implemented its own fiscal adjustment measure of 28,000 billion liras. These were not the only measures of this magnitude: the Dini government (1995) passed a measure of 20,000 billion liras of cuts; the Prodi government (1996) an adjustment measure of 60,000 billion liras, including the pension reform, new fiscal restrictions and the "tax for Europe" levied on all incomes (Ferrera and Gualmini 2004, 70). The "austerity therapy" managed to decrease the budget deficit (but with new revenues mainly coming from (regressive) VAT taxation), public debt, inflation, and interest rates. Nonetheless, the effects of austerity therapy also had a strong impact on domestic social cohesion by triggering recession (1992–1993), a decline in investments and productivity, wage stagnation, and growing inequalities. Unemployment grew, in the North, from 6.9 to 7.7 percent between 1993 and 1997, and in the South from 17.5 to 21.7 percent in the same period (Graziani 1998, 185). Unemployment, precarious jobs, and reduction of real salaries are important effects of the recession and accompanying restructuring (Simonazzi 1999, 79).

Elsewhere (Cozzolino 2019a), I remarked that the 1990s can be conceived as the moment of *consolidation*, in and beyond the state, of the neoliberal order. This is also the period of the strong deceleration of GDP growth, with mediocre growth rates thereafter.[14] Therefore, the permanent deflation of the Italian economy not only ended up in the long-term deterioration of public finance, especially whenever a financial crisis occurred (1992, 2008, 2011–2012), but also increased inequalities dramatically from this time onwards. For instance, Alvaredo and Pisano report an "increasing pattern in top income shares since the mid-1980s, mainly driven by top wages and self-employment income [. . .] the late 1980s and early 1990s were years of unequal growth [*and*] the years that followed combined rising income concentration with a lower growth rate" (2010, 628). Thus, the social bases of Italian democracy started to be seriously undermined, and to enter a permanent critical phase after the global financial crisis of 2008–2009 (chapter 7).

IN LIEU OF A CONCLUSION: AN INTERPRETATION OF NEOLIBERAL TRANSFORMATIONS OF THE ITALIAN STATE

In this final section, I provide an interpretation of the neoliberal hegemonic project "Italian-style." In outlining an interpretation of the Italian transition, I start by dealing with a compelling interpretation developed by Stefano Palombarini (2002; see also Revelli 1996) through regulationist (Boyer 1990) theoretical lenses. Palombarini's argument, in brief, is that in the 1980s the dominant social bloc comprised a social alliance between large private industry and financial rent, the core of the *pentapartito* consensus. The alliance, however, broke up in the early 1990s for one main reason: the consensus machine of the 1980s—based on large budgetary deficits and public debt—entered a crisis driven by changes in the productive system (especially SMEs and from the late 1980s also large firms). In fact, the profitability of the capital invested *in productive activities* had declined due to the weight of passive interest (2002, 65–71). The rupture of the social bloc (due to the contradiction between financial rent and industry) led to the political crisis of 1992, which was therefore due to *endogenous* factors. Palombarini's interpretation of the Italian transition, by aptly zooming in on the centrality of social blocs, has the merit of overcoming commonsensical and reductionist interpretations based on the revolt of an undetermined "civil society" against the corruption of the political elites of the time (e.g., McCarthy 1996). Nonetheless, the regulationist approach also suffers from several specific theoretical limits such as functionalism and structuralism. By discussing these limits, I try to develop a more holistic interpretation of the establishment of neoliberal hegemony in Italy and, in light of this, of the changes that occurred during the 1980s and 1990s.

First of all, this approach regards historical change in rather "automatic" and functionalist terms that materialize especially in the ways in which the social dimension interacts with politics; in so doing, either the social bloc is manufactured by ruling political forces, or political change is mechanically determined by a modification occurring in the ruling social bloc. By downplaying the role of sociopolitical agency, moreover, the regulationist approach not only misses the dialectical relation between civil society and political society but also overlooks fundamental dimensions such as discourse and ideology—that is, the battle over the *significance* of social phenomena *and* the discursive construction of the "solutions" to the perceived crisis (Hay 2004, 44). Another limit of this approach can be detected in the overtly domestic/endogenous view of change, which misses the relevance of transnational dynamics such as the unfolding of global capitalism during the 1980s and 1990s (Bieler and Morton 2018). In chapter 5, I also argue that we can understand some of the characteristics of the Italian transition only by taking into account the memory of the conflicts and turmoil in the 1960s and 1970s, which were later exploited by state representatives to pursue a widespread cultural battle revolving around the ordoliberal "culture of stability" (chapter 5).

In developing an alternative reading of Italian neoliberalization, I maintain that by zooming in on the political agency in the state, it is actually possible to provide for a better comprehension of the characteristics of the Italian neoliberal transition and, more broadly, of the relation between neoliberalism and the state. In what follows, I take into account four main *intertwined* dimensions that help to explain the turning point: (a) the political economy; (b) the state and state apparatuses; (c) collective memory and political identity; (d) transnational and supranational factors.

With respect to the political economy dimension, I have already taken into account the important changes that took place in the early 1990s. Here, I wish to remark that in the 1980s the foundations of the neoliberal finance-led model of capital accumulation were laid, and which strengthened in the decades that followed. From this perspective, the 1990s seems to be substantially in line with the tendencies that arose in the previous decade: along with the falling wage share[15] (Davanzati et al. 2019, 932–933) and less antagonistic industrial relations,[16] Italian governments started to achieve permanent surpluses in the primary budget (i.e., net of interest) through massive cuts in public expenditures since 1992. In terms of the monetary policy regime, it is also worth noting that the "divorce" between the BI and the Treasury introduced a more autonomous and, above all, *non-accommodating* monetary policy towards wage earners, actually anticipating the shift of monetary policy sovereignty to the European Central Bank in the 1990s.

The second dimension concerns the state. The political economy shifts—wage moderation, non-accommodating monetary policy, low inflation, supply-side measures—were accompanied by a process of *reconfiguration* of state apparatuses. The BI is a prominent actor in this process given its cognitive resources, plus its critical transnational linkages which rendered it the national offshoot of the *international* neoliberal epistemic community. Crucially, the BI provided key "human resources" in other segments of the state between the late 1980s and mid-1990s. Guido Carly, governor of the BI (1960–1975) was also, as minister of Treasury (1989–1992), involved in the Maastricht Treaty negotiations. Carlo A. Ciampi, also governor of the BI (1979–1993), was the prime minister of the first full technocratic government in Italy in 1993–1994 and Treasury minister for several years in the second half of the 1990s (centre-left governments), ending his *cursus honorum* as president of the Republic (1999–2006). Lamberto Dini was general director of the Treasury (1979–1994) and prime minister of the second full technocratic government of Italian history (1995–1996). Mario Monti, prime minister in the third full technocratic government (2011–2012), was dean of the Italian private business school, Luigi Bocconi, head or member of several Italian reform commissions for the liberalization of financial markets during the 1980s, and European Commissioner for the Internal Market DG (1995–1998) and Competition DG (1999–2004).

Thus, neoliberalism as a hegemonic project in Italy emerged during the late 1970s and 1980s within a specific segment of the state mainly revolving around the "party" of the BI and Treasury (see Dyson and Featherstone 1996). This group, that I termed earlier a "technocratic collective intellectual," aptly exploited the window of opportunity opened by the crisis of 1992 to modify power relations *in* the state and, *through* the state, in society as a whole. Recalling the words of Poulantzas, "the political field of the state (as well as the sphere of ideology) has always, in different forms, been present in the constitution and reproduction of the relations of production" (1978, 17). In this regard, Guido Carli meaningfully stated that "our agenda at the table of the Inter-Governmental Conference on European Union represented an alternative solution to problems which we were not able to tackle via the normal channels of government and parliament" (quoted in Dyson and Featherstone 1996, 272). This last passage is particularly important, and can be compared with the words of Tommaso Padoa Schioppa, likewise vice director-general of the BI (1984–1997), member of the executive committee of the European Central Bank (1998–2006), and minister of the economy in a centre-left Italian government (2006–2008). Schioppa writes that

> the decision, *highly political*, to join the European monetary system was determined by the purpose of gradually entrusting to the constituency of markets the necessary stimulus to correct the behaviour of private and public entities [. . .] If the constraint of nominal exchange rates [. . .] managed to push the enterprises to seek competitive gains through the compression of real wage instead of price increases [. . .] *to discipline public institutions turned out to be much more difficult.* (1997, 54; quoted in Simonazzi 1999, 78; emphases added)

Thus, after 1992–1993 crisis, processes of state reconfiguration tended towards the concentration of power in the state (especially the executive), along with a gradual marginalization of a more autonomous role for parliament and of parties[17] as collective agencies. In line with Gill's "new constitutionalism" (1998) thesis, the early 1990s marks the transition from the "Republic of parties" to a political system more insulated from popular democratic forces and processes, in which the strengthening of executive powers and technocrats is a prominent factor (see chapter 6).

The third analytical dimension concerns collective memory and Italian identity, which also relates to the European integration process (more in the next chapter). Adopting a medium-term perspective, the cycle of class struggles lasted much longer in Italy than in other countries and, at the same time, was not just confined to the enterprise (or to the parliament) but expanded to society as a whole. The memory of the conflicts of the 1960s and 1970s, as well as of "fiscal instability" and growing public debt, combined to construct the commonsensical imaginary of *endemic* Italian instability and, accordingly, the necessity to introduce South of the Alps the culture of stability[18] typical of the North of Europe. In other words, at stake was the image of a country perceived to be unable to achieve a condition of stability and "normality" on her own. This, I argue, was further amplified by the historically weak legitimation of the Italian state. Formed not through a revolutionary process but, following Gramsci, as a case of passive revolution, the new Kingdom of Italy reproduced the notable and manifold differences among the different regions of the Peninsula, which *have actually remained* the specimen of Italian history. Hence, the manifold divisions and endemic conflicts are rooted in the precarious basis of the Italian state and its historically weak legitimation. At the same time and importantly, European integration (as I noted earlier) played a fundamental *cognitive* and *discursive* role in representing the external anchor to finally *stabilize* the country. This explains the generally strong support for European integration in the 1990s and 2000s.

The last element concerns the international dimension and global capitalism. Italian production, as I remarked earlier, was integrated into European markets from the very beginning of the post-war period, to the extent that the "economic miracle" was led by exports. In terms of exports, Italy is the first export economy in the Euro area by small business size (10–49 employees) and the third by medium (50–249 employees) and large (250 or more employees) business size (OECD 2019). The integration of finance and production significantly improved in the 1980s and 1990s, following transnational dynamics. For instance, in 1980 the outward stock of FDI amounted to 1.54 percent of GDP. In 1990 this had increased to 5.11 percent, in 2000 to 14.89 percent, in 2010 to 23.2 percent, and in 2017 to 28.66 percent. The inward stock of FDI likewise notably grew from 1.87 percent of GDP in 1980 to 10.73 percent in 2000 and then to 22 percent in 2017 (Unctad). Finance, as I noted above, was at the forefront of the Italian insertion into international markets especially through the privatization of public debt (Graziani 1998, ch. 9), which enhanced the direct influence of creditors on the political economy (Cozzolino 2019b). But, this is also a period of sustained financialization on the part of Italian firms (Davanzati et al. 2019), furthering the insertion of the Italian economy into global financial relations. Yet, the question of transnational/international relations, as I argued in the previous chapter, cannot be confined to the (clearly fundamental) structural changes in global capitalism but concerns also the political and ideological dimension rooted in global neoliberal hegemony in the aftermath of the collapse of the Soviet Union (Gill 1993; Cox 1993). In other words, it is equally wrong to frame the transformations of the state either as determined by exogenous factors (European integration, the global political economy) or by endogenous elements (national social blocs, political crises). The transformations of the nation-state, in terms of both ideas/ideology and state-system, are indeed part and parcel of the *dialectical* interaction between international and national structures, processes, and agencies.

Concluding, the early 1990s can be conceived as a war of movement, a blizkrieg, within the state. Institutional changes, ideas, material, and immaterial resources that had already emerged during the war of position of the 1980s proved to be key when a window of opportunity opened in the first half of the 1990s. Without framing that specific juncture and its pre- and post-historical development, it is not possible to understand the nature of contemporary crises in Italy. The next chapters deal with the discursive construction of the neoliberal state to understand how Italian state representatives legitimated the reform of economy and society (chapter 5), the strengthening of executive powers and how it was related to the introduction of neoliberal and austerity policies (chapter 6), and eventually the contemporary crises of the Italian state, which I conceive as the intensification of the imbalances that have accumulated since the period discussed in this chapter (chapter 7).

Chapter 5

The Discursive Construction of the Neoliberal State in Italy

In this chapter, I analyse the discursive construction of the neoliberal state in Italy since the late 1980s through the analysis of the discourses of the political forces in the government. Thus, while in the previous chapter I provided a critical history of the Republic, here I go into greater detail regarding the forms and strategies of legitimation of neoliberal transformations. The state, let me emphasize once again, is a privileged perspective from which to comprehend the broader changes occurring in a society. On the one hand, the terrain of the integral state is a key field for competing sociopolitical groups to seek societal hegemony, and hence to legitimate and impose their own versions of "common sense." On the other, the struggle to impose a certain idea of state, with both its ideological integuments and effects, is a critical factor in the legitimation and naturalization of a project of societal transformation, as neoliberalism actually is. As I have already argued, the idea of the state as "disinterested servant of the common interest" (Jessop 2015, 18) possesses an intrinsic ideological nature and power (Abrams 1988). Hence, by deconstructing the social construction of the (neoliberal) state, it is possible to understand the specific discursive strategies through which the transformation of a social order, with its unequal relations and forms of domination, is legitimated.

On more empirical grounds, this chapter provides for new materials for understanding the characteristics of Italian neoliberalization. It sheds light on the key juncture of the early 1990s as the moment for the consolidation of the neoliberal discourse, the main elements of which have sedimented heavily since then, and reconstructs how they have evolved until the present. At the same time, the analysis explores the construction of the external constraints that legitimated the processes of economic restructuring and state transformation. In particular, such constraints are international finance and European integration, the latter being fraught with polysemous meanings (more below). Another feature of this chapter is the analysis of the strategy of legitimation of permanent austerity, an extraordinary case of how austerity is naturalized as a necessary therapy to heal and improve the economy. I call this strategy the "political economy of sacrifice and promise." This chapter, moreover, while stressing the substantial policy continuity between governments of different political orientations (e.g., technocratic, centre-left, and centre-right), zooms in on the centre-left governments to emphasize how these proved to be the main sponsors of European integration and neoliberal modernization. I define this peculiar strand of neoliberal discourse as "neoliberal-progressive Europeanism." Finally, in the conclusions I discuss depoliticization—the second face of technocracy—as a strategy that informs the construction of the neoliberal integral state and aims to strip society of its material class fractures and political conflicts, thus fostering a conception of society as a single, conflict-less marketplace.

A CRITICAL DISCOURSE ANALYSIS OF NEOLIBERAL TRANSFORMATIONS OF THE ITALIAN STATE

The transformation of the idea of state is an extremely relevant aspect of the legitimation and naturalization of neoliberal ideology. Hence, "the idea of state becomes a crucial object of study" (Abrams 1988, 77) to help us explore how political forces can redefine the idea of state and, consequently, to deconstruct the construction of neoliberal semiotic order (in our case in Italy). According to Bob Jessop, "'semiotic systems [. . .] frame individual subjects' lived experience of an inordinately complex world and/or inform collective calculation about that world. They [. . .] constitute the semiotic moment of a network of social practices in a given social field, institutional order, or wider social formation" (2010, 344). More specifically, the analysis zooms in on the discursive construction of the state from a political economy perspective. Through the Critical Discourse Analysis approach,[1] I study the main fiscal and economic policy document enacted by the Italian government, that is, the *Documento di Programmazione Economico-Finanziaria*[2] (DPEFs) [Economic and Financial Planning Document]. The corpus of the analysis comprises twenty-nine Documents enacted every year from 1988 to 2017. Such documents are relevant insofar as we find not only state representatives' *desiderata* of social change but also their specific policy choices and the legitimation of such choices, vis-à-vis both the international and the domestic context. The presentation of the findings follows several criteria, both content-based and temporal, with the aim of deconstructing the main elements of neoliberal discourse in Italy. More specifically, the study is organized in the following subsections:

(I) The discursive definition, by policymakers, of (i) the characteristics of the juncture of crisis and transition of the early 1990s,[3] and (ii) the fundamental question of the external constraint (see Diodato 2014; Moschella 2017). More specifically, I conceive the external constraint as constituted by two interlinked factors: international finance and European integration, both of these provided with important symbolic elements. The analysis of the intertwined dynamic of crises and external constraints is key for understanding the call for action to reform the Italian economy and to legitimate permanent austerity.

(II) The specific discursive forms of legitimation of *risanamento*, that is, permanent austerity, which can be conceived as the backbone of the Italian political economy from the early 1990s. I define the overall strategy of legitimation of permanent austerity as "the political economy of sacrifice and promise."

(III) The post-2008 phase. Here, I explore if, and to what extent, the crisis represents another opportunity to further the process of neoliberalization and to (re)impose austerity discipline.

(IV) The cross-party analysis of the discursive legitimation of neoliberal economic reform and austerity. While the findings generally confirm the strong support among all governments for supply-side policy programmes and fiscal restraint, they also show strong support for European integration by the centre-left. In this section, thus, I describe in detail what I term "neoliberal-progressive Europeanism."

(V) Eventually, by emphasizing the transformations of the idea of state from the post-war Republican state to the neoliberal era, I show the key elements of the construction of the neoliberal idea of state.

EARLY 1990S CRISES AND EXTERNAL CONSTRAINT(S): THE CALL FOR ACTION TO REFORM ITALIAN SOCIETY

A crisis juncture may represent an opportunity for political actors to try to impose a definition of the situation/problem and outline the call to take action to resolve the problem(s). Borrowing again from Jessop, crises are "potentially path-shaping moments that provoke responses that are mediated by semiotic-cum-material processes of variation, selection and retention" (2010, 346). The element of *semiosis*, that is, the production of meaning, is particularly important. External constraints and structural-material circumstances, per se, do not impose a direction to social, political, and economic change. It is the situated agency of political forces, particularly in and through the state, that—in dialectical relation with social forces in civil society—articulate and legitimate the desired direction of change, attempting to make this appear a *natural* and *necessary* process.

To understand the shift in the Italian political economy in the last decades—in terms of both policy choices and discursive legitimation—it is necessary to explore the late 1980s and the early 1990s. Italian state representatives framed or, better, crystallized the characteristics of the Italian "economic disease" and outlined the pathway to be "necessarily" taken to heal the economy and avoid major negative consequences. The early 1990s crisis, moreover, strengthened a path-dependency that only in recent months was (albeit very contradictorily) put in question.[4] Before presenting the elements of the empirical analysis, it is important to emphasize the interlocked dynamic of the external constraints and domestic crises,[5] which *jointly* are represented, by political forces, in terms of exceptional circumstances that put the Italian economy under pressure, the latter being depicted as "weak" in their own right.

From the first DPEF (1988–1992), indeed, a sense of weakness, exceptionality and vulnerability frames, in state representatives' discourse, the Italian economy. The joint dynamic of the financial conditions of the Peninsula—in particular the debt burden—and of the external constraint represented by financial markets were considered factors contributing to a weak international position for Italy. "The worsening of public accounts, along with the resurface of the external constraint, highlights the fragility of the situation, and exposes our country to financial instability."[6] The situation of emergency is strongly emphasized, and constitutes the call for action to reform the country. Also, this moment is framed as the "last call" to reform the country and as an opportunity not to be missed—prompting a sense of urgency. "It is not rhetorical to talk about emergency. Available data signal the urgency to take action to ensure the structural adjustment of public finance. A failed improvement or, even worse, a further deterioration [of the situation] would *definitely* compromise the achievement of the objectives, while, on the contrary, reversing the trend would trigger the virtuous cycle of risanamento"[7] (emphasis added).

Crucially, this moment is portrayed in terms of "either/or": either "modernizing" the country through the "right reforms," or compromising definitely the pathway to healing the national economy and, as a consequence, sliding backwards towards instability. The technocratic government led by Carlo A. Ciampi emphatically wrote, in the Document issued in 1993, that "junctures of bifurcation characterize countries' economic and political life: to choose one way or another is an *irreversible* choice which marks, in the years to come, the perspectives and quality of welfare and growth of future generations"[8] (emphasis added). Importantly, in none of the Documents analysed do we find examples of possible alternative; hence, narrowing the cognitive spectrum in terms of the policy solutions judged to be feasible. As such, the structural adjustment of public finance and neoliberal reforms are the only options put on the table to recover the Italian economy. The overall and unquestioned political economy choice is thus strengthening the country's position in the global economy by improving competitiveness and "credibility" vis-à-vis financial markets (see also Cozzolino 2019b). A variety of supply-side measures are presented as necessary and urgent reforms, ranging from income policy (that is, wage devaluation), privatizations, scaling down the public sector's role in service provisions, cuts in public expenditures, and empowering the control of the executive on budget measures.[9]

International finance is particularly important for framing the sense of weakness, emergency, and vulnerability that marks, in state representatives' discourse, the Italian context. The liberalization of financial markets, in particular, is depicted as a source of pressures and potential instability. "The necessity to reduce the financial reliance of the public sector on financial markets is stronger because of the international evolution of financial integration."[10] In the previous chapter, I analysed the fundamental paradigm change revolving around public finance, financial integration, and public debt that occurred in the early 1980s. What is worth noting here is that after such a paradigm shift in Italy and the liberalization of financial markets, "credibility" to financial creditors became the main concern of policymakers, which put *risanamento,* that is, permanent structural adjustment of public finance, at the top of the political economy agenda (more on this below). Credibility can be conceived as a mix of neoliberal orthodoxy and permanent fiscal adjustment. Financial creditors became, thus, the principal interlocutors of Italian state representatives; on the other hand, decreasing interest rates became the main policy target to decrease the cumbersome public debt. In this respect, the consequences of a failed adjustment of public finance are portrayed, in momentous terms, as something that would negatively affect future generations:

> Renewing confidence in the Italian economy would reduce the exorbitant difference between our interest rates and those of our international counterparts [. . .] *This is what markets expect from us.* If [structural adjustment] would not happen, the difference between our interest rates and international rates, far from diminishing, would rather increase. This would worsen the future dimension of the adjustment, and therefore the overall cost of stabilization.[11]

This juncture, importantly, is a path-shaping moment as it strengthened the sense of structural weakness of the Italian economy, the necessity and urgency to take action in terms of permanent fiscal restraint and of scaling down the public sector, while also implementing "structural reforms"—that is, neoliberal policies. Now, before exploring the fundamental question of *risanamento*, it is important to consider the "other" external constraint; that is, European integration, and how state representatives framed it.

EUROPEAN INTEGRATION AS MULTIFACETED AND POLYSEMOUS EXTERNAL CONSTRAINT

European integration can be conceived as the "other" external constraint. And yet, if compared to international finance, "Europe," in the political and public discourse the synonym of the European Union, emerges as an umbrella symbolic reference under which several intersubjective meanings are constructed and naturalized. In fact, the European Union is not only portrayed, by Italian state representatives, as a constraining factor on the national political economy but also as a *superior standard* of market civilization. Above all, "Europe" became a means to achieve the permanent stabilization of the Peninsula.[12] As we will see below, "to be European" implies attaining a superior and dynamic model of market economy, capable of improving the quality of domestic institutions and *rescuing* Italy from backward southern standards.[13] "Europe," in fact, is key for understanding how state representatives' discourses aimed to legitimate and naturalize austerity and neoliberal reforms (especially, as I show, by centre-left governments)—also by discursively resorting to the "necessity to be more competitive": "integration with other European countries requires political economy choices [. . .] consistent with the worsening of the degree of competition on all markets."[14]

Generally, from the first DPEF European integration is portrayed as a constraining factor, and, at the same time, as a process without which Italy would fail to stabilize her economy. The potential exclusion of Italy from the kernel of the European system is portrayed as a problem for Italian society as a whole. "When determining the budget policy in the three-year period between 1991 and 1993, we shall take into account the European constraints, or we might be excluded from the European System of Central Banks. This would be plainly in contradiction with the pro-European Italian aspirations."[15] While, on the one hand, potential limits or contradictions of the internal market are neither considered nor discussed, on the other the possibility of failing to access EMU is framed as a serious destabilizing factor.

> The consolidation of public finance is indispensable not only to access the Monetary Union, but also to strengthen the national economic development in conditions of stability. Without the perspective of the Monetary Union, the

purpose of public finance adjustment would be much harder: the expectations of the exchange rate of the Lira would be unstable, with major consequences for the level of interest rates and the cost of debt.[16]

Also, in this case, state actors resorted to the discourse of weakness and vulnerability of the Italian economy, further strengthening this image by comparing Italy to other countries. "At a time when the pro-European aspirations pursued over the past fifty years come to a realization, Italy experiences increasing difficulties to govern the public finance within the accession criteria,"[17] let alone the public debt: "[w]hile the majority of European countries is not far from this target [60 percent of GDP/debt ratio], our public debt has exceeded 120 percent of GDP."[18] The invocation of "accession criteria" reinforces the call to take action to pursue fiscal adjustment, hence favouring the massive cuts in budget expenditures that I documented in the previous chapter. There is, therefore, a direct mutual relation between European integration and the adjustment of public finance, or, seen differently, European integration is invoked as a source of legitimation of permanent austerity at the domestic level. In the months before EMU accession, we read in the Document enacted in 1997 that "[t]he government pursues two fundamental objectives of economic development: (I) the accession to the European Monetary Union; (II) the adjustment of public finance. These are two purposes that feed off each other via the fall of interest rates."[19] Ten years later, despite the contradictions already in place which then erupted after the crisis of 2008, the centre-left government of the time maintained that "the European convergence process, the accession to the European monetary union and the introduction of the Euro have been the fundamental anchor to pursue the financial stability of our country, laying down the premises for the sustainable growth of our economy."[20]

European integration is not only invoked to pass unpopular measures at home. Crucially, "Europe" is also portrayed, especially during the 1990s and under centre-left governments, in positive if not enthusiastic tones. This aspect, often overlooked in the analysis of the political rhetoric surrounding European integration, is extremely important for understanding a fundamental aspect of neoliberal hegemony in Southern Europe—and, at the same time, the recent crisis of European integration (chapter 7). Meaningfully, "Europe" is discursively framed as a *dynamic, prosperous* and *progressive market civilization*. Thus, it emerges as a superior and modern economy, an anchor to both *modernize* and *stabilize* the Italian economy and society. "[Our policy programme] will determine a higher and more competitive productive base, in line with what is established in the Maastricht Treaty, which imposes also measures of structural adjustment of the public sector and labour market institutions."[21] In state representatives' discourse, European integration is framed as a *qualitative* process of change which—under conditions of market freedom, improved competitiveness, and public finance stability—would eventually render Italy a "properly European" country with a higher, more competitive, and stable economic growth. "Europe, which is the frame of reference of this Document, is profoundly changing: on the basis of monetary and budget stability, it is projecting the establishment of a more competitive economy, oriented to higher growth." In what is, perhaps, the most emphatic passage of the DPEFs about the European Union, we read:

> The Economic and Monetary Union is a fundamental step to the realization of the great European project whose foundations were laid fifty years ago with the Treaty of Rome. This is a political and economic project that will affect future generations, modify the structure and perspectives of the whole of Europe and of the world through it. For Italy, to access the European Economic and Monetary Union goes even beyond prestige and contingent benefits. It means concurring to the formation of the "quality" and "characters" of the new institutions [. . .] If the policy address outlined by this government will find broad acceptance, it will be possible to say that the harsh pathway begun in early 1990s will arrive at its conclusion. It has been not an occasional effort, but a deep and permanent modification of the behaviour of Italians: the stability culture would have prevailed.[22]

Italian accession to EMU is solemnly saluted, in the DPEF of 1999 issued by the centre-left government, as the most important achievement of the 1990s. The efforts of *risanamento* and reform, in this juncture of strong confidence in European integration, are portrayed as a painful but eventually successful pathway. An optimistic vision of the future characterizes the tone of the Document, while the confidence in markets and financial stability—this is the global momentum of progressive neoliberalism—is at its highest. Furthermore, reading the following passage now, in a time of rising neo-nationalism and euroscepticism, gives a sense of the broken promise of European integration as a path towards economic prosperity and stability.

> This Document is presented [. . .] on the eve of the birth of the Economic and Monetary Union. Italy will be part of it. She will outline, organize, and manage the European economy. She will share the responsibility [. . .] The awareness of the European goal marked the beginning of an unprecedented virtuous cycle in the past thirty-years [. . .] The commitment followed the decision to be part of EMU, and the reforms that made such task credible, have been rewarded: our confidence in the Italian economy to be able to accelerate *risanamento* has transformed into the confidence granted by the markets, and, afterwards, by our partner countries [. . .] The decision to achieve EMU membership by January

> 1, 1999, has determined the government agenda, and has set the conditions to implement the macroeconomic and structural policies to boost economic growth within the context of the Stability and Growth Pact [. . .] This implies the commitment of all the productive forces of the country, of the entire Italian system. Italy is going to participate to the creation of Economic and Monetary Union by bringing stability and vitality, to find a possibility of increased and more durable growth of wealth and employment.[23]

THE POLITICAL ECONOMY OF SACRIFICE AND PROMISE: THE LEGITIMATION OF PERMANENT AUSTERITY IN ITALY

Risanamento, namely the permanent structural adjustment of public finance through the reduction of public expenditures, is the backbone of the Italian political economy throughout the period considered in my analysis. It is not only a political economy strategy but also a cognitive framework that regards, directly, *Italian identity*. Moreover, it is related to the transformation of the idea of state, and, at the same time, to the reconfiguration of state system.[24] The importance of this analysis, of the discursive legitimation of permanent fiscal restraint, is of paramount relevance for understanding how a specific political economy strategy is not only legitimated as a technical, neutral and unavoidable necessity, but also as a pathway eventually leading to a better and more dynamic-cum-stable society.

The characteristics of austerity "Italian-style" are intriguing for a number of important reasons. First, the longitudinal coherence of this policy choice throughout the timeframe of the analysis. Second, the coherence, across the entire party system, of the discursive frame of austerity as an unquestionable necessity. Third, the specific discursive strategies of legitimation of permanent austerity, which involve the relation between southern and northern Europe. Fourth, the gap between the perception of southern fiscal profligacy, with the necessity to amend such *original sin*, and the reality, in Italy, of the attainment of budget surpluses from the early 1990s. Fifth, the ongoing denial of the need to publicly discuss, or even recognize, the permanent austerity therapy as a cause of poor growth and structural imbalances.

Let's briefly recall the orthodox rationale that sustains fiscal adjustment. Against the background of higher debt costs and therefore higher public debt levels, a country "needs" to embark on a programme of structural fiscal adjustment to become credible vis-à-vis financial markets and thus to decrease the level of interest rates, to achieve a balanced growth led by markets and not by the state (whose task, incidentally, is to supervise the market mechanism). This said, as I already showed here and elsewhere (Cozzolino 2020), with respect to the Italian case there is a remarkable and somehow interesting gap between the narrative of "Southern fiscal profligacy" and the reality of massive cuts in the state budget from 1992 onwards (Ferrera and Gualmini 2004, 70). The cumbersome Italian debt does not derive from "uncontrolled spending" but from the accumulation of *passive* interest rates,[25] which also represent a case of "reverse distribution" from taxpayers to the owners of financial assets and of increasing inequality (see Chapter 4; Graziani 1998; Palombarini 2002).

The question, then, is how Italian state representatives managed to impose and legitimate such a process of permanent restraint, which has deeply impacted Italian economy and society in the face of the growing systemic failures of this strategy. To capture the overall discursive framework of the austerity paradigm, I define the legitimation strategy of Italian policymakers as *the political economy of sacrifice and promise*. While the sacrifices are solicited to "heal" the economy, the promises are represented by a future of stability, prosperity, and growth. Moreover, a crucial, yet dramatically unexplored question is that, almost between the lines, there is a sense of instability and exceptionalism that marks the South, and Italy in particular, hence characterizing the unequal relation with Northern Europe. By anchoring Italy to "Europe," that is, to the North, the culture of stability will eventually prevail in the South, too. At the same time, there is another conundrum related to austerity discourse. While many DPEFs acknowledge the poor growth of the Italian economy from the early 1990s, fiscal adjustment is neither considered nor mentioned as a potential cause of stagnation and imbalances. This allowed for the ongoing legitimating and naturalizing of austerity (also after 2008) as the solution to the problems that, to a great extent, this policy already helped produce.

Let's take a closer look at the discursive legitimation of permanent *risanamento*. Concretely, *every* DPEF analysed mentions the *risanamento* strategy (more than once[26]) as urgent and necessary. While the external constraints and the crises of the early 1990s represent the material and cognitive framework within which, as noted above, the call to take urgent action is initially framed,[27] this also triggered a cognitive and discursive path-dependency through which *risanamento* is framed and legitimated thereafter. In other words, the analysis confirms that *the necessity of fiscal adjustment recurs longitudinally and with no significant variations across the party system throughout the period considered*. Hence, financial stability is a first, important source of the legitimation of austerity. "Risanamento of public finance is our main objective [. . .] Fiscal consolidation will push away the risks of financial instability and unsustainability of the public debt."[28] As a centre-left government maintains by resorting to the "TINA" discursive frame, "there is no alternative to continuing risanamento policy. Pursuing this with determination, despite the difficulties, will strengthen the credibility of our country."[29] Furthermore, this process is framed as permanent and irreversible, with existential implications for Italian society as a whole. In this respect, it is also worth noting that a sense of ineluctability also surrounds European integration: "it is necessary and urgent to create the conditions in Italy to access the Monetary Union in a *permanent* and *irreversible* way."[30] Importantly, after the 2008 crisis and despite the imbalances determined by *this* strategic political economy choice, *risanamento* is portrayed as the only and necessary pathway to heal Italian economy: "[t]he crisis has put under pressure public finance [. . .]. It is essential, in this regard, to restore a credible and solid risanamento pathway for the post-crisis period"[31] (more on the post-2008 period later).

Risanamento discourse has fundamental *cultural* integuments. In other words, it is a means to "discipline" southern profligacy and render this part of Europe closer to the stability culture of the North:

> If the address outlined in this Document will find broad acceptance, the long and painful pathway begun by Italians in 1992 will come to a conclusion. It has not been an occasional effort, but a *deep and permanent modification of the behaviour of all Italians: the culture of stability will have prevailed.*[32] (emphasis added)

In a Document of two years later, we read that the "risanamento of budget and public finance is the most important structural reform achieved in these years. It is necessarily destined to change profoundly—it is already changing—the functioning of our economy, and, in a context of monetary stability such as that deriving from the single currency, *it will change the behaviour, habits, expectations, and perspectives of the Italians*"[33] (emphasis added). In direct relation to the culture of stability, Italian state actors also legitimate austerity in terms of a duty with *moral* implications. "The country has accepted to undertake the pathway of risanamento, despite the adverse conditions [. . .] Such *bloodless revolution* which has occurred in the behaviour, ways of life, and aptitudes [of the Italian people] not only helps us to undertake the choice of risanamento, it makes this a duty." Even under the first Berlusconi government (1994), *risanamento* is pictured as "our moral—rather than just political—duty."[34]

Risanamento is not just a difficult yet necessary process of economic and cultural change. There is also a positive side to it: the promise. The dimension of sacrifice is legitimated, in fact, by envisioning a stable and prosperous economy in the future within the European integration process. More to the point, *to be finally European* is within Italy's grasp. It is the culture of stability that, through the sacrifices of *risanamento*, will finally allow Italy to leave, albeit imaginatively, the tumultuous, unstable shores of the South. "Today's sacrifices, fully sustainable by our economic system, will avoid negative effects on the socio-economic context, and will set the foundations to improve the welfare of future generations."[35] This frame also recurs after the sovereign debt crisis (2011), when the technocratic government led by Mario Monti wrote, in the DEF of 2013, that

> An adjustment of such a magnitude, furthermore made in short time and in a condition of economic *weakness* and stress in financial markets, cannot but happen with heavy sacrifices and harsh social and economic consequences in the short period. Data testify the economic downturn and the growth of unemployment and social unrest [. . .] This Document demonstrates that the reforms can really change the growth performance of our Country [. . .] This is the [political economy] strategy that our Country needs to exit a crisis that is going on from way too long.[36]

This last passage summarizes some of the main traits of austerity discourse in Italy: the sense of economic weakness, the constraints represented by the tensions in financial markets, the necessity of the sacrifices, and the promise of future growth. And yet, the more important and critical element is *never* present: the relation between the structural decline of the Italian economy and permanent austerity. The final step to deconstruct the political economy of sacrifice and promise is to explore a collateral but fundamental point, namely the systemic effects of permanent fiscal adjustment on Italian society and how they are framed—more accurately hidden—in the DPEFs. Generally, the outcomes of the deflationary impact of permanent fiscal restraint are fully acknowledged in many Documents. "Evidences of decline manifested throughout the 1990s. [. . .] During the 1990s, the main economic indicators testify an increasing gap between our competing partners and us."[37] Also, the long-term decline of the Italian economy is entirely recognized:

> Growth [from the 1990s] has been far from that of the previous decades, and lower than that of other industrialized countries. The growth of GDP, which was around 3.6 and 2.9 percent respectively between 1971–1980 and 1981–1990, fell to 1.6 percent between 1991 and 2000, and to 0.5 percent in the last five years. Even potential growth, which during the 1970s was around the 4 percent of GDP, has gradually reduced in the following decades to 1.3 percent (average) in the first years of the 2000s.[38]

Is the acknowledgement of such systemic failures a call to abandon, or at least rethink or even discuss permanent austerity? Not exactly. While, indeed, the effects of permanent *risanamento* are acknowledged, *austerity is never considered or mentioned as a potential cause of Italian decline*. This made it possible for austerity to be imposed, again and vis-à-vis the recession, as the necessary pathway to heal the Italian economy. In other words, the removal of *risanamento* from the range of debatable issues has granted its resilience over time. This is particularly evident after 2008, when the structural imbalances of the European integration emerged violently and were amplified by the imposition of further austerity therapy and neoliberal reforms (Pradella 2015; Cozzolino 2020).

The Global Crisis of 2008 and the Sovereign Debt Crisis of 2011: A New Call for Austerity Therapy

In the final lines of the previous section, I emphasized that the DPEFs recognize the imbalances and flat growth of the Italian economy. And yet, they never related, either directly or indirectly, such poor performance to permanent austerity. This allowed Italian policymakers to impose prolonged austerity despite its own failures, further imposing it as the solution to such failures. The "stickiness" and resilience of the austerity discourse is even clearer after the 2008 crisis and after the sovereign debt crisis in Southern Europe (2011), a factor that brought the country to its knees.[39] Indeed, despite the negative impact of both these crises on the country's social cohesion, austerity is resolutely confirmed as the pathway to heal the country. Also, and importantly, the nexus between crisis, weakness/vulnerability of Italian economy and pressures of international finance is entirely reproduced, especially after the 2011 crisis.

> Towards the end of 2011, Italy found itself in a situation of vulnerability vis-à-vis international markets due to the state of public finances and the conditions of the real economy. For a decade or more, the economic and productive system has been experiencing a slow but steady decline, marked by flat growth rates and loss of competitiveness, in turn due to the stagnation of productivity and an unfavourable business environment, plus other structural weaknesses that have slowed down the adjustment to a more dynamic and competitive global context.[40]

Despite this situation, Italian policymakers re-legitimated *risanamento* as the necessary pathway to heal the economy *as if it had not been the backbone of the Italian political economy over the previous three decades.* As in the early 1990s crisis, when the main traits of *risanamento* discourse were outlined and framed, the juncture 2008/2011 helped to strengthen *risanamento* discourse without substantive changes in the overall discursive framework or among political forces. The principle of the balanced budget was even inserted into Italian constitution in 2012 under the technocratic government of Mario Monti, backed by a large coalition of centre-left and centre-right parties (see chapter 7). Of course, under this government the emphasis on the necessity of austerity was defended in even stronger terms:

> The action of the government aimed to maintain financial stability while relaunching the economy through relevant structural reforms. Notwithstanding the unfavourable international economic context, *risanamento* was pursued with determination in view of the achievement of the balanced budget in structural terms by 2013 [. . .] *Risanamento* action [finally] introduced and implemented the balanced budget principle in the Constitution.[41]

While, in substantive terms, this reform of the constitution was coherent with the strategy pursued in the previous decades, on the other hand it sanctioned the orthodoxy of *risanamento* by putting it in the constitution. In chapter 7, which is devoted to the contemporary crisis of Italian state, I will return again to this key juncture by arguing that the establishment of Monti government, along with further austerity therapy, eventually resulted in the (mature) crisis of the image of "Europe" in Italy.

NEOLIBERAL-PROGRESSIVE EUROPEANISM: ITALY'S CENTRE-LEFT AND ECONOMIC RESTRUCTURING

While it is normal to expect that centre-right politicians stand in favour of free markets, reduction of taxation on wealthy households, and against the direct intervention of the state in the economy (as we indeed read in the DPEFs[42] enacted by centre-right governments), by contrast, it is via enquiring into the choices of the centre-left, and how they are legitimated, that is possible to assess the extension and penetration of neoliberal hegemony and culture across the entire Italian political spectrum. In this section, I show in particular the transition of centre-left discourse towards the neoliberal position. This transition is consistent with the international change of some mainstream strands of the left in the 1990s and with the demise of social democracy (among others, see Streeck 2013). However, I argue that the Italian case concerns the strong relation between the centre-left and European integration more specifically. In other words, the left associated its political identity and discourse with "Europe" and this latter's specific form of neoliberal modernization. I call this peculiar strand of neoliberal discourse as *neoliberal-progressive Europeanism* (more below). Most importantly, such a discourse deserves special attention especially to understand, and put in its place, the evolution and crisis of post-2008 politics—a question that I analyse extensively in chapter 7.

Therefore, this section provides for an in-depth exploration of the discursive strategies displayed by the centre-left to legitimate its strategy. The first centre-left government during the Second Republic occurred in 1996[43] while, in 1998, a government was led for the first time by a former communist, Massimo D'Alema. In total, the centre-left, through various coalitions and under different leaderships, governed from 1996 to 2001, from 2006 to 2008, and from 2013 to 2017 (see the Appendix). In total, the centre-left produced eleven Documents. An important part of these (from 1996 to 2000) were written immediately before and after the Italian accession to EMU: hence they echo the pro-Europe enthusiasm of the time. The other two were outlined before the Great Crisis (2006–2008), while all the others were written in a time of consolidation of austerity, "secular stagnation" and crisis (2014–2017). In the analysis, I zoom in on especially the first bloc of DPEFs, since in those Documents it is possible to identify the core of what I conceptualize as a form of neoliberal-progressive Europeanism. Neoliberal-progressive Europeanism can be conceived as a combination of confidence in the market economy and the culture of fiscal stability, coupled with the progressive allure of European integration process as *the* anchor to modernize and stabilize Italian economy and society, and as set on the path of democracy and prosperity. Neoliberal-progressive Europeanism emerges as an *ideological junction* between the global expansion of neoliberal hegemony in the 1990s and the post-Maastricht phase of European integration. In Italy such a junction was mainly sustained by the centre-left.

In terms of political economy choices, the range of policies put on the table by the centre-left is a coherent set of supply-side measures (the so-called "structural reforms"). Market liberalization, flexibilization of the labour market, wage moderation, *risanamento*/fiscal consolidation through restructuring the public sector, tackling inflation, emphasis on competitiveness and entrepreneurship, and programmes of privatization represent the core measures of centre-left political economy, along with the reconfiguration of state intervention.[44] The following passage, among many others, is particularly effective for capturing "the new spirit of capitalism," as Boltanski and Chiapello put it (2005), and how this was fully embraced by the left:

> the privatization of public enterprises, the liberalization and re-regulation of markets, the reduction of the constraints to entrepreneurship, flexibility of labour markets, and the modernisation of public administration will contribute, along with public finance consolidation, to a new phase of growth in conditions of stability.[45]

Against the background of the cross-party pursuit of neoliberal reforms and austerity measures, the real difference between the centre-left and the centre-right governments (the latter permanently under the leadership of Silvio Berlusconi) is how they frame and resort to "Europe" as a symbolic reference.

While in the DPEFs outlined by centre-right governments, "Europe" is portrayed as a constraining force that must be (reluctantly) taken into account,[46] by contrast the tones of the left are strongly pro-European. European integration, here, is not only pictured as a constraining force, but above all it is strongly marked by a *progressive*, *dynamic*, and *modern* allure. As I earlier demonstrated by showing several long textual extracts from centre-left DPEFs (all from centre-left governments; see fn. 23 and 24), what characterizes the rhetoric of centre-left governments is the unquestioned and strong adhesion to the stability culture, clearly embodied by "Europe," and the challenge to render the South closer to northern standards. In this last respect, the relation between the South and the North is mostly under the radar; yet, implicitly, it is the South that needs to be adjusted, or better *normalized*, by following the northern (and signally German) culture. Intriguingly, such a relation is made explicit just once. The DPEF of 1997 (Prodi government) stated that Italian participation to EMU implies "assuring, in the European construction, the equilibrium between the mid-European (*mittel-european*) component and the Mediterranean component, which represents the foundation of the nature and history of our continent."[47] And yet, while it is not clear what kind of *cultural* features characterize the Mediterranean component, by contrast, the dimension of the stability culture is ever present.

Thus, the support for European integration came, in Italy, mainly from the left, and mainly as a mix between the neoliberal confidence in free markets and the ordoliberal pre-eminence of financial stability, in turn strengthened through the construction of the image of a South perpetually "eccentric" compared to northern stability. It is no surprise, then, that in conditions of the Great Recession of the late 2000s and later sovereign debt crises, the decline in the political legitimation and support for the European Union, increasingly perceived as a coercive and non-democratic force, began to drag down many social-democratic political forces across Europe, and the Italian left among these (see chapter 7).

FROM THE REPUBLICAN STATE TO THE NEOLIBERAL STATE

So far, I have analysed how state representatives legitimated and naturalized neoliberalization and accompanying austerity measures over a period of three decades through several rhetorical strategies. The final question is to understand, in this background, how the idea of state has changed from the post–World War II period to the present; that is, to explore the backbone of the neoliberal integral state project. The state, as Pierre Bourdieu remarked, is "the viewpoint on viewpoints" (2014, 28). In a way, it is the underlying ideological and cognitive force that represents the polity. The battle for the imposition and transformation of a determined idea of state—*what the state is, what the state ought to be, what the state does, what the state ought to do*—is the pivot through which a concrete conception of the world is legitimated and naturalized through the aforementioned "state effect." Once again, by redefining the cognitive, cultural, and ideological characteristics of the integral state, ruling forces try to legitimate, in parallel, changes across society. To throw light on this, I now briefly compare the evolution of the idea of state between the post-war Republican era and the neoliberal epoch. In relation to the first period, I will present the idea of state as it emerges in the constitution. Let me note, incidentally, that the comparison aims to show two different historical moments and their peculiar conceptions of the state. To avoid simplistic and misleading views of the Keynesian period, however, it is also worth highlighting a few important caveats: (i) the "early neoliberal" growth model after World War II and how the narrative of the "economic miracle" veiled the anti-labour policy in the late 1940s and 1950s; (ii) the contradictions of the Italian political system, dominated by Christian Democracy; (iii) the achievement of labour, welfare, and social rights only due to the cycles of workers' struggles in the 1960s and 1970s (see the previous chapter).

The Republican constitution is the main document through which I shed light on the post-war idea of state. The constitution of 1948 (especially in the first three articles) is the condensation of a broader agreement among all anti-fascist political forces of the time and, as such, reflects a common understanding about the nature of the Republican state. Let's start by saying that, under the fundamental article 3, the constitution stipulates that "[t]he Republic recognises to all citizens the right to work, and *creates* the conditions to make this right effective. Every citizen has a duty to undertake, according to their possibilities and choices, an activity or function to contribute to the material and spiritual progress of society" (emphasis added). Under article 2 (second paragraph), the constitution sets forth that "[i]t is a duty of the Republic *to remove* the economic and social constraints that, limiting the effective freedom and equality of citizens, prevent the full development of human beings and the participation of all workers in the political, economic and social organization of the Country" (emphasis added). Under article 1, another fundamental article to understand the idea of state, we read that "Italy is a democratic Republic founded on labour. Sovereignty belongs to the people, which it exercises within the forms and the limits established by this constitution."

Generally, three main elements stand out through the reading of these articles. The first is the recognition of the centrality of labour as an organized force in society; the second is the *proactive* role of the Republican state, and the third is the dimension of participation. All of these are functional to each other. The Republican state is, in fact, a proactive state that *creates* the conditions, and *removes* the obstacles, to foster the participation of *all workers* in the political, economic and social organization of the country. After the corporatist experience of the fascist regime, which prevented an autonomous organization of the labour force and banned political parties, the Republic, whose material configuration was based on a substantial equilibrium between the forces of labour and capital (especially from the late 1950s), sanctioned the autonomy of workers' organizations (art. 39), the right to strike (art. 40), and of political parties in the parliament. The element of political participation is particularly important, and represents one of the main differences with the neoliberal idea of state. In fact, the political authority of the new Republic institutions was rooted in the constitutional enlargement of participation to all productive forces. By formally recognizing the sociopolitical confrontation through the *autonomous* agency of the organizations of workers and capitalists to achieve compromises between different interests, and by establishing channels of political struggle through free parties in the parliament (within a shared framework of common rules and principles), the Republic sanctioned the principle that the socioeconomic policies were left to be determined by social and political forces; in other words, the space for different political economy worldviews was formally and substantively allowed.

Now, let's try to frame the neoliberal idea of state by returning to the analysis of the DPEFs. Generally, as stated in a DPEF issued by the centre-left government in 1997, "[t]he privatization of assets owned directly and indirectly by the state [. . .] is an important element of the transition towards a more competitive system," as "[t]he State, in a context of stable development of the economy, based on open markets, competition and deregulation, is no longer in charge of the management of enterprise activity, but just of governing and monitoring the respect of market rules."[48] *Risanamento* is directly linked to the redefinition of the general purposes of the state. "Risanamento of public finance can succeed only if the state exits from the direct management of economic activities, by nature better fulfilled by the free market."[49] The "market" (and its virtues and properties) thus represents the main cultural, symbolic, and ideological reference to legitimate the reform of the state. The market is framed as an intrinsically effective, dynamic, and rational system. Thus, while the state has to (de)regulate and protect the free market, it has also to change, *with respect to its own functioning*, by mimicking the functioning of the market economy. The reform of the state "in the name of the market" (Bruff and Starnes 2019) and of market-oriented "rationalization" is legitimated as the key strategy to improve the mechanisms of state action, in particular by making this "'smaller, less costly and characterised by higher returns' in terms of efficiency."[50] Rationalization is thus another keyword to understand the legitimation of public sector reform. As well as the case of *risanamento*, rationalization recurs in all the Documents analysed. More specifically, in policymakers' discourse the word rationalization indicates the reform of the public sector (and of public spending) according to the market-oriented cost–benefit approach. The reform applies to a number of areas ranging from public services, health system, education and research, taxation, pensions, public employment, and public administration, and it clearly accompanies austerity therapy.

> The possibility of achieving the targets of spending reduction through rationalization and saving depends on the commitment of all the subjects involved. In the middle-term, it is necessary to potentiate the interventions of rationalization started in the last years, reducing the free supply [of services] to some categories of citizens, and increasing the contribution of citizens [through indirect taxation] to the production of public services.[51]

An important direct outcome of this is represented by the stress on the reform of state budget procedures in the 1990s.[52] The reform can be conceived as the point of conjunction between the *redefinition of the general purposes of the state and the reconfiguration of state apparatuses*. Indeed, while the reform of the state budget is legitimated through the political economy of *risanamento* and the necessity of "rationalizing" public expenditures, in concrete terms it provides for a reduction of the scrutiny role of the national parliament, while at the same time improving the decision-making power and independence of the executive and economic ministries. By referring to the comparison to "other countries" (symbols of stability and balanced budgets), the following passage summarizes the *desiderata* and the rationale of budget reform.

> Budget procedures in countries that have lesser public deficits and public debt stock are characterized by the following requisites: the decision on the overall entity of state budget is taken before the discussion of the Documents in the parliament; Parliament's powers to increase public expenditures are limited to the level already decided before budget procedure; a substantive degree of independence of the Treasury minister, so that s/he can lead the process responsibly and effectively, both in the government and in the parliamentary procedures; the prohibition to change budget levels during the year.[53]

As this last passage (among many others[54]) makes clear, the neoliberal integral state project targets directly the structure of the state and state procedures to foster a process of hierarchical centralization of decision-making. In this respect, if the legitimating factor around the birth of the Republican state was based on political and social participation by all production and social forces across Italy, by contrast the construction of the neoliberal state put forward an idea of state as modelled on the culture and ideology of the free market economy, depoliticizing the agency of state institutions and excluding the possibility to pursue different political economy alternatives. Hence, besides the *formal* continuity of legal and constitutional order between these two conceptions of the state, neoliberal hegemony has substantially *re*founded the state on new cultural, ideological and material bases.

CONCLUDING REFLECTIONS: THE CONSTRUCTION OF THE NEOLIBERAL STATE BETWEEN SOUTHERN EXCEPTIONALISM AND DEPOLITICIZATION

In this chapter I shed light on the strategies of discursive legitimation of the neoliberal transition in Italy from the late 1980s to present. The first factor that emerged from the analysis of state representatives' discourse is the image of southern/Italian exceptionalism and, accordingly, of European integration and austerity as the means to discipline the country by imposing northern/European "normal"—that is, *normalizing*—standards. Another key discursive strategy is what I defined as the political economy of sacrifice and promise, conceivable as rhetoric based on the necessity of collective sacrifices for the recovery of the economy to achieve economic prosperity in the future, and in so doing, systematically and purposefully neglecting inequalities and structural imbalances produced by permanent austerity and neoliberalism. A further element I shed light on is what I identified as a distinctive form of neoliberal-progressive Europeanism; that is, a combination between trust in the free market economy and ordoliberal culture of stability along with the progressive vision of the European integration process, which characterized in particular the centre-left discourse and is currently in a deep crisis (see chapter 7). More broadly, the analysis of the DPEFs has also demonstrated the substantive continuities in political economy choices by centre-left and centre-right governments, actually constituting a "greater neoliberal political centre" (Cozzolino and Giannone 2019; for a brilliant account of the moral dimension of neoliberalism and the left in Italy see Muehlebach 2012). In chapter 7, I will show extensively how, after the crisis of 2008, the consensus towards European institutions and Europeanism as a political option entered into a deep crisis.

In general terms, the cultural shift based on the new ethos of market economy, entrepreneurship, and competitiveness provided for the general cognitive framework for the construction of the neoliberal "integral state." Yet there is also another factor that help us to frame better the broader strategy through which neoliberalization and permanent austerity were legitimated and naturalized as necessary choice. This factor is depoliticization, a political category

(Mouffe 2005) well-suited to catch the essence of the overall discursive framework that sustained neoliberalism and austerity (Giannone 2019, 60–70; De Nardis 2017). In general terms, depoliticization is a rhetorical strategy that aims to remove the partisan nature of political (and political economy) choices by appealing to technical or external factors—such as European integration or international markets (Burnham 2001; Flinders and Wood 2014). In so doing, "political choices conditioned by the market acquire the character of necessity and invevitability" (De Nardis 2017, 343). At the same time, depoliticization is also a form of legitimation of political power and policymaking (Giannone 2019, 62). This latter justifies its actions by resorting no more to general political visions of society but to the—supposed—objective, neutral, measurable "economic rationality" and technocratic expertise.

The Italian case, in this respect, has proved to be an extraordinary case since experts and technocrats, rather than providing for the economic expertise as generic "organic intellectuals," were members of the government (prime ministers, top officials in key ministries) on several occasions—and mostly when a financial crisis erupted—and provided a critical cognitive framework for legitimating austerity and neoliberal policies. In so doing, they granted a sort of "legitimation surplus" for unpopular economic measures in a country in which the political class has been heavily discredited since the early 1990s. Therefore, while generally depoliticization is "a process whereby state managers may seek to place at one remove the politically contested character of governing and in so doing paradoxically enhance political control" (Burnham 2014, 189), in Italy it was particularly effective over time thanks to the joint action of depoliticization and technocracy. Moreover, in such a strategy the dimension of external constraints is of critical importance since it constitutes, as my analysis of DPEFs has shown, the framework for the imposition of the mantra of "there is no alternative." By appealing to external factors—international finance and especially European integration—state representatives could off-load their responsibilities, and, at the same time, remove austerity and neoliberal measures from debate on the causes of macroeconomic imbalances, with the consequence of strengthening their overall control over the national political economy and also of the marginalization of dissent and alternatives. Thus, in the words of Fabio De Nardis:

> a discursive de-politicization determines the convergence of preferences into a single, albeit diverse, cognitive construction of reality (frame for public actions). It is no coincidence that the prevailing paradigm in the contemporary liberal political economy has been narrated in the form of a "single thought" [there is no alternative] demonstrating a clear cultural hegemony of transnationalized and financialized capitalism. (2017, 344)

To conclude, in this chapter I took into account the fundamental dimension of legitimation and naturalization of political economy choices through the redefinition of the idea of state. Yet and crucially, ideas and discursive strategies are accompanied by key transformations in the apparatuses of the state, and signally in the form of *executive strengthening*—the topic of next chapter. The social construction of the state and the institutional system, despite being analytically distinguishable, are part of the same processes of neoliberal transformations.

Chapter 6

The Rise of the Executive State and the Crisis of Parliamentary Democracy

Discussing the growth in the production of decree-laws in Italy during the 1910s and the 1920s, Sabino Cassese reports that, between 1915 and 1921, a total of 2,945 decrees was enacted, adding that "based on the practices of the liberal-authoritarian state, the future protagonists of the fascist state did confer an enormous power to the executive" (2016, 210–213; in chapter 8, I will focus on Gramsci's analysis of the transition from the liberal regime to the fascist state). More than one hundred years later, the question of the rise of executive powers in the state has emerged once again, clearly under different overall conditions but, in a way, always-already within the precarious relation between capitalism and democracy. In fact, "[t]he problem of the relation between market and democracy has emerged everywhere in Europe. Market integration requires centralization of decision-making power in a wide range of political economy policy domains" (Monti 2012, 18; own translation). The words of Mario Monti, prominent member of the Italian "technocratic collective intellectual" from the 1980s and prime minister of the fourth technocratic government of the Peninsula (2011), help us to frame the central question of this chapter: the *concentration* of power *in* the state and, more specifically, the strengthening of executive powers with specific relation to neoliberalism. In the previous chapter, I analysed the *construction* of the neoliberal state, and the specific forms and patterns of legitimation of neoliberalization and accompanying austerity policies by zooming in on the Italian state representatives' discourses. In the present chapter, I broaden the analysis by looking at the transformations of some of the key segments of the institutional apparatus of the state: the executive, the national parliament and the supranational institutional complex of the European Union.[1]

Below I analyse, for the first time in the literature, the longitudinal evolution of the legislative production with specific respect to political economy policy domains. More specifically, the source of the analysis is the legislation enacted in Italy from 1976 to 2015, now gathered and analysed in my *Political Economy Legislation Dataset*.[2] In general terms, "legal structures are excellent indicators of shifts in the democratic systems" (Obendorfer 2015, 28) as they reveal the underlying mechanisms, actors, and procedures through which decisions are taken and implemented. For instance, decisions regarding policy and policy implementation can be more hierarchical or more horizontal (namely, in this last case, based on discussion, mediation, real participation, and the possibility for dissent not only to be expressed but to also be able to challenge the *status quo*); insulated from public discussions and scrutiny or being kept accountable; grounded in ordinary procedures or enacted through emergency legislative tools in a permanent state of exception. In this respect, by coining the category of "new constitutionalism," Stephen Gill noted that the mechanisms of neoliberal governance increasingly relied on the separation of "economic policies from broader political accountability in order to make governments more responsive to the discipline of market forces and correspondingly less responsive to popular-democratic forces and processes" (1998, 5; see also Giannone 2019). Yet while Gill's theory aptly stressed the increased responsiveness of governments to market forces, the question of the separation between economy and political accountability needs to be clarified. Actually, rather than a general separation of economic policies from political accountability, I show that in Italy there is an unprecedented mobilization of specific apparatuses of the state to implement neoliberal and austerity policies and neutralize possible alternatives. In other words, the making of the market economy requires not only permanent market-making intervention from the state (Bruff 2011b; van Apeldoorn et al. 2012) to promote processes of neoliberal restructuring but also, and more importantly, processes of centralization and insulation of decision-making to fast-track the policymaking (e.g., through decree-laws) and marginalize alternatives and dissent within and outside the state.

Hence, the aim is to show the correlation between the relentless strengthening of executive powers and the implementation of neoliberal and austerity policy. Once again, the Italian case is particularly interesting for two main reasons. The first is that, as I argued in chapter 4, the post-war Republican constitution assigned the primacy to elected assemblies (the parliament) and parties, so the process of executive empowerment represents a transformation in the state de facto, namely without major constitutional changes, thanks to the agency of political forces in the state. The second is that, as the empirical analysis will confirm, a dramatic rise in executive-sponsored legislation is found especially in the early 1990s, that is, in connection to the establishment of technocratic executives, more insulated from parties and especially less accountable towards the electorate. This also triggered a path-dependent process that has characterized the entire period of the Second Republic up to the present. In the conclusions, I will discuss the question of executive strengthening as a key *political* factor of the neoliberal transformation of the state.

EXECUTIVE STRENGTHENING, EMERGENCY LEGISLATION, AND NEOLIBERALIZATION

The shift of power resources from parliament to executive is not, in Europe, an epiphenomenon of the post-Maastricht European integration process, despite the fact that this advanced phase of integration has empowered both national and supranational executives (Obendorfer 2015; Bonefeld 2015; Wigger 2019). Already in 1978, Nicos Poulantzas noted that "the relative distinction between legislative and executive power is becoming less sharp: through a process correlative with changes in the nature of such regulation, the power to fix norms and enact rules is shifting towards the Executive and state administration" (1978, 219). In what follows, I present a descriptive statistics-based analysis of political economy legislation and, through this, I assess the transformations in the Italian state's institutional system. The timeframe of the study embraces the period from 1976 to 2015. Partly anticipating the findings of the research, the analysis confirms that, over the entire timeframe of this study, processes of executive strengthening have appeared since the late 1970s/early 1980s, along with earlier processes of neoliberal economic restructuring. Also, such a process has been reinforced over time in parallel with the marginalization of the national parliament.

With specific respect to the research process, by gathering data from different types of laws enacted with regard to several different political economy policy domains, I present evidence of the relation between the evolving role of state institutions and the making of the national (and supranational) political economy. Generally, the legislative function is usually associated with the elected assemblies, while the government can enact legislative measures only in exceptional cases and usually through decree (legislative tools also known as "order," "ordinance," or in French, "ordonnances"). By analysing, for instance, the quantity of decrees enacted in a specific period of time, it is possible to assess the evolution of the executive's law-making activity. More in detail, the statistical analysis of the frequency through which emergency legal measures are used with *specific* regard to the national political economy allows us to understand the executive's particular role in processes of economic restructuring. At the same time, the analysis of ordinary law allows us to assess how the parliamentary legislative output evolves over time in relation to policymaking, and thus also the centrality of parties as collective agencies. Let me remark, in this respect, that the evolution of parties and the party system is another fundamental element of the analysis, and in some respects deserve an entire chapter in its own right. "Presidentialization" in the state parallels the crisis of parties as collective organizations and element of mediation between civil society and the state; in other words, processes of presidentialization and personalization of party politics coexist, and are mutually reinforcing of, presidentalization in the state (see Poguntke and Webb 2005; Passarelli 2015; Calise 2015). This process has also been aptly portrayed as "the democracy of the leader" (Calise 2016).

Returning to the present analysis, here I present data concerning the legislative activity of the executive and of the parliament; also, I include the domestic legislation that transposes EU law, so that three institutional sources of legislative production are taken into account. The analysis, and the presentation of the findings, is organized along the following subsections:

(I) An historical overview of executive strengthening in Italy in the late 1980s and 1990s, with a brief discussion of key reforms of the executive apparatus.
(II) Presentation of data about the overall legislation, to provide for an overview, and periodization, of the institutional transformations in Italy from 1976 to 2015. Also, this section zooms in on the historical trends of the longitudinal frequency of the main law typologies: ordinary law, decree-law, and legislative decrees.
(III) A specific focus on key political economy policy domains. Specifically, the so-called structural reforms (more below), public finance, local and regional finance, labour legislation, and EU legislation.

THE REFORMS OF THE ITALIAN EXECUTIVE IN THE 1980S AND 1990S

In Italy, presidentialization is associated with the rise of executive powers by means of improved organizational and law-making capacity, especially from the 1990s (Calise 2005; Musella 2019; Criscitiello 2019; Vercesi 2019). Generally, increases in executive-sponsored legislation already appeared in the 1980s, even if only in the 1990s the legislative activity of the executive acquired a new dimension and relevance. In relation to this last point, several key reforms paved the way to the strengthening of executive apparatus and its leverage on the national political economy. The first and most important reform was enacted in 1988, with the law no. 400. The aim of the bill was to channel policymaking activity into one main institutional centre, the executive, backed in its policymaking action by the economic ministries (unified, in

2001, in one single ministry for the economy and finance). This reform also established two important supporting institutions: the under-secretariat of the government and the general secretariat, both under the direct authority of the prime minister. The main innovation of the 1988 reform was the introduction of the "confidence question" (which is different from the "no-confidence" vote[3]). Specifically, the executive can *impose* the confidence question on the parliament in relation to specific law proposals, so as to reduce the risk of a parliamentary rejection of the bill. In this case, the executive warns its parliamentary majority that it will call for new elections in case of a negative vote on the bill covered by the confidence question. At the same time, this legal mechanism serves to fast-track the approval of the specific bill, and to cut down the time allocated for discussion and, relatedly, to the amending power of parliamentary forces (Criscitiello 2004, 2019). The question of confidence is particularly relevant, as it significantly empowered the executive against the parliament and parliamentary scrutiny. Importantly, the executive started to resort to this means of "pressure" on parliament especially from the early 2000s, and systematically after 2008. Currently, parliamentary discussion of key reform bills is consistently cut down through the ordinary resort to confidence question.

Through the bill introduced in 1988, moreover, the prime minister obtained the power to convene the council of ministers, to block the act of a minister and to ask for a collegial discussion in the council, and to nominate the under-secretariat of the government. Importantly, while this reform sanctioned the primacy of the chief executive *within* the council of ministers, it also imposed *the primacy of the executive's policy priorities over those of the parliament*, so that through "the change in the rules regulating the parliamentary agenda, both on the floor and in committees, the government has become able to impose its own bills far more effectively. The ratio of laws originating in the parliament and laws passed by the government has consequently shifted dramatically towards the latter" (Calise 2005, 92; see also Criscitiello 2004, 77). Importantly, with respect to the legislative dimension, the reform also established several policy structures to coordinate and enforce the legislative power of the executive, in particular the department of legal and judicial affairs. "The law-making power of the government acquires through this law also a formal centrality [. . .] For the first time, the law-making instruments of the executive, starting from regulations, were causally related to the administrative reorganization" (Criscitiello 2004, 98; own translation).

Almost ten years after the 1988 reform, two new reforms, enacted by the centre-left in 1997 (Prodi government) and in 1999 (D'Alema government) improved the organization of the executive branch as a part of a broader strategy of public sector reform. Incidentally, let me remark that in the previous chapter I stressed that the centre-left espoused market ideology and permanent austerity, also via the uncritical support for the European integration process. Here, it is worth noting that the centre-left also supported the strengthening of the government in light of the "necessity" to improve "governability" (I return to this concept in the chapter's conclusion). A recent and most relevant part of this parabola was the constitutional reform proposed in 2016 by the centre-left government led by Matteo Renzi, which (among other things) aimed to enhance significantly the policymaking power of the executive by outlining an improved procedure to enact decree-laws. However, in the referendum held in 2016 this reform of the constitution was rejected by 60 percent of those who voted (leading to Renzi's resignation).

But let's return, now, to the specific reforms of the centre-left in the late 1990s. The law no. 59 of 1997 aimed at reinforcing "the autonomous function of impulse, direction and coordination of the president of the council." This measure made the presidency structure at the same time (a) lighter, with respect to its infrastructure, (b) more autonomous from other ministries, and (c) more incisive with respect to imposing the overall policy. The following centre-left cabinet led by Massimo D'Alema in 1999 made another substantive advancement in executive strengthening and reorganization by enacting a legislative decree that reorganized the cabinet and public administration more broadly (law no. 303). This reform provided for (i) the introduction of independent agencies, which obtained the authority of regulating key policy areas such as market competition and telecommunications; (ii) the transformation of prefectures into territorial offices of the government; (iii) the promotion of financial responsibility of the whole infrastructure of public administration and of the government, and (iv) the transformation into departments of the great majority of ministries. This last reform concentrated and strengthened even further the decision-making power of the cabinet, to the extent that the chief executive gained control over every area and instrument of policymaking (Criscitiello 2004, 111). The reforms of 1988, 1997, and 1999 were important steps in the reconfiguration of the executive apparatus and public administration. This process was clearly strengthened by the European integration process and by the EMU more specifically, which favoured the centralization of decision-making and coordinating power of the prime minister's office and its technocratic infrastructure. "In Italy, the 'technicalisation' of ministerial staff proceeded apace during the 1990s, particularly in ministries (like the Treasury) most exposed to the policies of financial convergence required by European Monetary Union (EMU)." At the same time, "'[t]echnicalisation' also involved the Prime Minister's Office, which equipped itself with a staff of policy makers to coordinate EU policies centrally" (Fabbrini and Donà 2003, 37; Barbieri 2003). Yet the strengthening of the Italian executive occurred also as a *praxis* based on the systematic resort to decree-laws, as I now discuss.

POLITICAL ECONOMY LEGISLATION AND STATE TRANSFORMATIONS: A GENERAL OVERVIEW

Many studies take into account how domestic legislation changed over time, framing the use of emergency measures from the early 1990s (Capano and Giuliani 2001; Musella 2019), the rise of legislative decrees (Kreppel 2009), the evolution of the role of parliament (Chimenti 1992; De Micheli and Verzichelli 2004), the weight of EU legislation in domestic law-making activity (Borghetto et al. 2012), and the use of emergency legal instruments and mechanisms during the global crisis (2008-2011) (Calvano 2014).

As noted earlier in the chapter, the present study analyses the longitudinal evolution of legislative production with specific respect to the political economy, gathered in the *Political Economy Legislation Dataset.* For reasons of space, in this section, I concentrate my attention on two key sets of data (for the analysis of all the findings see Cozzolino 2018c). The first regards the general tendencies of legislation according to the type of law, that is, ordinary law, or the law originating from parliament; decree-law and law of conversion, a legal instrument in the hands of the executive; legislative decrees and EU law (this enacted via legislative decrees). The second set of data zooms in on key political economy policy domains: macroeconomic ("structural") reforms, public finance, local and regional finance, labour law, and several other domains covered by EU law.

Ordinary Law and the Prolonged Crisis of the Italian Parliament

As already noted in this book, the Republican constitution assigned to the parliament a central position within the institutional system, marking a rupture with the single-party, executive-led fascist regime. Therefore, elected assemblies formally owned the legislative power and, accordingly, the ordinary law (or parliamentary law) was designed to be the main instrument of legislation (art. 70 of Italian constitution). So how did ordinary parliamentary law evolve through the analytical timeframe considered by this study? Generally, in the period from 1976 to 2015 ordinary law accounts for the 40 percent of the entire legislation produced in Italy. It is the highest legislative instrument used in domestic policymaking. Yet, *it is also the one characterized by the most intense, steady, and quantitatively relevant decline*. This will be clearer by looking in detail at specific historical moments and junctures. During the 1980s and until the early 1990s, the use of the ordinary law, even if already characterized by a decreasing trend, was still considerable. For instance, it achieved a mean of 57 laws per year (4.7 per month) between 1976 and 1990.

The first remarkable decline of parliamentary law-making occurred in the early 1990s (table 6.1).

As I showed in the previous chapter, this juncture is characterized by a number of key political and economic events that, on the one hand, legitimated and naturalized *risanamento* and neoliberal measures as the solution to Italian economic malaise. On the other, they favoured a process of centralization of power in the state, especially through the agency of technocrats. In more practical terms, the power shift from parties in the parliament towards the executive apparatus (and, within the party, towards the leadership; see Calise 2015) helped produce a remarkable decrease in the levels of ordinary parliamentary legislation (and, as we will see in next section, a rise in emergency legislation). For instance, from 78 ordinary laws enacted in 1991 regarding the political economy, the total number of parliamentary laws dropped to 35 in 1992, 27 in 1993, 14 in 1994, and, respectively, 9 and 6 in 1995 and 1996, before increasing slightly in 1997—though never reaching the earlier levels. Importantly, the second remarkable fall occurred after 2008, when this legislative instrument became definitively marginal during the years of the sovereign debt crisis. According to the data, from a mean of 14.4 laws per year between 2001 and 2005, the use of ordinary law dropped to a mean of 5 laws per year between 2006 and 2010 and 6 between 2011 and 2016 (table 6.1).

Currently, parliamentary law is relegated to an absolute marginality in quantitative and qualitative terms. In quantitative terms, the fall of ordinary law vis-à-vis the legislative production of the executive—and of the European Union—reveals several important tendencies to help us understand the evolution of contemporary democracy within neoliberal capitalism: first, the formation of law in the parliament through political debate, conflict, and mediation over alternatives has paved the way to forms of fast-track imposition of measures through the executive apparatus. Second, the national parliament has no relevant decision-making power regarding political economy

Table 6.1 Trends in Political Economy Legislation (yearly mean)

	Ordinary Law	*Law of Conversion*	*Legislative decree (dom)*	*Legislative decree (EU)*
1976–1980	62.2	27.4	–	0.2
1981–1985	61	27.4	–	0.4
1986–1990	43.2	20.4	5.6	0.2
1991–1995	32.6	24.2	7	15.6
1996–2000	26.6	20.4	33.6	14.4
2001–2005	14.4	23	21.4	14.4
2006–2010	4.8	11	11.2	16.2
2011–2015	5.8	13.4	10.2	17.6

Source: Own elaboration. Data taken from normattiva.it.

policy domains or policymaking more broadly. Actually, it mostly ratifies executive decisions.

Executive Powers and Emergency Legislation

The Italian constitution stipulates that the legislative power ordinarily belongs to the parliament (art. 70). Yet, it provides also that in *extraordinary* cases of *necessity* and *urgency* the executive may enact, under its direct responsibility, provisional measures endowed with "force of law": the decree-laws (art. 77). According to the constitution, decree-laws ought to be presented to the Chamber of Deputies and to the Senate during the same day of their adoption by the executive, and then must be converted into law by both Chambers within a period of sixty days. The conversion occurs through a dedicated legal act, the "law of conversion." Importantly, while the effects of decree-laws are immediate, if it is not "converted in law" by the parliament within sixty days, the decree loses its legal effects after its initial enactment by the executive.

This kind of legislation, also labelled "emergency" and/or "urgency" legislation, strengthens the policymaking role of the executive in the parliament as decree-laws allow the executive to impose its priority over the parliamentary agenda (Musella 2012, 2014). Moreover, as decree-laws are immediately productive of effects, the Italian constitution requires that such legal instruments must be enacted, first, in "exceptional circumstances"; second, that decree-laws must have a direct and organic link to such "exceptional circumstances." More specifically:

(a) The extraordinary/exceptional nature of the event is the precondition for the adoption of decree-laws. In theory, in such exceptional events the government issues the emergency legislation for reasons of necessity and urgency. Therefore and generally, the Italian constitution states that the executive cannot issue legislation on an ordinary/normal basis.

(b) According to the constitution and to a key ruling of Italian Constitutional Court (1996), decree-laws ought to be homogenous with respect to their content. The homogeneity concerns the field/domain (that is, a decree-law cannot contain measures of different policy areas or with respect to different situations), and/or needs to be linked to the specific and exceptional circumstance being invoked. Therefore, and in theory, executives cannot legislate in different policy domains through single decree-laws and in ordinary circumstances.

Let's turn, now, to the quantitative analysis of decree-laws. A remarkable number of studies concerning the use of emergency decrees usually recognize the unprecedented and daily resort to this type of law from the early 1990s. Indeed, the use of decree-laws skyrocketed under technocratic governments in the first half of the 1990s. Technocratic executives, twisting de facto the constitution, resorted to decree-laws on an ordinary basis to enact measures in a great variety of policy domains. However, the data collected and presented in this study show that the rise of decree-laws began in the mid-1970s, during the crisis of the Keynesian welfare state, increased during the 1980s, and then skyrocketed from the early 1990s. Between 1975 and 1976, the laws of conversion (in this case concerning not just the political economy but the overall law-making activity) increased from 18 measures to 51, and maintained higher trends afterwards. Importantly, fiscal policy and structural reforms are the fields in which the use of decree is more frequent (more on this below).

Figure 6.1 shows the trends concerning decree-laws and laws of conversion from 1948, that is, when the constitution entered into force, to 2016. From 1976, and then during the 1980s, the use of decree-laws started to increase remarkably. As already noted, the technocratic executives in the first half of the 1990s used decree-laws to legislate on daily affairs, clearly beyond (and against) the "extraordinary cases of necessity and urgency" required by the constitution. At the same time, given the frequency in the resort of emergency legislation, the rate of successful parliamentary ratification declined, producing a mismatch between the number of decrees adopted and the number of laws of conversion effectively approved. As displayed in figure 6.1, the higher the resort to decrees, the lower the approval capacity of the parliament (see in particular the years between 1979 and 1996). Between 1992 and 1996, this trend acquired outstanding features, with 1,381 decree-laws passed versus 299 laws of conversion eventually enacted, thus a rate of successful approval of one law of conversion for 4.6 decrees.

Coming to emergency legislation regarding specifically the political economy policy domains, and taking into account just the laws of conversion,[4] it is worth noting that the highest rates of law of conversion occurred from 1976 to 1985. Several factors explain this. First and importantly, between the late

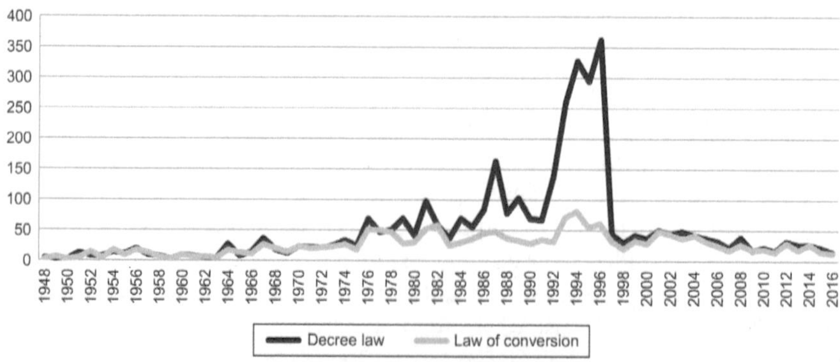

Figure 6.1 Decree-Laws and Laws of Conversion (1948–2016).

1970s and the mid-1980s the beginning of the use of decree-laws was related especially to fast-tracking measures to tackle the oil crisis and the fiscal-economic restructuring of the period, namely when the government's deficit started to increase (chapter 4). Given, however, the lesser total number of decree-laws enacted compared to the early 1990s (figure 6.1), the rate of success in the conversion of decrees in laws (of conversion) was higher. Second, as I noted before, from the early 1990s Italian governments, especially technocratic, enacted an unprecedented amount of (hundreds of) decrees, thus provoking a flection in the rate of conversion—by the parliament—of these into laws. Moreover, along with the decree-laws, the government started to resort to legislative decrees (more below), so that it could rely on two legislative channels for policymaking.

It is also important to note that in 1996 a ruling of the Constitutional Court censored this practice as anti-constitutional, generating a decrease in the use of decree-laws—even if these started to increase again between 2001 and 2005 (Berlusconi government). During the post-2008 crisis and sovereign debt crisis (2011), there is no overall increase in the rate of laws of conversion compared to other periods analysed. However, as I argue below in relation to the analysis of the specific policy domains, this legislative instrument actually increases in key areas like "structural reforms" and public finance. In other words, it is true that the political-economic legislation declines *in general*, but importantly the agency of the executive is selectively addressed to those domains concerned by austerity policies and neoliberal measures (Cozzolino 2019a). It is worth stressing another tendency related to emergency legislation. While the total number of decree-laws decreases over time, and in particular after 2008, their *internal* dimension grows as they have become "maxi-containers" of measures enacted in a large number of fields and policy areas (more below).

Legislative Decrees and EU Legislation

The last legislative tool to analyse is legislative decree (*decreto legislativo*). According to article 76 of the Italian constitution, the legislative decree is a law approved by the executive after a mandate issued by the parliament through a specific law, that is, the delegation law (*legge delega*). *Legge delega* outlines the general framework for the *decreto legislativo*, while the executive establishes the content and specific measures of the decree.

Throughout the First Republic, the use of legislative decrees was almost non-existent (Kreppel 2009; Musella 2014). The first legislative decrees started to be enacted from 1988, and during the 1990s they became the main legal instrument for economic and especially institutional reforms (under the aegis of the New Public Management; see Capano 2000). Importantly, legislative decrees are also the principal legal instrument through which EU legislation is transposed into the domestic system. Methodologically, the analysis of legislative decrees is split into two subgroups.

(a) Domestic legislative decree, namely those originating exclusively within the national context;
(b) Legislative decrees that transpose EU legislation—to which I refer here as *EU legislation*—therefore originating from another institutional source.

The methodological choice of "separating" the two sources of *decreto legislativo* is aimed at analysing, empirically, the EU as a source of legislation, thus exploring the evolution of the policymaking role of three peculiar institutions: the parliament, the executive, and the EU.

Turning now to specific quantitative assessment, the use of legislative decrees started to become relevant and systematic in the 1990s. In general terms, legislative decrees constitute 28 percent of total legislation, but within an analytical timeframe of twenty-eight years (as the first legislative decree actually appeared in 1988). In this framework, 15 percent of legislative decrees are adopted exclusively in the national context, and 12 percent transpose EU legislation. Importantly, while domestic legislative decrees increase in the five-year period between 1996 and 2000 but thereafter begin a steadily declining tendency, EU legislation marks a rising trend throughout the period considered. Even more importantly, while the overall legislation (i.e., all types of law) declines throughout the period of this study, the EU is the only source of legislation that increases steadily, now becoming the principal source of policymaking (see table 6.1 and figure 6.2).

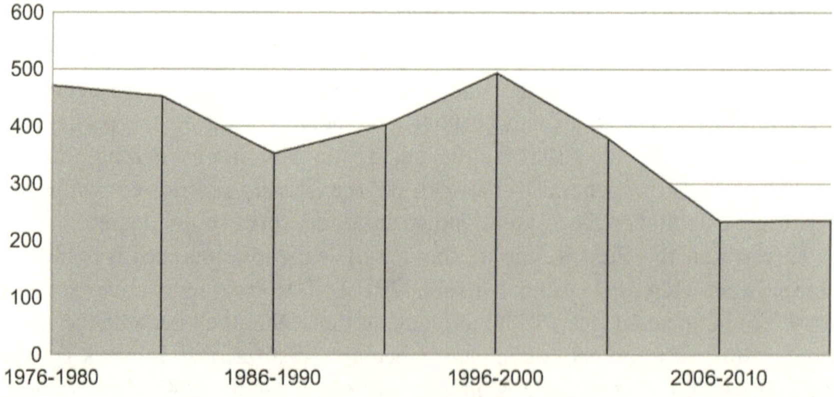

Figure 6.2 Political Economy Legislation (1976–2015).

GENERAL PATTERNS OF POLITICAL ECONOMY LEGISLATION: A FIRST ASSESSMENT

Table 6.1 displays the yearly mean of political economy legislation from 1976 to 2015. In light of this and of the analysis done so far, now we can draw some preliminary conclusions on the historical trends of legislative production in political economy.

First, the parliamentary legislative production, in general and particularly with respect to political economy policy domains, displayed a relentlessly declining tendency throughout the period analysed, in particular from the 1990s. Parliament can be currently considered to be marginal in relation to the quantity and quality of political economy legislation. It is worth stressing, moreover, that junctures of decline in parliamentary policymaking occurred during the periods of the main fiscal crises of the Italian Republic (1992–1993, and 2007–2008).

Second, the longitudinal patterns of the executive's legislative production shows that it started to prevail over parliament's legislative activity from the early 1990s, in connection with the transition from the First to the Second Republic, under technocratic governments and along with the introduction of the majoritarian electoral system. From this moment, the output difference between the executive's and the parliament's legislation continued to grow steadily, with the consolidation of the first and the marginalization of the second.

Third, data concerning decree-laws show that their highest frequency occurred in the first decade, while the lowest rates are found over the last decade. Why? There are two main explanations. The first is the already-mentioned tendency, qualitative and "internal" to decree-laws, to use these as a sort of "general containers" of many policy measures. In other words, while the number of decrees decline, the content of single decrees expanded. Second, there is a general overall reduction of legislation in political economy (see figure 6.2). Such a reduction is explained by the decline of ordinary law and the internal/qualitative expansion of decree-laws, plus the increasing visibility of EU legislation. However, if we analyse the ratio among types of law, within the mentioned trend *the law-making activity of the executive outnumbers that of the parliament by four times* (table 6.1). Crucially, the intervention of the executive, as the next section shows, becomes increasingly selective towards structural/neoliberal reforms and fiscal policy, especially by resorting to the aforementioned "maxi-decrees," while declining in all the other political economy policy domains (e.g., infrastructures, energy policy, agriculture and fishery, industrial policy, etc.; see Cozzolino 2018c, for a general overview).

At the same time and in contrast to the overall decline in legislative production, EU legislation increased (table 6.1, figure 6.3). Thus, along with the

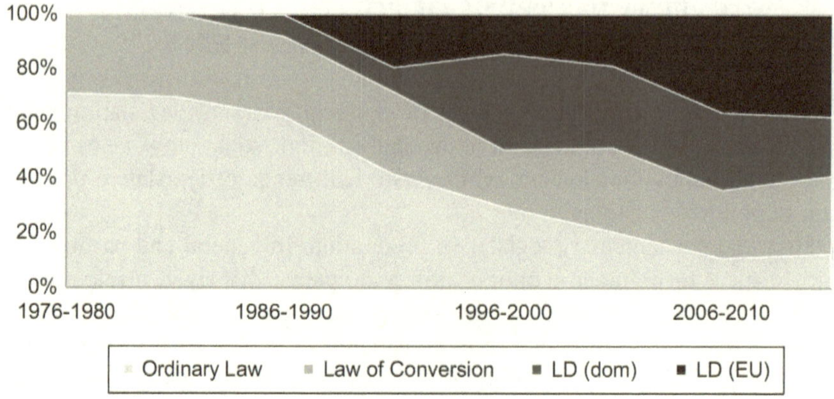

Figure 6.3 Ratio between Law Types (1976–2015, %).

marginalization of the parliament and the "selective intervention" of Italian executives, there is another institutional dynamic to be considered in the making of the domestic political economy: the growing direct impact of EU law (see figure 6.3).

In the last decade of the study (2006–2015), the EU counts as the second source of legislation, with an output *three times higher* than that of the national parliament of Italy. In terms of single law types, EU law also outmatches the law of conversion and the domestic legislative decree. Concluding, in the last decade covered by the research, the legislative production concerning the political economy has increasingly shifted towards the EU and domestic executive, with a drastic marginalization of parliament.

NEOLIBERALIZATION BY EXECUTIVIZATION: AN IN-DEPTH ANALYSIS OF KEY POLICY DOMAINS

In this section, I analyse data concerning several fundamental political economy policy domains: macroeconomic ("structural") reforms, public finance, regional and local finance, and labour policy. I then complement the analysis by providing data of EU legislation with specific respect to market liberalization, in particular financial activities and public services.

Neoliberal Reforms via Executive Powers

Let's start with the key domain of macroeconomic-structural reforms. As noted by Crespy and Vanheuverzwijn (2019) with respect to European economic governance, the notion of "structural reforms" actually points—as "empty signifier"—to neoliberal policies and ideas. In this study, I gather under the label "structural reforms" a range of neoliberalizing measures aimed at changing the productive structure of Italian society by strengthening the supply-side. This includes measures to enhance the scope of markets and competition, tax breaks for enterprises and collateral measures to improve firm competitiveness, reduction of labour costs, subsidies for entrepreneurship, and liberalization of productive activities.

In quantitative terms, the distributional frequency of laws in this domain shows the crucial role of executive powers in implementing neoliberal measures. Importantly, such an enhanced role for the Italian executive appears in the early 1980s, and then strengthens through the whole period under scrutiny. The data demonstrate that there is a clear-cut prevalence of laws of conversion—except for the five-year period from 1996 to 2000. More specifically, while ordinary law accounts for 19 percent of total legislation and the *decreto legislativo* for 12 percent, the laws of conversion constitute 70 percent of the legislation in this domain (see figure 6.4).

With respect to the historical trends of legislative production, the in-depth analysis of law-making activity reveals a growing tendency in two discrete and long periods: from 1981 to 1995, and from 2001 to 2015. In the second period, legislative output is higher compared to the first phase of increases between 1981 and 1995. Moreover, after the global economic crisis in 2008, and the sovereign debt crisis in 2011, overall legislative output increased further and reached its highest peak. While fourteen measures were passed through laws of conversion during the heights of the crisis (2007–2010), the post-crisis period (from 2011 to 2015) saw the consolidation of the trend with the enactment of further twenty-two measures (figure 6.4). Importantly, ordinary legislation in this policy domain is actually negligible, hence testifying to the strong marginalization of parliament.

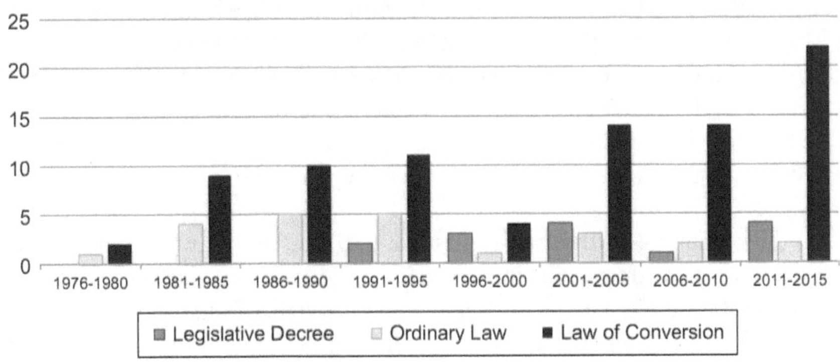

Figure 6.4 Structural Reforms (1976–2015).

Public Finance Legislation: Austerity by Exceptional Means

Public finance is the backbone of the national political economy. The previous chapter has already analysed the discursive strategies that legitimated *risanamento*, namely permanent austerity, naturalizing this political economy choice as an unavoidable and necessary policy. This section offers a different but interlocked perspective by analysing how the consolidation of public finance is enforced in legislative terms. I consider dispositions concerning spending mechanisms, fiscal adjustment measures, financial stability bills, and budgetary reforms.[5] More specifically, I gather all the measures concerning public finance (especially spending cuts) introduced outside the annual budget laws provided for by the constitution. In so doing, it is possible to appreciate in detail the role of executive agency in relation to the fiscal policy and, above all, fiscal consolidation. Yet, it is also worth noting that also the ordinary financial and budget laws experienced a quantitative decline over time (Cozzolino 2018c), coupled with (1) the limitations to parliamentary forces to amend the entity of budget measures introduced during the 1980s (see chapter 4), and (2) the close surveillance and monitoring of the European Commission with respect to fiscal policy, especially after the 2011 crisis.

In relation to the longitudinal frequency of legislative production, during the first five-year period of this study (1976–1980) the measures in public finance were generally rare, also given the role of the parliament in determining budget measures. In the following five years—a period which can be considered as the beginning of the first phase of fiscal consolidation—the overall measures quadrupled, especially due to the resort to decree-laws. Importantly, the Italian executive started to pass decree-laws to enact fiscal adjustment measures (especially in the health system and welfare). From the second half of the 1980s, the use of the decree-law for purposes of fiscal adjustment grew consistently. By contrast, the single ordinary law passed in this period is law no. 400 in 1988 (analysed earlier), which introduced the reform of budget procedures and tightened the control of the executive vis-à-vis the parliament. In conjunction with the consolidation of neoliberal policy and austerity in the 1990s, the use of decree-laws for *risanamento* purposes grew further (figure 6.5). Fundamental measures of fiscal consolidation and reduction-cum-restructuring of public spending passed mainly via emergency legislation.

At the beginning of the twenty-first century, ordinary law disappeared as a legislative tool for public finance. *Risanamento* action thus occurred, on institutional grounds, via the enhanced legal activism of the executive, while parliament became a mere ratifying (or delegating) institution. On the other hand, the use of the legislative decrees in this policy domain is relatively marginal, but nonetheless several legislative decrees introduced important

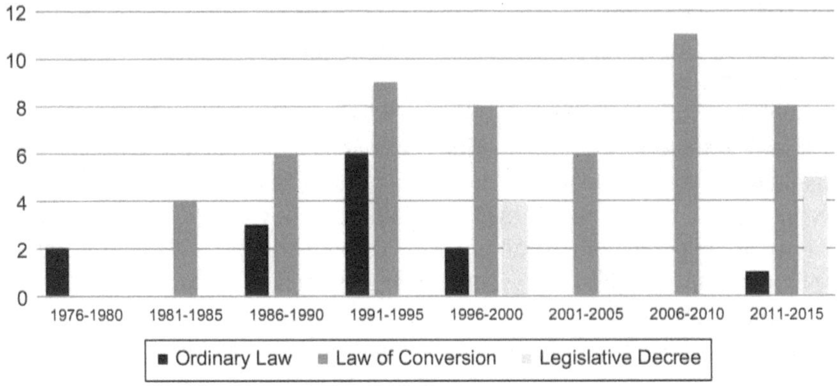

Figure 6.5 Fiscal Consolidation (1976–2015).

general reforms of the state budget and spending mechanisms, especially in the periods from 1996 to 2000 and from 2011 to 2015. Statistically, the law of conversion stands out as the legal instrument that recurs with the highest frequency—68.5 percent of the overall legislation—followed by ordinary law (17 percent) and legislative decree (14 percent) (figure 6.5).

In the last decade, the legislative production continued to increase. This trend materialized soon before the global crisis, when in 2006–2007 several decrees enacted important measures of fiscal consolidation (e.g., 248/2006, 286/2006). However, it is after the breakout of global economic crisis and sovereign debt crisis that policymakers systematically and exclusively resorted to emergency legislation and legislative decrees to pass austerity measures. Meaningfully, the single ordinary law passed in the crisis period is a collateral measure of the reform of the constitution that, under the Monti government, introduced the balanced budget principle (2012).

Regional and Local Finance: Fiscal Adjustment from the Late 1970s

Regional and local (i.e., municipality level) finance is actually the first policy domain in which the executive resorted to decree-laws to introduce measures of fiscal consolidation. In fact, as soon as the fiscal crisis of the Keynesian state appeared in Italy in the 1970s, the first large-scale application of austerity measures (1977) was punctuated by a series of decrees aimed at reducing public expenditures at regional and local levels. The use of decree-laws to regulate these levels of public finance continued in the following decade, when they were used to pass a series of extraordinary measures concerning in particular local spending. In relation to the role of the parliament, between the late 1970s and during the 1980s, ordinary law was used mainly to introduce general dispositions concerning the coordination between the budget of the state and that of the regions (figure 6.6).

After this first phase of fiscal adjustment, from the early 1990s new trends in legislative production arose. First, ordinary law became absolutely marginal, while the frequency of decree-laws also decreased. The legislative decree, on the other hand, turned to be the main instrument of law-making activity in regional and local finance. Throughout the 1990s, the Italian executives, influenced by the hegemony of New Public Management (Capano 2003), employed legislative decrees to pass several major reforms on public administration, taxation, education, pension, and health systems. Local spending was part of this "permanent cycle of reform" (Capano 2003, 787), which aimed to implement "fiscal federalism," and thus to ration the financial transfers to local government. The reform also aimed to strengthen the fiscal autonomy of local government within the framework of the EU's Stability and Growth Pact (1997), and to introduce a business-oriented mentality in the public sector and in public administration.

After a decline in the overall volume of legislative activity from the early to mid-2000s, the legislation on local and regional finance grew again in the last decade, especially in the 2011–2015 period. In this historical juncture, the content of policymaking was likewise addressed to enhance fiscal federalism (in this case, also at municipal level) and to reform the local government budget. In terms of legal mechanisms, from the early 1990s to 2015, decree-laws and legislative decrees were the only types of law utilized. They account for, respectively, 45 and 34 percent of total legislation, while it is only 21 percent for ordinary law. The role of the parliament with regards to local finance policymaking, from the 2000s onwards, considerably shrank and can be considered marginal.

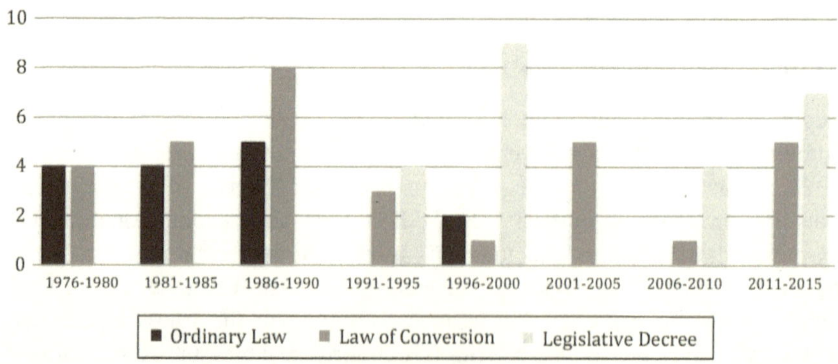

Figure 6.6 Regional and Local Finance (1976–2015).

Labour Policy

Labour law is extremely relevant for understanding the underlying structural class patterns of state reconfiguration and neoliberalization. As I noted in chapter 4, from the early 1980s and especially during the 1990s Italian policymakers reacted to the cycle of workers' struggles of the 1960s and 1970s by means of wage deflation and "flexibilization" of the labour market. In this section, I turn to analyse the legislation in the labour policy domain. Also, in this case, the aim is to assess how policymaking is related to the evolution and change in state apparatuses. More specifically, I present data concerning: (a) labour market, wages and general economic benefits linked to wages (labour policy); (b) legislation in recruitment, professions and careers; (c) labour, welfare (indirectly linked to wages) and pension schemes.

In relation to the first sub-domain, that is, general labour policy, the prevalence of legislative production is concentrated in the first decade of the timeframe. The overall number of legal acts in the five years from 1976 to 1980 is double compared to those enacted in the period from 1991 to 1995. Importantly, the fall in labour legislation is mainly related to the decline of ordinary law and thus of parliamentary activity in labour regulation (see figure 6.7).

With specific relation to the content of labour policy, from the mid-1970s and until the late 1980s the majority of policy measures in the domain concerned the decrease of labour costs and the gradual reduction of economic benefits linked to wage schemes. In fact, while the legislation concerning economic benefits experienced a fall throughout the 1980s, from 1991 to 1995 the technocrats started an intense period of policymaking activity. This revolved around the restructuring of the labour market (the aforementioned abolition of *scala mobile,* that is, wage indexation to inflation), the reduction

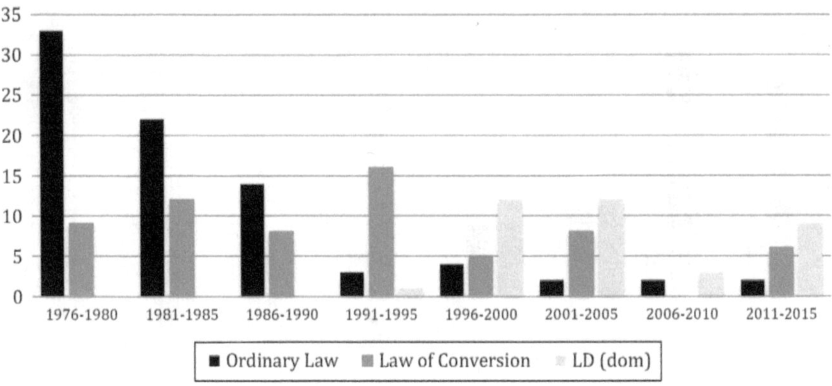

Figure 6.7 Labour Policy (1976–2015).

of labour costs and, especially from mid-1990s, the introduction of several important reforms of labour contracts, particularly via legislative decree (e.g., Law no. 196/1997, implemented by the centre-left government, which introduced several types of temporary labour contracts). Thus, from mid-1990s, and in the next decade, legislative decrees and decree-laws were (almost) the only legal tools used to issue measures in labour market.

With respect to the other two domains, "recruitment, professions and careers" (figure 6.8) and "labour, welfare and pensions" (figure 6.9), the trends in law-making activity are similar to general labour policy. In relation to the first group, between the mid-1970s and the late 1980s state intervention was addressed to recruit and/or stabilize the employees in the enlarged public sector (military and police, public education, health system, diplomacy, telecommunications), and to regulate career and career progressions. From the early 1990s, public intervention concerning recruitment and careers

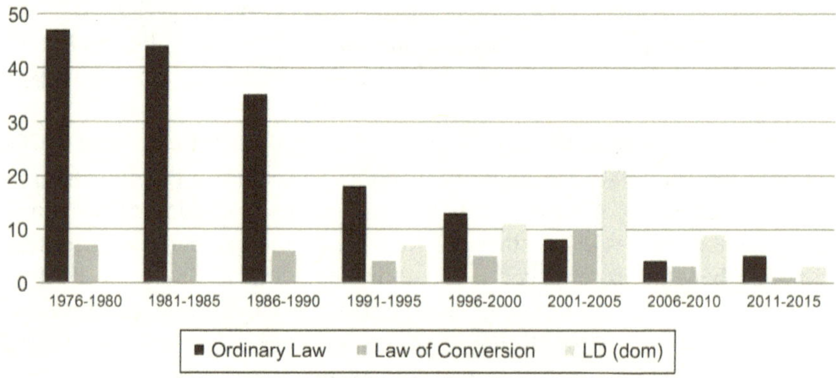

Figure 6.8 Recruitment, Professions, and Careers (1976–2015).

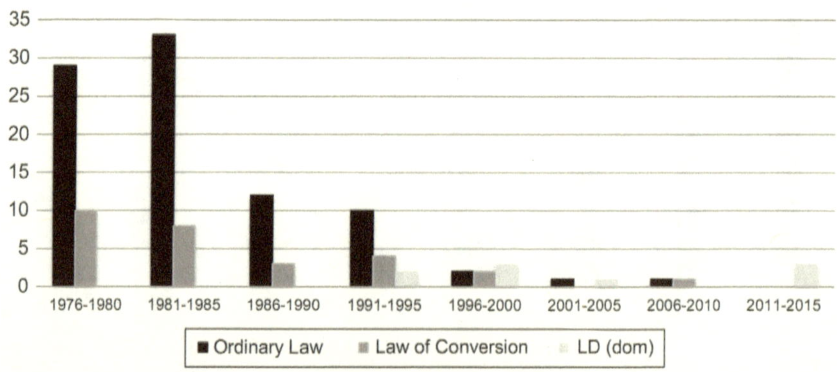

Figure 6.9 Labour, Welfare, and Pensions (1976–2015).

started to decrease, with the exception of the five-year period from 2001 to 2005 under the Berlusconi government, and decreased again after 2006. Ordinary law was gradually substituted, in particular, by legislative decrees.

Eventually, the legislation concerning labour, welfare, and pensions is even more remarkable, in terms of the decrease, compared to the other policy domains that have been analysed. Here, the global law-making activity dropped in three discrete periods: in the second half of the 1980s, in the second half of the 1990s, and eventually from the beginning of the new millennium. Thereafter, the legislative production became, in fact, absolutely marginal, confirming the global reduction of state intervention regarding labour, *with the notable exception of specific labour market reforms aimed at "flexibilizing" the labour market.*

EU LAW AND THE ITALIAN POLITICAL ECONOMY

This section provides for a general assessment of EU law and the Italian political economy, especially with respect to those policy domains where it is particularly relevant in quantitative terms compared to domestic legislation. Along with the analysis of EU legislation, this section also reflects on the broader EU governance framework and how it empowers the national executive on the one hand, and furthers neoliberalization and accompanying austerity policies on the other.

In relation to EU law, it is worth stressing, first of all, that the total weight of European legislation in the Italian legal system has increased, especially over the last decade (figure 6.3), as has occurred in all the other EU member states (Brouard et al. 2012). Currently, the EU is the second most important source of legislative production: behind the executive, ahead of parliament (figure 6.3). Moreover, given the overall decrease of domestic legislation with regard to the political economy (figure 6.2), and the parallel growth of EU law, national and supranational legislation are steadily coming closer together in quantitative terms (table 6.1). In this respect, the overall output of domestic legislation—all types of law considered and all the political economy policy domains—between 1976 and 1981 amounted to more than 450 bills, while between 2011 and 2015 it fell to 150 bills. On the other hand, EU legislation started to be relevant only from the early 1990s, when ca. fifty bills were transposed into the Italian system, but then grew thereafter: in fact, between 2011 and 2015 the total number of EU laws transposed into the national system amounted to 100 bills, significantly bridging the gap with the Italian state as source of legislation and policymaking (Cozzolino 2018c, 216).

Now, the question is to assess in which policy domains EU law is more relevant, especially in quantitative terms. According to the data collected from normattiva.it, EU legislation has grown, especially from the mid-1990s and especially in terms of market re-regulation and harmonization. EU legislation increased in areas such as "harmonization of common market" (where it constitutes almost the totality of bills enacted in the period of the study); "sanctions, bans and prescriptions on tradable goods" (where it constitutes the only source of legislation enacted from the mid-2000s to present); "firm governance" (where national legislation has shrunk since the mid-2000s); "health controls on food, plants and animals" (where EU law has been almost the only source of legislation from the mid-1990s), and "consumer protection." In relation to economic and financial activities, EU law has increased in particular in areas such as "liberalization of public services" (figure 6.10), "energy policy," "payment system," "credit system," and "liberalization of financial activities" (for the last of these, see figure 6.11), with a parallel marginalization of national legislation (Cozzolino 2018c).

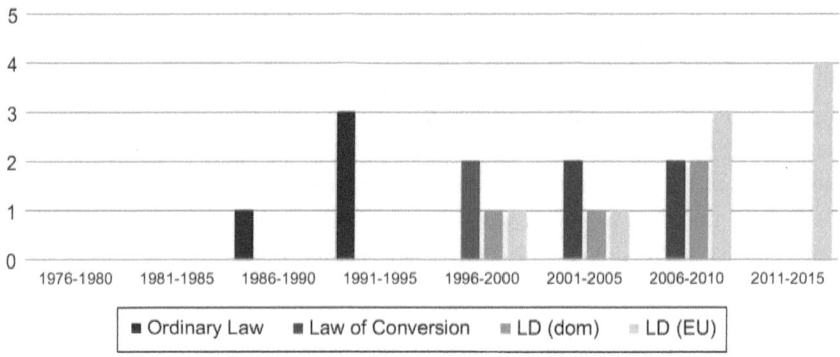

Figure 6.10 Liberalization of Public Services (1976–2015).

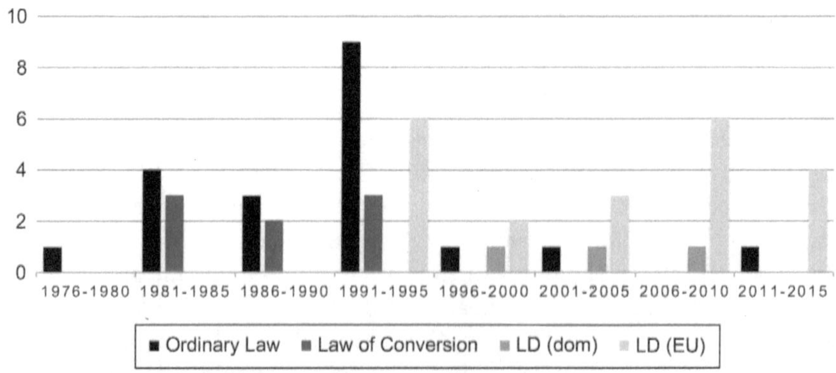

Figure 6.11 Liberalization of Financial Activities (1976–2015).

Concluding, the EU is increasingly relevant as a source of direct legislation regarding the Italian political economy. However, it is important to emphasize that key policy areas (like labour law) are still regulated by the member states but within a hierarchical centralization of policymaking agency through an increasingly integrated *national-supranational executive structure*. In fact, EU economic governance must be considered the framework whereby measures concerning public finance and budget rules, structural reforms, and labour policy are outlined in their main guidelines, and then implemented via executive channels. In this last respect, European integration deserves some further remarks. Especially after the Maastricht Treaty entered into force in 1993, the EU has moved towards a rules-based system, hence reducing the space for political economy alternatives to those enshrined in the Treaty, in the Stability and Growth Pact (1997) and in the recent Fiscal Compact (2013). The Italian economist Padoa-Schioppa (already mentioned in chapter 4 as a prominent Italian "technocratic collective intellectual" and minister of finance in 2006) defined EMU as a depersonalized "collective prince" (1994, 151, in Bonefeld 2017, 137), in which monetary policy is not subjected to political influence and, by being rules-based and expert-led, becomes "credible" especially with respect to market operators and creditors. Thus, on the one hand "[m]onetary union removes the conduct of monetary policy from the direct pressures of national labour markets" (Bonefeld 2017, 137). On the other, the EU is neither a proper fiscal union nor a political union: it is a monetary union that "emphasises market rule as the formative power of European society and recognises the role of the national state in securing market order" (ibid., 139) and, above all, improves competitiveness through permanent wage restraint.

Crucially, rules-based governance in the EU, far from being agent-less, actually empowers the European Council and, especially after the 2008 crisis, the European Commission—namely, the supranational executive—as the key actors of EU politics and law-making (Obendorfer 2015), along with the European Central Bank. In addition, and as already noted in the previous two chapters, the (apparently neutral) expertise of technocrats provided for a "surplus legitimation" for austerity and neoliberal policies, thus restricting further the space for mass democracy (see also Streeck 2013). In this regard, two key elements emerge. The so-called "democratic deficit" of the Union is not a collateral effect of the integration process but derives from the very design of its institutional architecture (Bonefeld 2015). It is, in other words, a political project in which the centrality of parliamentary sovereignty (at national and supranational levels) retains a marginal position from the outset, as I document with respect to the Italian case. Second, the supranational responses in the post-2008 period of multiple crises can be seen as a case in which the "procedures followed, the institutions involved in policymaking, as well as the policies approved at the European level for getting out of the crisis have exacerbated the already serious democratic deficit of the Union" (Giannone 2015, 101). For instance, the "six-pack" regulation, while empowering the Commission's powers of supervision, sanctioning and surveillance of Member State fiscal policy, has also promoted a joint mechanism of "de-democratization of politics" and "de-politicization of the economy" (ibid., 103) due to the automaticity of its procedures. Importantly, others have also found—especially against the background of the state of emergency that unfolded after the crisis of 2008—an increasingly authoritarian rule inscribed in the legal order of EU governance due to the growing discretionary powers of its executive actors and given the resort to exceptional legal practices (Kreuder-Sonnen 2016, 2018; see also Sandbeck and Schneider 2014, 2018). In chapter 7, I will return to this issue, and analyse the political consequences of the increasing involvement of the European institutions—with its austerity and neoliberal policy orthodoxy—in Italian politics, one of the reasons for the rising influence of eurosceptic parties and euroscepticism more broadly.

CONCLUSIONS: THE RISE OF THE "EXECUTIVE STATE" IN ITALY AND THE DECLINE OF LIBERAL DEMOCRACY

In chapter 2, I noted that one of the main problems with debates about state transformation, either from a "declinist" perspective or from a state-centric one, is to overlook the *internal* shifts of power *in* the state, and how these are directly related to the furthering of neoliberalization processes and regular (re)impositions of austerity policy. By contrast, I argue that the internal redefinition of powers among state institutions is one of the defining elements of the neoliberal reconfiguration of the state and, accordingly, one of the most crucial aspects of the making of "neoliberal democracy" (Giannone 2010). Of course, the redistribution of power in the state in favour of the executive is not unique to Italy. For instance, by drawing on legal and constitutional scholarship, Saskia Sassen has stressed that the internal redistribution of power in the U.S. state in favour of the executive branch of government began under the Reagan administration. Comparing the period of the New Deal with Reagan's neoliberal counterrevolution, Sassen writes that "[t]he transformations of the New Deal involved the Congress as a key player [. . .] whereas today's shifts of power inside the state mostly do not. Indeed, today's accumulation of powers is concentrated in the executive and has reduced the political participation of the Congress" (1998, 172). Others, from a political science perspective, have analysed the emergence of "presidentialization"—namely, when "the head of government and party leadership as a whole has become more prominent" (Passarelli 2015, 1)—in comparative perspectives in many democracies worldwide (Poduntke and Webb 2005).

This scholarship, however, often postulates (albeit implicitly) an external and indirect relation between state transformations and "global factors," hence overlooking the nature of neoliberalism as a political project. For example, Sassen contends that "[t]he redistribution of power within the state is a consequence of changes in both the national and international political economy but is also constitutive of those changes" (1998, 170–171). This, while holding true in general, implies (albeit implicitly) that the range of transformations in the state is a sort of automatic "consequence" of the changes occurring in the national and international political economy. By contrast, it is important to remark that this is the *effect* of processes of neoliberalization as a transnational hegemonic project: hence the outcome of the dialectical relations between internal/international structures and agencies in a specific historical period. The case of the transformations of the state can be seen as the political project to reduce the spaces for the representation of different social forces within state structures, thus restricting in particular the potential for political economy alternatives that would limit the scope for capital accumulation and reproduction to be articulated.

Clearly—in Italy and beyond—state transformations and neoliberal policies encountered a significant amount of resistance. One of the agents of such resistance in Italy was the Constitutional Court, which tried to safeguard the centrality of the parliament and the principle of political representation, especially after the turning point of the 1990s (Research Department of the Constitutional Court 2017; Troisi 2019). On the other hand and importantly, while parties were themselves defined by the gradual personalization of politics (Calise 2016) and increasingly became bureaucratic agencies secluded from civil society, many movements arose outside the state and the (increasingly marginal) parliament. A case in point is the movement for the defence of public water services, which in 2011 led to the victory in the referendum against the privatization of water services (Bieler 2021; Marotta 2019). The victory, however, was opposed first by the right and then by the centre-left Democratic Party that undermined the popular will by fostering a new cycle of privatization of water services. The movement nonetheless managed to continue an important grassroots battle for new democratic institutions and for the defence of the commons against privatizations (Micciarelli 2018; Muehlebach 2018), envisioning a possibility to create a better future for all and to overcome widespread political apathy and unproductive (i.e., reactionary) resentment (see also chapter 8).

The dynamics of decision-making centralization took specific forms according to the national conditions and context and the given national and international processes. In this regard, for instance, the agency of technocrats in the Italian state is a prominent example of a particular case of neoliberalization. Interestingly, the contemporary classic of conservative thought *The Crisis of Democracy*, written by S. Hungtington, J. Watanuki and M. Crozier on the behalf of the Trilateral Commission (1978), gives a more direct view of the neoliberal interpretation of democratic crisis and how to resolve it. In brief, their analysis start with the recognition that the advanced industrial democracies (the United States, Western Europe, and Japan) were threatened by forms of widespread political contestation/delegitimation and an overload of "social" demands and pressures on governments (along with the stagflationary conditions of the 1970s). Hence, while commending the increasing number of technocratic and policy-oriented intellectuals (p. 7), they also wrote that the only viable response to the democratic stalemate was to improve the *governability* of democracy. The improvement of "governability," I argue, occurred by means of the depoliticization of society on the one hand, and through the transformation of the liberal-democratic state form on the other (chapter 5). This means that, in practical terms, the *purpose* of transformation of the state through the empowerment of specific decision-making apparatuses can be regarded as a *pre*-emptive attempt to restrict the spaces for mass democracy, especially after the cycle of conflicts in the 1960s and 1970s and the incursion of the masses into politics.

The main point raised by this chapter and demonstrated empirically is that the use of emergency legislation and, accordingly, the empowerment of the Italian executive runs in parallel to the unfolding of neoliberal restructuring since the 1980s and consolidated during the 1990s. Therefore, it is a long-term process and not just the outcome of emergency politics of post-2008 phase, even though the last decade has opened a new window of opportunity to empower further the national and supranational executives. Importantly, the current marginalization of parliament has come to its mature phase. Looking at the data presented in this chapter, it is possible to conclude that the Italian parliament has, currently, neither a substantive nor an autonomous role in policymaking, mediation and negotiation, elaboration and implementation, or amendment. In other words, its current function is to ratify executive decisions in a wide range of policy domains, especially those pertaining to the political economy. In fact, according to a publication of the Research Department of the Constitutional Court, the government—and the prime minister in particular—has "de facto seized the legislative function [. . .] through the resort to emergency legislation, which now largely predominates within the entire legislative production" (2017, 20). Moreover, after the global crisis of 2008 a further array of legal mechanisms—such as the abuse of "maxi-decrees" or the imposition of the confidence question on multiple occasions—have marked a step forward in limiting parliamentary discussion, legislative powers, and compromise-seeking. Hence, the form of state has shifted towards a de facto executivized regime, as the heralds of neoliberal counterrevolution suggested by stressing the importance of governability. But governability, conceivable as a technocratic utopia, has turned into an illiberal dystopia, seriously undermining the authority and legitimation—especially against the background of the social crisis of 2008—of national and European institutions (see chapter 7). Chapter 8 returns to the contemporary organic crisis of the neoliberal era and its novel authoritarian manifestations.

Chapter 7

Society, Territory, Politics

Understanding Contemporary Crises in Italy

In this chapter, I analyse the social, territorial, and especially political consequences of neoliberalization and austerity in Italy by zooming in on the post-2008 period. The global financial crisis of 2008 represents a turning point in the history of neoliberal capitalism and a step forward in the process of institutional change (see also chapter 6). As noted by Wolfgang Streeck, "after what has happened since 2008, no one can understand politics and political institutions without closely relating them to markets and economic interests, as well as to the class structures and conflicts arising from them" (2014, xv). Yet the political turmoil and the social imbalances of this phase are often analysed in isolation from the broader neoliberalizing patterns unfolding from the previous decades; moreover, even when considered together, the "economic" and "political" factors still tend to be treated as separate dimensions interacting only externally with each other. By contrast, this chapter will ground the contemporary evolution of Italian politics in the structural changes consolidated from the 1980s onwards, thus zooming in on the dynamics strengthened after the global crisis of 2008. My argument is that only by looking into the structural imbalances of neoliberal and austerity politics, and their socio-territorial effects, is it possible to achieve a more comprehensive and holistic understanding of the contemporary Italian context. Moreover, the analytical effort to look jointly at society, territory, and politics is justified—as we shall see in greater detail below—by the fact that these dimensions actually represent three intertwined factors of the contemporary Italian crises.

Thus, while the previous chapters reconstructed the historical roots of neoliberalism within and beyond the state (chapter 4), and zoomed in on the manifold dimensions of state transformations (chapters 5 and 6), here I take a closer look at the evolution of the domestic political system. In line with the theoretical and empirical approach underpinning my method of enquiry, I consider historical changes in terms of the dialectics between socioeconomic factors and politics. I also take into account the societal effects of neoliberalism by zooming in on the labour market reforms and their impact on Italian society. Usually, in many mainstream political science accounts labour is only loosely (if ever) taken into account. By contrast, in this analysis the labour market reforms—and their consequences—are key for understanding the evolution of political relations in Italy since the early 1990s and especially post-2008.

In addition, I assess how the socioeconomic crisis unevenly spread over the Italian territory, thus increasing the divide between the North and the South. With social and territorial factors in mind, I turn to analyse the evolution of the country's politics after 2008 by shedding light on two key tendencies. The first is the crisis of the consensus regarding what I termed neoliberal-progressive Europeanism (chapter 5), especially after the experience of the technocratic executive led by Mario Monti in the early 2010s. I corroborate my argument with regard to electoral trends before and after the euro crisis period. The second main tendency is the rise of eurosceptic, populist, and radical right political forces such as the Five Star Movement (FSM) and The League. Here, I analyse in detail (i) the rise of these political forces against the background of the Italian socioeconomic crisis, and (ii) the populist government itself (FSM–The League 2018–2019), paying particular attention to its relationship with European institutions. In the concluding remarks, I provide a critical and comprehensive interpretation of the tendencies and contradictions immanent to contemporary social and political relations in Italy.

THE SOCIOECONOMIC CONTEXT: NEOLIBERAL REFORMS AND THE DISRUPTION OF THE SOCIAL FABRIC

The impact of several decades of permanent austerity and neoliberalization, particularly after the global crisis of 2007–2008 and in the wake of the sovereign debt crisis of 2011–2012, brought many segments of the Italian working and middle classes to their knees. Especially women and young workers were the social groups most severely hit by the crisis, with the rise to unprecedented levels of poverty and inequalities. In this section, I look especially at the tendencies within the labour market, which is one of the main drivers of this process. The rise of social inequalities, on the other hand, is the other key issue to be considered.

The Italian labour market has been reformed several times over the last decades. Among others, the Treu package (1997), the Biagi reform (2003), the Monti reform (2012), and more recently the Jobs Act (2014–2015) have deeply reshaped the overall employment conditions and, accordingly, the wage levels. The general aim of such reforms was to improve labour market flexibility by introducing atypical and fixed-term contracts, and by making it much easier to dismiss workers. While employment levels actually grew up to the 2008 crisis, the main and long-term consequences of this model materialized in two main directions: the segmentation of the labour market and the squeeze on salaries (Pianta 2020, 14). The segmentation of labour markets was driven by the massive resort among employers to short-term and atypical contracts, which led to the rise of precarity, especially among young workers and women. These contracts, besides dragging down the salary level, also offer lower coverage for unemployment benefits and smaller social contributions (Ciccarone e Saltari 2015, 235). The latter reduces "non-wage" labour costs but, as the former shows, at the expense of placing workers at the margins, and sometimes even outside, the welfare system. Before and especially after the Jobs Act reform, the number of part-time and poorly paid jobs increased dramatically, equalizing the working conditions downwards across the labour market as a whole. Part-time jobs, for instance, increased by 38 percent between 2007 and 2018, while the number of "involuntary" part-time posts (i.e., people obliged to accept this kind of contract due to the lack of full-time jobs) grew from 38 percent (of the total number of part-time contracts) to 64 percent in the same period. Women and young people constitute 71.6 percent of this segment of the workforce (Censis 2019).

Wage deflation is the main consequence of the labour market reforms. In this regard, it is important to emphasize, first, that the squeeze on salaries has been the main strategy implemented by policymakers in the name of improving the country's overall competitiveness on the global market. As a consequence, "the increasing labour supply resulting from international production restructuring, immigration, and neo-liberal labour market and welfare reforms put an increasing pressure on the employed workers" (Pradella 2015, 13). With specific respect to the Italian case, prior to the introduction of the Maastricht Treaty and the establishment of the Economic and Monetary Union, Italian firms mostly relied on monetary devaluation—that is, of the Lira—to improve their international market share. After the loss of monetary sovereignty in the early 1990s, the main policy strategy put in place to bear the increasing competitive pressures deriving from neoliberal globalization consisted in a focus on the devaluation of labour via labour market adjustments and corporate restructuring more generally—given also a very low propensity to invest in technology by Italian firms. Thus, in the period from 1992 to 2012 the labour share of GDP decreased by 5 percentage points (Ciccarone e Saltari 2015, 232). Squeezing wages through labour market segmentation aimed, therefore, to make Italian supplies cheaper and to attract foreign investments and capital. For instance, a much-criticized government leaflet issued by the Renzi government (2016) urged foreign investors to invest in Italy due to the "competitive wage level" of Italian engineers, comparatively lower than in the other European countries. As a result, several decades of ongoing wage deflation and flexibility "increased precariousness, limited the innovation and skill content of the working force and, ultimately, reinforced the irregular labour market rather than reducing it" (Talani 2017, 266; Ciccarone and Saltari 2015). These trends also "reinforced the most embedded tendencies of the Italian labour market, in particular the dualism between the north and south of the country and the porousness between the formal and the underground economy" (Talani 2019, 114; more on this later).

As noted earlier, the labour market can act as a source of structural inequalities, these latter driven in particular by "lower wages, higher profits and financial wealth" (Pianta 2020, 14). Generally, high unemployment levels, plus part-time, atypical, and temporary jobs led to extreme difficulty for precarious workers to earn a steady income, in turn a key factor for explaining the growth of economic inequalities and of the working poor (Istat 2016, 212–213). Actually, Italy is characterized by one of the most unequal distributions of income and wealth in Europe, a trend that strengthened from the mid-1980s after the reduction of inequalities during the 1960s and 1970s. Moreover, especially from the early 1990s inequalities have grown in Italy more than in other European countries (Istat 2016), in terms of disposable income (Alvaredo and Pisano 2010; Albertini 2013; Francini et al. 2016) and net wealth (Dagnes et al. 2018). For instance, empirical findings on the long-term trends of income distribution confirm the position of labour in the process of neoliberal restructuring (Pradella 2015). The data show, in fact, a rising income differential of blue-collar families vis-à-vis white-collars, and, on the other hand, that *within* the service class there is a growing gap between "high" and "low" class fractions. In other words, the average earnings of the managerial class in particular started to increase during the 1980s and improved dramatically thereafter (Albertini 2013; see also Duménil and Lévy 2011, for a global perspective on this); compare this to positions at the "low" end, such as in retail or hospitality. The Italian case testifies that since the 1980s and especially during the 1990s the labour market constituted a major source of the increase in inequalities, even more than those deriving from capital income and rents (Francini et al. 2016, 5, 25–30). Thus, the national share of income has dramatically shifted towards the richest households since the early 1990s. According to a study by the Bank of Italy (2018), in 2016 the national share of net wealth held by the bottom 30 percent of the households amounted to 1 percent, while the richest 30 percent of households held 75 percent of the share of net wealth. Within this, the top 5 percent held a staggering 40 percent (Bank of Italy 2018, 4).

The growth of the wealth share of the rich and affluent, however, is only a part of the story. Once again, it is by looking at the working conditions that we can derive a clearer picture. In this respect, two of the most significant trends which strengthened over the last decades in Italy are the growth of the working poor and the rise in poverty levels, which are directly linked to one another. By looking at Western European state interventions in promoting neoliberal and austerity reforms before and especially after the 2008 crisis, Lucia Pradella (2015) aptly related this trend to the long-standing (and growing) use of atypical, precarious, and low-paid jobs. In the years of the economic crisis in Italy (2008–2013), several factors accompanied and even strengthened the trend: (i) the quantitative expansion of atypical and lower-paid employment; (ii) the erosion of the bargaining system under the Monti government (2012); (iii) a decrease in social protection expenditure; (iv) a collateral polarization in working time between full-time employed and part-time jobs (Pradella 2015, 11–12). The working poor and high unemployment levels are directly related to the rise of poverty levels. In this respect, it is worth citing a passage from the study of the Bank of Italy to understand the extent of the issue. Generally, a household is financially poor if it would not have sufficient resources to avoid the risk of poverty for at least three months. Actually, we read that

> In 2016, 44 percent of the population found itself at this level of vulnerability, a share that is still much higher than that recorded in 2006 [. . .] Wealth poverty is more concentrated among persons at risk of income poverty: around 85 per cent of persons with equivalent income below 60 per cent of the median do not possess sufficient financial resources to cover an emergency [. . .] With the start of the financial crisis, the incidence of financial wealth poverty rose faster than at risk of income poverty. This led to a rapid rise in the share of persons who fall under both categories—from 15 per cent in 2006 to almost 20 per cent in 2016—after remaining essentially stable for the previous 10 years. The effects of the extended crisis therefore seem to have been more severe when both income and wealth are considered. (Bank of Italy 2018, 12)

The poverty gap[1] increased between 2006 and 2018 from a ratio of 0.333 to 0.408 (OECD 2019d). Today, five million people live in a condition of absolute poverty, while nine million people live in a condition of relative poverty (Istat 2019).

The worsening of the social fabric had a deep impact on the perspectives and feelings of Italians. According to a recent Censis report (2019), 69 percent of Italians feel a sense of instability about the future, 17 percent feel pessimistic, and only 13 percent are optimistic. Sixty-nine percent of Italians think that social mobility is blocked. Unemployment and the economy are top of Italians' worries, respectively 44 and 31 percent against an average of 21 and 16 in the EU. The concerns about the material conditions overtake those about immigration, "only" 22 percent. This situation, in addition, also worsened the mental health and stability of the population. For example, the consumption of anxiolytics and sedatives increased by 23 percent in three years (2015–2018), while 69 percent of the people consulted regard Italy as an anxious country. Significantly, this figure rises to 76 percent among poorer classes. After a decade of prolonged crisis, Italian society appears embittered, rancorous, less trustful towards the political classes, and generally less tolerant.

The Territorial Dimension of the Crisis

Prior to analysing how several decades of socioeconomic restructuring redefined the Italian political landscape, it is worth briefly turning to the territorial dimension of the crisis. In fact, if in the last two decades Italian economic conditions have been characterised by "extensive impoverishment, causalisation and high unemployment" (Pianta 2020, 14), this is especially true for the Southern regions.

Yet, this is an element often overlooked in analyses of the Italian political context, and yet it represents one of the main hallmarks of the Italian nation-state—almost as if the country is made of two different states. The current territorial discrepancies, which have grown since the 1990s, intertwine with long-term factors rooted in the fragile bases of the Italian state (chapter 4), with the dynamics of the integration of the Italian economy into the European space, and eventually with the geopolitical decline of the entire Mediterranean area (Rossi 2013). More specifically, while the Italian working population as a whole suffered from economic crisis and restructuring, the effects of these manifested in strongly uneven terms across Italian territory. What is worth noting is that after a decline from the 1960s to mid-1980s, the territorial gap between the North and the South started to increase from the 1990s (Rossi 2012) and, more intensely, from the crisis of 2008 onwards (Svimez 2019). If, as noted previously, social class inequalities have generally grown throughout the Peninsula, poverty levels for southern regions and the islands are generally three times higher compared to the rest of the country, to the extent that the Italian Mezzogiorno is among the poorest regions in the EU.

Since the global crisis, the GDP growth of Mezzogiorno has been in (almost) permanent stagnation and recently plunged into recession again. This economic growth differential compared to the North has thus continued to be persistent, and the same goes for productivity levels. Actually, the level of household consumption is 9 percentage points lower than the 2008 level, while the final consumption expenditures of Public Administration in the South contracted by 8.6 percent in the period 2008–2018 (against an increase of 1.4 percent in the North). According to Svimez calculations, in 2018 the investment in public works equated to 102 euros per capita in the Mezzogiorno versus 278 euros per capita in the North/Centre. This level in 1970 was, respectively, 677 and 452 euros. Unemployment is maybe the most worrying factor of the structural decline of Mezzogiorno. The South registered, in 2018, 260 thousand fewer employed people compared to 2008 (–4 percent; also due to mass emigration, as I argue below). The gap with northern regions has increased here, too, as the level there rose by 2.3 percent. The employment level among young people in the South (15–34 years old) is only 29 percent, a figure unmatched in Europe. Importantly, the Mezzogiorno has also been deeply hit by the working poor phenomenon. According to the latest Svimez report

> The qualitative worsening of the labour market—due to the increasing precarity—determines, especially in Mezzogiorno, the remarkable growth of absolute poverty even among those families in which there is a working person. In 2018 the impact of absolute poverty has grown in the South to 8 percent, while it was 7.2 percent in 2017 (5.6 and 4.9 percent, respectively, in the North and the Centre). It is *double that in 2008* [. . .] The growth of low paid jobs due to de-skilling of labour and the explosion of "involuntary part-time" contracts is among the main causes, in Mezzogiorno in particular, of why the even modest growth of occupation failed to deliver positive answers to the increasingly worrying social crisis. (2019, 28; emphasis added)

Due to persistent high unemployment, low wages and few job opportunities, the southern regions have also been characterized by a new wave of mass emigration. From the beginning of this century, a little over 2 million people have left the Mezzogiorno regions, mostly between 15 and 34 years old. An important segment of this active and young workforce that leaves the South is the skilled workforce with a secondary diploma (37 percent) and with a degree (31 percent). "This 'new emigration' is the effect of profound changes occurred in the Southern society, an area which is ageing and is not capable of keeping its youngest components—especially the age groups between 25–29 and 30–34 years old—both those with higher education and those trained in specific professions" (Svimez 2019, 22). As a consequence, there has been a steady decline in the active workforce and a dramatic ageing of the population.

In a context in which the social crisis intertwines with a process of territorial disintegration, my argument is that the socio-spatial fracturings of the Peninsula should be read within the broader disintegrating patterns of the European space, once again along the lines of the northern core and the southern "periphery." The richer regions of the North of Italy are globally more integrated into the core of European economic circuits, while the South has gradually started to go adrift. The dynamics of European market integration, in other words, accelerated the territorial fracturings of the country. On the other hand, the manifold spatial and territorial lines of fractures marking the Italian state were also sources of novel forms of politicization thanks to the agency of centrifugal political forces, especially in the North. In the words of the geographer Ugo Rossi (2012, 7),

> [w]hile the Southern Question became delegitimised owing to its own—perceived or real—failures, the same decades (the 1990s and the 2000s) have witnessed the rapid political ascent of the *Lega Nord* in the most prosperous parts of the country, fostering explicitly anti-Southern sentiments and calling for politico-economic devolution if not secession from the national state. Even though regional disparities between the North and the South of the country were persistent and in some respects even widened during these decades, the alleged Northern Question [. . .] has gained increasingly wide currency within the general public.

Since the 1990s, therefore, new political forces such as, in particular, Silvio Berlusconi's Forza Italia and The Northern League (currently "only" The League) combined to shift Italy's political axis towards the North. This was also due to the absence of a coherent project of social and territorial cohesion among the political elites, more preoccupied with restructuring the country's social relations of production along neoliberal lines than to reduce the regional divide. As a matter of fact, European integration, the euro, and globalization put a strain on the entire country but hit in particular the southern regions, the decline of which after 2008 became extremely worrying. In this context, and more specifically, the territorial axis of Italy's multiform crisis is a key dimension for understanding post-2008 Italian politics and the elections of 2018, an earthquake in the national political system.

FROM SOCIETY TO POLITICS: POST-2008 ITALIAN POLITICAL RELATIONS

Financial Crisis, Technocracy, Austerity: Italian Politics Back to the Future

The date of August 5, 2011, is a highly symbolic moment in the perilous waters of Italian politics after 2008. On that day, the president of the ECB Jean-Claude Trichet, with his anointed successor Mario Draghi, sent a (secret, at the time) letter to the Italian government, led by a centre-right coalition with Silvio Berlusconi as prime minister, urging it to take immediate action and implement an ambitious programme of structural reforms and fiscal consolidation to restore the trust of international creditors and financial markets. This letter constituted an unprecedented involvement of EU institutions in Italian politics, and to a large extent marked the opening of a new chapter in the country's political relations. Let's analyse in greater depth the dynamics of such transition.

The global financial crisis plunged Italy into a mix of (still-enduring) stagnation, while also triggering a phase of instabilities in the country's economy and finances. Such instabilities exploded during the second crisis of this period, namely the sovereign debt crisis in 2010–2011. Due to the pressures of financial markets (Sacchi 2015) and given the lack of a common European financial firewall (Moschella 2017), the "spread crisis" put increasing pressures on the Berlusconi government and, after its resignation, led to the establishment of the third technocratic executive in Italian history. This executive, headed by Mario Monti—a former president of the private Bocconi University and a previous European commissioner for competition—had as its main goal the restoration of Italy's "credibility" in the eyes of financial creditors. In terms of state transformations, moreover, the establishment of the government should be also seen as a further twist of formal constitutional procedures, as it was born without "officially declaring the government crisis [i.e., the crisis of the confidence between the executive and parliament], the early end [of the legislature], or calling for regular elections to attain the formation of a new government" (Calvano 2014, 7; Cozzolino 2019a). As indeed the EU president Herman van Rompuy made clear, "the country needs reforms, not elections" (reported in Culpepper 2014, 1265). Let me also mention three other important institutional and political factors in this turbulent period. First, the establishment of the Monti government saw the unprecedented direct political involvement of the president of the Republic, Giorgio Napolitano, in this case amounting to a significant shift in his constitutional and political powers (Tebaldi 2014; Pasquino 2018, 348–349). Second, this government massively resorted not only to decree laws, as I documented in the previous chapter, but also to a wide array of exceptional legal measures aimed at constraining the power of parliament to scrutinize and amend (Cozzolino 2019a, 346–347). Third, the technocratic executive was backed by a large coalition comprising the Democratic Party (centre-left), the Union of the Centre (centrist), and Berlusconi's the People of Freedom (centre-right)—a factor that undermined popular support for such political forces in the long-run (more below).

Now let's return to the ECB letter and clarify its main points, to give a sense of the involvement of European institutions in Italian politics and of the scope of such involvement. The letter envisaged an ambitious and wide-ranging programme, spanning from the political economy to industrial relations, the state budget and the public administration. In particular:

1. The ECB recommended the implementation of a "comprehensive, radical and credible" strategy of structural reforms, including the liberalization of local public services and professional services through a "large-scale" privatization programme;

2. In relation to the labour market, the ECB first of all urged Italy to reform the collective bargaining system by decentralizing it to the level of the firm, to "adjust salaries and working conditions according to the specific necessities of enterprises," and to make the local/enterprise level "more relevant" than others (i.e., the central/national level, in which unions retain greater bargaining power). Second, the ECB also urged the Italian government to reform labour law to make dismissals easier;
3. In relation to fiscal consolidation, the ECB urged the government (1) to implement a more ambitious plan of public finance adjustment to achieve the balanced budget by 2013 "through cuts in public expenditures"; (2) to reform the pension system by raising the retirement age in the private sector, and reduce the cost of labour in the public sector "if necessary by reducing the stipends"; (3) to introduce a mechanism of automatic reduction of the public deficit by implementing "horizontal cuts in discretionary expenditures" whenever the deficit exceeds the prearranged level;
4. Finally, the ECB urged reform of public administration to improve efficiency and the "capacity to comply with the necessities of enterprises," and even to "abolish or melt together some intermediate levels of the public administration as the Provinces."

Importantly, the (former) presidents of the ECB urged the Italian government to introduce such measures *by decree*, thus bypassing parliament: as shown throughout this book, a practice long established in Italy, and now set to become even more significant. Also, the letter stated that "it would be appropriate to *reform the constitution* to make more stringent the budgetary rules." After Berlusconi's resignation due to the joint pressures exerted by financial markets and European institutions, the Monti executive "quickly adopted the ECB letter—and the structural reforms it prescribed—as its roadmap" (Sacchi 2015, 85). As a matter of fact, and despite being in power for only one year and five months (November 2011–April 2013), the Monti government introduced a wide range of structural measures such as, in particular, the reform of the labour market and pensions; the reform of the constitution to introduce the balanced budget principle; the automatic fiscal adjustment clause through the increase of VAT tax; widespread cuts in public expenditures. The main point to emphasize, however, is the governing style of the Monti executive, characterized by a strongly decisionist aptitude based on the imposition of austerity measures and structural reforms. The unelected Monti government, in fact, "did nothing to conceal blatant distaste to trade unions" (Sacchi 2015, 85) and rejected forms of compromise-seeking among social parties (especially unions and political parties) (Culpepper 2014). In terms of political relations, as aptly noted by Stefano Sacchi, Monti was strongly backed by European institutions rather than by domestic social and political actors. Above all, Sacchi adds, during the adoption of the labour reform "[t]he development of parliamentary work was constantly and closely monitored by EU institutions and international economic organizations, which had regular contacts with the policy-makers involved" (2015, 87). Moreover, "[w]here EU involvement in domestic politics and policymaking really looms up [. . .] is on the surveillance dimension. EU institutions carried out frequent and pervasive monitoring of Italy's commitment to the agreed structural reforms, from adoption to implementation" (ibid., 88–89).

Having framed this, the question, now, is to understand what the main political consequences have been from this period, also with reference to the consensus towards the European institutions and European integration. Let's start by saying that in the 2013 general elections, while the "European elites continued to support Monti and his reform plan," as Culpepper noted, "Italians [. . .] emphatically rejected Monti's newly formed political party at the polls" (2014, 1265). Despite the discourse based on "modernization versus the status quo" (see Caterina 2019), the technocratic political option largely failed in its first test of democratic politics and thus to achieve a broader consensus. In this context, however, especially the role of the EU is of primary importance to understand the new structuration of the political cleavages. In chapter 5, I analysed how the discursive-symbolic mobilization of "Europe" in Italy was *the* key through which austerity measures and structural reforms were legitimated. In the euro crisis juncture, this strategy achieved its peak due to the (i) quantum leap forward in the direct involvement of European institutions in Italian politics, (ii) the coercive/decisionist approach on the part of both the EU and the domestic technocratic government. Thus, it is in this phase that the EU started to *consolidate* as an increasingly relevant and structuring cleavage in Italian politics, clearly the backdrop to the already-analysed widespread social and territorial imbalances and inequalities.

However, there is only one way to go from the peak: down. The perception of Monti as a figure embedded in European technocratic circuits rather than a national political leader combined to undermine the EU consensus in Italy, which has now become to be one of the most eurosceptic countries in Europe (Volpi 2018). In addition, this crisis of the consensus affected especially the centre-left Democratic Party (PD), and led to the exhaustion of what I have termed "neoliberal-progressive Europeanism"; that is, the view of the European integration as a parabola set on the path of progress towards democracy and prosperity. Most importantly, it is in this context that populist forces such as the FSM and The League achieved an unprecedented level of popular support.

Beyond the Second Republic? The Crisis of Neoliberal-Progressive Europeanism

The general elections of 2013 and especially of 2018 constituted the overcoming of the political system based on the alternation between two coalitions of centre-left and centre-right (Bull and Pasquino 2018), a system that had marked Italian politics since the establishment of the Second Republic in the early 1990s. Below I discuss the magnitude of this fundamental transition, as well as the declining trends in electoral participation, a key element for understanding the erosion of mass democracy. As noted above, the political consequences of the early 2010s affected especially the centre-left and its neoliberal-progressive Europeanism. In this respect, are the data gathered from the electoral arena consistent with my argument? To what extent can the elections of 2013 and 2018 be conceived as a *structural* shift in the axis of consensus?

While the centre-left and centre-right *coalitions* achieved, respectively, 29.55 and 29.18 percent of the vote in 2013, the FSM alone took 25.56 percent, becoming the first Italian party in terms of electoral size. As a result, given the novel tripolar nature of the outcome, it was difficult to form a stable government. The expedient of the large coalition—masterminded by the president of the Republic, Giorgio Napolitano (see Pasquino 2018)—managed to be a (temporary) solution to the stalemate. Thus, from 2013 to 2018 Enrico Letta, Matteo Renzi and Paolo Gentiloni (all members of the PD), respectively, led three coalition governments in alliance with centrist (like Mario Monti's Civic Choice) and centre-right parties (Garzia 2019). Since in policy terms such governments did not manage to improve substantively general economic conditions, the 2018 elections definitively changed the political landscape and thus signalled the need for broader societal change. Three factors stood out. The first was the rise of the FSM, which achieved 32 percent of the vote. The second was the rise of The League of Matteo Salvini, which unseated Berlusconi as the (so far) undisputed leader of the centre-right after more than twenty years. The third element was the collapse of the PD, whose electoral numbers are highly relevant. In 2006 L'Ulivo, the "father" of the PD gained, in absolute numbers, 11,930,983 votes. In 2008, even if the centre-right coalition prevailed by a handful of votes, the PD did even better with 12,095,306 votes. Five years later, however, the situation dramatically changed and the PD totalled 8,646,034 votes. Yet, the real collapse occurred in 2018, when the PD received 6,161,896 votes, thus halving its electoral size in ten years. Importantly, a study of the 2018 elections by the Italian Centre for Electoral Studies (LUISS University) reported that especially the upper social classes tended to vote for the Democratic Party (De Sio 2018). This left a window of opportunity for other parties (such as the Movement and the League) to win support from the impoverished and poorer classes. For instance, Pianta aptly notes (2020, 16) that The League gained consensus especially among the impoverished middle-classes, while voting for the FSM is strongly associated with income poverty and causalisation, conditions found particularly in the South (more below).

Turmoil and structural changes were not the only key factors in Italian politics: electoral participation is another relevant element for understanding the democratic disaffection. Generally, turnout in Italy has always been high (above 90 percent until the late 1970s), but there has been a downward trend that accelerated after 2008. In 1992 turnout was 87 percent and from 1996 to 2008 it averaged 82 percent, but it then decreased to 75 percent in 2013 and again to 72 percent in 2018, the lowest in Italian history. In absolute terms, compared to the elections of 2006, five million people chose not to vote in 2018. The European parliament (EP) elections show similar tendencies. Generally, turnout is lower compared to the national elections, yet there has also been a steady decrease in electoral participation. While in 1979, the first EP elections, turnout was 86.12 percent, twenty years later (1994) it fell to 74.65 (see figure 7.1). The last two elections (2014 and 2019) marked the all-time lowest shares, respectively, 58 and 56 percent (figure 7.1).

Politics, however, does not know empty spaces. The other factor to be taken into account is the rise of populism and euroscepticism in Italy, which has strengthened in the face of the crisis of mainstream political forces and of the consensus towards the European Union.

The Populist Turn: Eurosceptic Forces towards the Government

The Italian case is consistent with scholarship that has studied, in comparative perspective, the growing politicization of European integration, especially

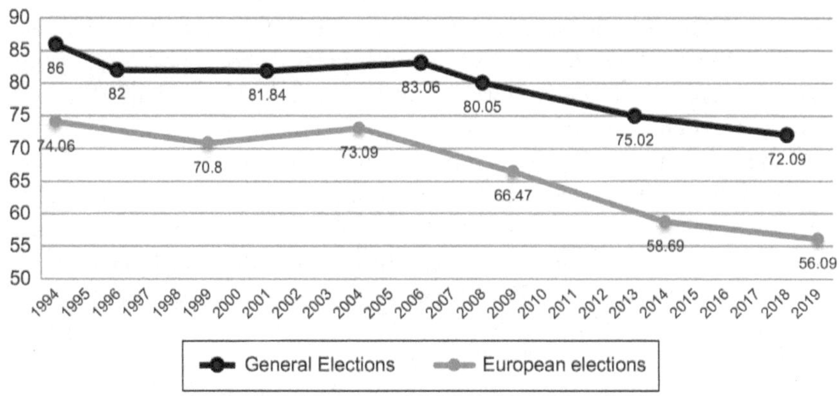

Figure 7.1 Electoral Participation in Italy (%).

during the euro crisis. Politicization is conceived, in general, as the "expansion of the scope of conflict within the political system" (Hutter et al. 2016, 7). In the case of European integration, it implies that the EU is a factor of increasing political polarization and conflict in the national political system. Specifically to Italy, I argued that especially the experience of the Monti government and the unprecedented direct involvement of EU institutions in the national polity led to a quantum leap forward in the politicization of European integration. Such a critical event is indeed confirmed by "the growing relevance of pro-/anti-EU policy for party competition in 2013 [which] constitutes the most important evidence of a change in the structure of the Italian policy space during the last 15 years" (Giannetti et al. 2017, 31; Cozzolino 2018b). Above all, it is true especially given the rise of populist and eurosceptic parties, prominently the FSM and The League, which increased their popularity in the context of the euro crisis and its aftermath. In what follows, rather than reasoning in the abstract about typologies of populism(s), I will focus my attention especially on the relevance of the anti-EU cleavage in Italy.

Let's begin with the FSM. Beppe Grillo, a comedian and blogger, founded the Movement in 2009 after two years delivering countless speeches in Italian squares against the "*casta*," namely the political establishment. The year 2011—and the establishment of the Monti executive—represented a critical moment in its upward trajectory (inter alia, Diamanti 2014; Natali 2014; Ceccarini and Bordignon 2016). It is worth stressing, in the first place, that the FSM managed to give voice to the increasing socioeconomic discontent and anxieties growing in Italian society during the euro crisis (Biorcio 2014; Conti and Memoli 2015). On the other hand, for the Movement it was easy to attack mainstream parties since these, by supporting the Monti government, proved to be "aligned and subordinate to the directives of the European institutions and to the disastrous economic recipes that the latter had imposed on the member states" (Tronconi 2018, 165). Not without ambiguous ideological stances typically summarized in the "neither left-wing nor right-wing" position, the Movement nevertheless started to express a fierce opposition against the "real existing" EU and austerity (Franzosi et al. 2015; Caiani 2019, 5–6). In the general elections of 2013, the electoral outcome for the FSM "constituted the most successful election debut for a political party not just in the history of the Italian Republic but in post-war Europe" (Tronconi 2018, 165). Since then, the Movement has become one of the main actors in the Italian political system and gradually but relentlessly consolidated its position up until the general elections of 2018, when it achieved one-third of the vote and went on to form the first entirely populist government of Italian history with the other eurosceptic party, The League.

The parabola of The League is even more relevant than the FSM's in terms of the anti-EU cleavage. Only recently The League abandoned the word "northern" in its name: inscribed in this change is one of the most interesting cases of political transformation. The Northern League (NL) was founded in 1991 by Umberto Bossi, and it is currently the oldest Italian party. The NL contributed to the crisis of the party system of the First Republic in the early 1990s just as much as the FSM to that of the Second. It was born to give voice to the northern Italian regions (especially small business) protesting against "Rome" (that is, the central state and its bureaucracy) and the corrupt political establishment of that time. Even more importantly, while the socio-economic differences between the South and the North can be considered the hallmark of the Italian state since 1861 (see chapter 4), only with the rise of The League in the early 1990s did these became a *political cleavage*. In this regard, the Northern Question became at least as important as the Southern Question, which had been a more familiar topic in Italian history (Cento Bull and Gilbert 2001). Especially from the second half of the 1990s, the NL's key objective was the creation of Padanian nationhood, namely an autonomous state comprising the Northern Italian regions and the Po valley. "Padania," borrowing from B. Anderson, became an "imagined community" with its invented tradition made of symbols, ancestors, heroes, and rituals (Biorcio 1999). Above all, it managed to foster a new anti-southern prejudice by portraying the "productive North" as structurally exploited by the South, in turn pictured as "lazy," corrupt and living on the welfare financed by the northern regions—and since history does not lack irony, this discourse is nowadays often reproduced by Northern Europe against the Southern countries. The NL's propaganda therefore argued that "the fundamental source of this misrule was the unitary Italian state, which had proved incapable of governing Italy's highly diverse territorial reality and which was in the hands of a corrupt, largely southern, political class that was guilty of neglecting the rights of northern citizens" (Brunazzo and Gilbert 2017, 628).

Given its "ethno-populist" and sub-regional nature, the NL never managed to gain much support outside its "nation." Moreover, it enjoyed varying electoral fortunes. During the 1990s it performed well, on average around the 8–10 percent of the total vote (with a 17–20 percent in the northern regions). From the beginning of the 2000s, the party entered a period of electoral downturn despite being a stable member of the centre-right alliance in several Berlusconi governments. The tables, however, were turned after 2013: a Copernican revolution in the party. While in the general elections of 2013 the NL obtained only 4 percent of the vote, in 2018 it jumped to 17.35 percent, now rebranded as "only" The League.

To understand such a leap forward, it is necessary to focus on the transformation of The League under the leadership of Matteo Salvini since 2013. Umberto Bossi had begun to lose his grip on the party in 2012, when a scandal concerning the mismanagement of public funds by some of his closest collaborators and family members was denounced in the press. After a short ad interim period, Salvini took the upper hand in the first-ever primary of the party, winning with a crushing 80 percent against Bossi's poor 12 percent. As part of this leadership transition, The League's political strategy also changed. Historically, it had accepted only passively the external constraints imposed on the Italian government by the EU (Brunazzo and Gilbert 2017, 625). Yet, already during the Monti government the party was declaring a fierce opposition against "the technocrats" and Brussels (despite voting in favour of the reform of the Constitution in 2012, a typical example of the party's frequent lack of consistency). This move became definitive after the 2013 elections, in which NL performed poorly, with the support for the FSM pushing Salvini to embrace the eurosceptic hard-line, even overcoming the FSM's comparatively mild euroscepticism. Therefore, the EU became the main political target of The League and substituted Rome as *the* political enemy.

In other words, the national/European cleavage replaced the North/South internal cleavage. Most importantly, the opposition against European integration became the vehicle to shift the party's ideological line from its historical ethno-regionalism into a full-blown nationalism (Albertazzi et al. 2018). The struggle to retake the "lost" sovereignty back from Brussels—so-called "sovereignism"—entered into The League's political discourse along with other typical radical right elements such as the fight against immigration (portrayed in the terms of an "invasion"), the obsession with security, the primacy of the national interest, and the defence of the "traditional family" and of Christian values (Caiani 2019, 10–11). "Italians first!" became the principal party slogan. Most importantly, when serving as Minister of the Interior from 2018–2019 Salvini fostered an overtly authoritarian style of political relations, showing a strong intolerance and irritation for political opposition, especially in relation to immigration. Eventually, this mix of anti-establishment rhetoric and euroscepticism bore fruit: The League became, with the general elections of 2018, the first party of the Italian right.

Populists in Government

The 2018 general elections can be considered, even more than in 2013, as an earthquake in the Italian political system (Schadee et al. 2019). For the first time two populist parties, the FSM and The League, went on to form a government. The "government of change"—namely how Salvini and Luigi Di Maio (the new leader of the FSM) portrayed their coalition—was also based on a "contract" of government through which the two parties agreed on a common political and policy programme. Giuseppe Conte, a private law professor, was appointed as prime minister to mediate between the two parties. Before analysing the populist government in detail, a brief overview of the results of the 2018 elections may provide for a sense of the extent of such a change. First of all, while for the left this was "the worst electoral performance since the return of democracy after the Second World War" (Pasquino 2018, 354), the outstanding result for the FSM was driven especially by its expansion in the Centre and South, respectively, +7 and +20 percent of the vote compared to the 2013 elections. In the first section, I already emphasized the territorial dimension of the Italian crisis and specifically the southern context. To a great extent, the Movement captured the desire and need for a radical change in an area severely hit by rising poverty levels, thus gaining the support of the disenfranchised and marginal fringes of Italian society. On the other hand, The League achieved its best ever result, in parallel with the worst ever performance of Berlusconi's revamped party Forza Italia. Moreover, while consolidating its overall position in northern regions, The League penetrated the "red zone," namely the central regions of Italy (as Tuscany and Emilia-Romagna) in which the left had deep roots; eventually, through a sort of red herring party list ("We with Salvini") it also managed to reach (albeit with modest results) the South, a previously forbidden zone for this party.

Let's analyse, now, the populists when in government. In general, despite this government's life being particularly short due to the abrupt decision of The League to break the alliance (more on this below), a number of factors are of great interest. I shall take into account three of these (for a more detailed analysis see Moschella and Rhodes 2020; Stamati 2020). The first is the policy dimension. In other words, to what extent did the populist government really represent a break with past neoliberalizing programmes? The second concerns the relation with the EU and financial markets, and the disciplinary constraints that soon reduced the government's space for manoeuvre. The third element is the recent (and current) new government alliance between the FSM and the PD.

In the first place, it is worth noting that both The League's and the Movement's success was possible thanks to a social and economic agenda aiming to break with austerity and boost economic growth. This was a difficult objective given "the very tight fiscal space available to it and the discipline imposed by bond markets and the EU institutions" (Moschella and Rhodes 2020, 3), and economic recession emerged at the beginning of 2019. However, the two flagship reforms of the government can be considered as a partial shift from the past. On the part of the Movement, its sponsored measure was the "citizenship income." This is a form of income supplement for poor households seeking (i) to fight poverty and social exclusion, and (ii) to reintegrate people into the labour market. Clearly, such a measure was tailored towards the stronghold of the Movement's constituency, the poorest southern regions. With respect to The League, its flagship measure was the pension reform ("Quota 100") based on an early retirement pension scheme.

Its aim was to reverse the previous reform enacted by the Monti government, which raised the retirement age.

These reforms involved an expansionary fiscal policy (especially the citizen's income) that followed an already harsh confrontation between the Italian government—with both parties united against Brussels—and the European Commission in October 2018. The Commission, indeed, rejected the 2018 budget due to what it judged to be infringement of the fiscal rules. Even though the government reduced its fiscal policy ambitions by the end of 2018, the introduction of the two aforementioned reforms in the early months of 2019 led to a second round of confrontations with the Commission. The Commission concluded in its May forecast that "[g]overnment spending is set to increase significantly following the introduction of the citizenship income and several provisions on pensions" (quoted in Moschella and Rhodes 2020, 4), and threatened Italy with triggering the excessive deficit procedure (designed to discipline member states, potentially through fines, with the aim of achieving a balanced budget). The situation escalated during the 2019 European elections, especially due to the anti-EU rhetoric of The League (more on this below). Importantly, tensions also arose in the financial markets. As I documented in the previous chapters, the large debt and high interest rates render the Italian economy structurally exposed to market-driven disciplinary constraints (notwithstanding its primary budget surplus since the early 1990). In this regard, the rating agency Moody's, for instance, downgraded Italy's from Baa2 to Baa3 due to the government's expansionary fiscal policy (Cozzolino 2019b, 152–154) in 2018, thus even before the introduction of the reforms. This led to a sudden increase in the spread level and, accordingly, of the rate of interest, reducing further the government's autonomous policy space.

As the external constraints constituted a pincer movement around the government, internal conflicts between the two parties soon arose. Earlier, I noted that The League took a radical eurosceptic position compared to the milder euroscepticism of the FSM, and the conflict with the European Commission started to polarize the parties' positions. The League pushed to breach the EU budget rules, thus forcing the Movement to take a more interlocutory position with the EU institutions. In the meantime, Salvini's strategy in Europe aimed to consolidate the alliance among eurosceptic and nationalist parties—comprising among others Orban's Fidesz party in Hungary, Le Pen's Rassemblemenent National in France, Alternative für Deutschland in Germany, the Party for Freedom in The Netherlands, and so on. This also pushed the Movement to move closer to pro-EU positions (for instance, the European parliament members of the FSM voted in favour of Ursula von der Leyen as the new president of the European Commission, provoking an internal rupture). The radicalization of the conflict with the EU yielded to The League an unprecedented result in the European elections. It received more than 9 million votes and became the largest Italian party. In contrast, by shifting towards more moderate positions the FSM halved its support in comparison to the elections of the previous year.

The European elections thus accelerated the already-deteriorating relationship between the two parties. After an informal/permanent electoral campaign held on Italian beaches during the summer of 2019, Salvini put the FSM on the spot and, in September, decided to break from the coalition and put an end to the government. In my view, rather than pushing for early elections and capitalize on the support for his party, Salvini sought instead to avoid the blame for the upcoming budget measure in October of that year. This would have implied *either* a move towards a decisive confrontation with the European Commission, *or* the abandonment of electoral promises to do away with austerity. Breaking the coalition proved to be the only viable exit strategy.

The demise of the Conte I government, however, did not put the legislature to an early end. After a short period, a new—unthinkable only few days before—alliance between the FSM and the PD was born, and thus a new parliamentary majority, confirming Giuseppe Conte as prime minister. Given the PD's entry into the government, relations with the EU improved as soon as the new government showed a more orthodox (and austere) stance towards fiscal policy. The government's budget measure of 2019 was characterized by a cut of "€2.7 billion from central government spending on goods and services. And notably there was nothing in the budget for critical sectors like research and education" (Moschella and Rhodes 2020, 10). Thus, after a tentative break with austerity that eventually proved to be more rhetoric than reality, the iron cage of austerity seemed to have taken the upper hand once again. However, the status quo was significantly shaken due to the Covid-19 crisis. While European states and supranational institutions have intervened with significant expansionary fiscal policies to avoid the collapse of the economy, it is still extremely uncertain whether the historical shift of the pandemic will mark a rupture with austerity and neoliberalism. As things stand (June 2020), it seems that, despite a number of measures and shifts—for example, the promised support for Southern European states and the permission granted for member states to run up large budget deficits—the prevailing view is that they represent the requirements of the exceptional current circumstances rather than anything more fundamental/long-term. Nevertheless, how this situation evolves in the coming years will be a fascinating research and political question, not least because Italy's population remains critical and sceptical of the EU.

CONCLUSION: MAKING SENSE OF CONTEMPORARY ITALIAN POLITICS

Post-2008 politics in Italy represents an extremely interesting case in terms of political change in times of socioeconomic decline. For many observers in the mainstream liberal field, the rise of populist forces is mainly related to the widespread ignorance that seems to characterize large parts of the Italian population. In other words, many Italians are unable to read a basic text, and accordingly cannot distinguish between real news and fake news. Given the propensity of the populists to produce and resort to fake news to foster the division between "the people" and "the elites," it follows that they have more chances to get their (simplistic) messages delivered to a broader audience. In my view, this interpretation of contemporary Italian politics is superficial, misleading, and self-righteous, and for two reasons. On the one hand, it neglects the socioeconomic context and how this made it possible for "eccentric"/anti-establishment forces to gain momentum and prevail vis-à-vis more traditional forces. Thus, it neglects the widespread need for change. On the other, it also neglects the historical roles of traditional political forces (of the centre-left and centre-right) and how their overall policy choices negatively affected Italian society as a whole. In contrast, I showed that only by looking at the long-term socioeconomic drivers of the crisis, is it possible to understand the reconfiguration of the political system.

In the analysis, I started by paying attention to the formation of the Monti government—conceivable as a turning point for Italian politics—and emphasized four factors. First, the substantial twist of regular democratic procedures and the imposition of this (unelected) executive; second, the decisionist style of this government, especially with respect to pension and labour market reforms; third, the unprecedented involvement of European institutions in Italian politics; fourth, the large coalition that backed technocrats in the government. The consequences of these factors were not long awaited—especially within the documented deepening of the social crisis—and the elections of 2013 and 2018 represented a sea-change in the Italian political landscape. Pro-EU parties (both on the progressive and conservative front) were swamped by the populist wave, and eurosceptic forces (both moderate and hard-line) gained the upper hand. Needless to say, the decisionist style of EU institutions—coupled with the EU deficit of democracy and legitimacy—and the austerity obsession undermined the image of the EU at the domestic level, while strengthening anti-EU/nationalist forces. In general, the absence of channels for (mass) democratic politics in the EU's multilevel governance structures to imagine and build political economy alternatives, led the EU itself to become *the* question that was put to the population rather than merely "economic" or "social" issues.

The analysis of the "yellow-green" populist government is extremely meaningful in this respect. While it is hard to argue that right-wing populism may really be an alternative to neoliberalism, it is still worth noting that measures such as the citizens' income and the pension reform (a timid expansionary programme) immediately triggered a counter-reaction from European institutions and international finance. This revealed, importantly, that even a minimal programme aiming to reverse (at least some aspects of) neoliberal and austerity orthodoxy does not find just internal obstacles but also, maybe especially—given the interdependency and power relations in the contemporary international political economy—powerful external constraints. However, while the populists in the government managed to capture the social malaise, it did not implement a coherent policy programme of change. Nevertheless, the parabolas of the FSM and of The League are further interesting signs of what appears to be a phase of consolidation of the process of the radicalization of politics in Europe. As regards the Movement, the shift towards moderate positions and the coalition with the PD dramatically undermined its level of support. On the other hand, the radical strategy of The League—and its mix of populism and authoritarianism—has led it to become the most popular party in the country, albeit in a context of extreme instability and rapid changes. For instance, during the Covid-19 crisis the personal popularity of Prime Minister Giuseppe Conte has increased, while that of The League—and of Salvini—has declined.

The rapidity of the rise and fall of leaders and parties, extreme electoral volatility, the vortex of international and domestic events, the ever-increasing crises of capitalism, and especially the capitalism-nature relation, make it very difficult to foresee a shift of Italian politics towards a possible stabilization. At the same time, representative democracy is put under pressures not only by the documented changes at the state level but also, maybe more recently, by the strengthening of authoritarian political cultures linked to the right. As I noted in chapter 6, the obsession for governability, conceivable as a technocratic utopia, has turned into an illiberal dystopia, seriously undermining the legitimation and authority of traditional (especially former social-democratic) parties, and national and European institutions. Yet the socioeconomic crisis is still fully in place—and destined to increase with the recession brought about by the coronavirus emergency. Thus, without a reversal of neoliberalism and austerity, Italian politics can at best buy time but will always be ensnared by crisis, as has happened with the populist governments.

Chapter 8

Conclusions

State Transformations, Decline of Democracy, and the Organic Crisis of Neoliberalism

Through the critique of the political economy of state transformations, this book has sought to provide for an anatomy of the neoliberal transition in Italy. Without adhering to either a "declinist" view of state powers or a reified account of the state-as-autonomous-force in society, the effort and the ambition of the book has been to theorize, and analyse empirically, the different dimensions of state transformations in the age of neoliberal globalization. By adopting a dialectical perspective between the state and society on the one hand, and between the national and the international on the other, this book has developed an alternative approach to understand and explain the neoliberal transformations of the state, and dovetailed these with in-depth analysis of the Italian case.

Earlier chapters addressed two interlinked spheres revolving around the "state question." The first dealt with theoretical reflections on the nature of the state and, in parallel, with the conceptualization of state transformations, which are actually two intertwined dimensions (chapter 3). The next contribution revolved around the empirical analysis of the transformations of the Italian state in light of the dual nature of the state and via a long-term historical perspective (chapter 4). More specifically, I analysed the qualitative changes linked to the socio-ideological construction of the neoliberal state through the exploration of Italian state representatives' discourses, tracing the redefinition of the idea of state within the neoliberal semiotic order "Italian style" (chapter 5). At the same time, I also analysed the transformations of a key segment of the state's institutional apparatus, the government/parliament complex (chapter 6). I showed that the transformations of the state in the neoliberal epoch entailed a process of centralization of power in the state, a marginalization of some democratic institutions (above all the national parliament), and, accordingly, a dramatic reduction of forms/spaces of mediation and expression of dissent/alternatives to neoliberal policy and ideology. This, moreover, occurred—especially in the post-Maastricht phase—against the background of the European integration process and as part of the overall strengthening of executive powers within the EU's institutional architecture. Finally, chapter 7 discussed the post-2008 period. By looking at the intertwining between society, territory, and politics, the chapter considered the contemporary Italian context. The aim was to provide for a broader and critical picture of some key political tendencies which have arisen in the Peninsula, and prominently (i) the crisis of neoliberal-progressive Europeanism (and of centrist parties more broadly) and, more broadly, of the consensus towards the EU in Italy, and (ii) the rise of populist-eurosceptic forces. The detailed analysis also reconsidered some key aspects of the contemporary crisis in historical perspective, thus avoiding flattening these tendencies to the present-day only and, above all, rooting the crises in the structural contradictions of the neoliberal paradigm.

This concluding chapter, by drawing on Gramsci's commentaries on the crisis of the 1920s, is a final reflection on the crisis of the neoliberal order and the increasingly illiberal transformations in the state. Yet before discussing this, in next section I summarize several critical points regarding the theory of the state and the conceptual reflections around its transformations, and the possibility to develop an alternative research agenda.

RETHINKING THE STATE AND STATE STUDIES: AN ALTERNATIVE RESEARCH AGENDA

Taking stock of the lively debates on the state and its transformations (chapter 2), a key aim of the book was to rethink the *problematique* of the transformations of the state in the neoliberal epoch. The critical point raised by this study is that it is not possible to deal with the issue of transformation without first examining the nature and the characteristics of this strange, ubiquitous, and multiform entity—the state. By drawing on Gramsci's theory of the state and critical international political economy scholarship, this book sought to systematize this body of insights concerning the nature of the state in capitalist societies and, at the same time, conceptualize the complex stratification of what we call "the state." Thus, only after the theoretical moment—and the examination of the stratified nature of the state—has it been possible to offer the analysis of its transformation in Italy and explore empirically the patterns of change. In turn and eventually, the methods of the research were part and parcel of how I conceptualized the object of the research. In other words, the choice of adopting a mixed-methods approach was justified by the purpose of analysing different and particular aspects—yet part of the same ontological unity—of the real and conceptual complexity of the state.

Let's try to sum up, now, some of the main theoretical and empirical points discussed by this book, while also reflecting on the extent to which they could be generalized in the study of the state to foster an alternative research agenda.

First, the state cannot be conflated with the government and, accordingly, reduced to a set of material capabilities. The integral state, as Gramsci taught us, cannot be understood in separation from the society in which it exists. Hence, the nature of the state as a condensation of social relations opens up the possibility (i) to rethink, in historical perspective, the genesis of specific forms of state as a stratification/condensation of social and spatial relations (and contradictions and conflicts) inherited from the past, and analyse these dialectically within the present forms and conditions—as the Italian case testifies in light of the transition from a strong parliamentary regime to one dominated by the executive. Therefore the study of the state is, ultimately, the study of its historical changes instead of the observation of a static picture; (ii) to rethink the actual form of state by including, dialectically, also civil society and therefore the agency of social forces; (iii) to identify in the dialectical relation between society and the state (conceived as a terrain of political agency) the engine of the transformations of the state, therefore in a non-deterministic or automatic way and also without falling into the reified account of the supposed "self-transformation" of the state; finally, (iv) to understand the world of states not as a conglomerate of interacting units (with certain material capabilities) but as national and transnational, vertical and horizontal institutionally stratified fields of action and conflict for (organized) social and political forces, these latter *unevenly* embedded into transnational capitalist relations of production.

Along with an integral concept of state in which state and society are equal partners, this book has also sought to intersect the Gramscian theory of the integral state with an in-depth conceptualization of the stratified ontology of the state, hence linking the social roots of state powers with an exploration of the complex nature of the state. In chapter 3, I argued that Gramsci's definition of the state—"the entire complex of theoretical and practical activities with which the ruling class not only justifies and maintains its dominance, but manages to win the active consensus of those over whom it rules"—already points to a stratified ontology of the state as a set of "theoretical" and "practical" activities rooted in social class agency. This has enabled my approach to depart definitively from a concept of the state as an autonomous unit in favour of a dynamic and process-oriented perspective, in its turn capable of retaining the analytical importance of the *relative* autonomy of the state field.

In more specific terms, the state can first of all be conceived as a social construction characterized by an intrinsic ideological power. This first nature of the state bears fundamental social and political consequences. Prominently, the state *appears* to be separated from society. As Marx wrote, "the political state appears to civil society in the same spiritual way of heaven to hearth" (2017, 49). The state seems to be the "disinterested servant of the community," thus fostering the *fictio* of a community of equals and, as a consequence, covering the real fractures and cleavages that cut across societies and divide humans along the lines of class, gender, race/ethnicity, religion, geography, and so on. So the state as undetermined abstraction has determined political consequences since it helps, as a socio-ideological construct, to justify, legitimate, and naturalize forms of domination and exploitation, usually through a degree of consensus on the part of subaltern classes—precisely the effects of hegemony.

While every state is a socio-ideological construct, every such construct possesses intrinsic specificities according to the local/national culture in which it is embedded. Once again, this represents another important factor as to why the state matters. Accordingly, it allows for studying similarities and variations in the construction of specific states in different cases and in light of different national cultures, and/or how and why specific ideas of states/political regimes spread across different nations and contexts. Through the in-depth analysis of the Italian case I showed that the redefinition of the idea of state is intertwined with a greater cultural battle that sought to modify "the behaviour, habits, expectations and perspectives of Italians" ([*sic*]; chapter 5) by means of market discipline. The North/South relation in Europe is likewise central. It is the South, eccentric and "not normal," that must be adjusted first of all through the permanent austerity cure to meet the Northern standards of market civilization: rescued by Europe, therefore, but only to finally become "European." Importantly, especially centre-left forces have fostered (and still do, to a large extent) such an image over the last decades. In fact, in discursive terms, neoliberal hegemony has mainly worked via a progressive view of the market economy (and entrepreneurship) as a dynamic and modern source of growth, stability, and wealth creation.

The second nature of the state concerns its specific institutional and organizational form. In theory, we can distinguish between authoritarian/despotic regimes, liberal-democratic regimes, hybrid regimes, different typologies of monarchy, and so on. In the Introduction of the book I noted, borrowing from Sartori (1982), that we can distinguish (among democratic regimes) between parliamentary regimes, presidential regimes, and semi-presidential regimes. While taxonomies can be misleading if they promote a static and reified picture of political and constitutional systems, they do possess the potential to have a powerful heuristic relevance if serving as cartography with which to trace processes of change and transitions from one form to another—processes in which, let me emphasize, politics and social relations more broadly always have the central place. In this respect, I showed that the Italian case is characterized by an institutional transition from a parliamentary regime to a de facto (that is, in absence of constitutional changes) presidential regime. This process occurred, it is worth noting, not as an automatic/necessary consequence of "globalization" but as an effect of trans/national class agency within and beyond nation-state apparatuses. Neoliberalism as a hegemonic project aimed, therefore, to forge the "entrepreneurial individual" and impose market culture just as much as it aimed to redefine (i) the idea of state "in the name of the free market" (Bruff and Starnes 2019) while, *in institutional terms*, (ii) to foster a centralization of power in the state to neutralize dissent and alternatives.

In this respect, Italy proved to be an extremely interesting case for several reasons. First and foremost, the decisive step forward in the neoliberalization processes came from the "technocratic collective intellectual," a political force located first within the technocratic apparatuses of the state—the Bank of Italy—and then capable of serving also as top-officials in the government (prime ministers, ministries of the economy) in key moments of the recent Italian history. From the early 1990s, technocracy provided the political authority when the "proper" political class (temporarily?) lost it. The experience of the technocratic government led by Mario Monti in 2011–2013 shows the extent to which this type of political agency is embedded into (while also rather unique to) Italian politics (chapter 7). Another relevant factor is that neoliberal policies were introduced by resorting, since the early 1990s, to an impressive number of decrees in a very short amount of time. This practice, introduced by technocratic governments in the early 1990s but later a path-dependent process, marked a fundamental twist of the Constitution and, more broadly, showed the intrinsic tension between the neoliberal project and representative democracy. In other words, the imposition of neoliberal orthodoxy revealed its illiberal core by marginalizing alternatives, spaces for negotiations and bargaining, compromises, and dissent (more on this below).

Returning to the conceptualization of the state, this book represents an effort to understand the theory and practices of the neoliberal state by enquiring into the redefinition of the (Italian) state as socio-ideological construct and the remaking of its institutional apparatus. As such, this integrated (and integral) and dynamic approach is suitable for a comparative research agenda capable of exploring the complex nature of the state, and its transformations, across different capitalist societies. The stratified ontology of the state, in the background of the state-society dialectical nexus, allows us to analyse the changes *of/in* the state. This research agenda can be a powerful tool with which to explore, in a comparative and critical perspective, the socio-ideological construction of the state within specific semiotic orders and (trans)national cultural environments, in parallel to assessing the evolution of states as institutional complexes (while also maintaining a dialectical relation with—national and transnational—class agency).

To summarize, the state as socio-ideological construct and institutional complex, and the integral state as dialectical nexus between social forces and political society, enables us understand that the integral state is *always* a *terrain* of conflict, intersections, and interactions among competing political projects and social forces. In other words, the state is hardly reducible to a machine of domination, to policymaking or to a mere instrument of the ruling classes. This is to say that, in contemporary (complex) societies the state, as Gramsci noted and Philip Abrams remarked, is a powerful factor of ideological cohesion/mobilization, and hence of consensus and legitimation. Today, tactical and strategic political concerns cannot avoid dealing with the "state question" in terms of forging an alternative common sense, articulating certain ideas of democratic state and popular democracy while also trying to advance into the "powerful system of fortresses and earthworks" of society.

THE ORGANIC CRISIS OF THE NEOLIBERAL ORDER: AUTHORITARIAN TRANSFORMATIONS IN/OF THE STATE?

Gramsci was an acute observer of the crisis of the liberal order during the 1920s and 1930s and, as a political opponent, witness to the transition towards the fascist regime at the cost of his own freedom and life. His reflections on the hegemonic crisis of liberalism, the changes at the state level, and the crisis of authority of the Italian political classes of his time represent a powerful heuristic toolbox, especially with respect to the category of *organic crisis*, to understand a moment of crisis and transition from one political regime to another (see Burgio 2014, in particular ch. 8; Martin 2015). Clearly, political categories ought not be applied mechanically beyond their historical context. Yet, in line with Morton (2007) and Bruff (2008), I contend that some concepts own a special heuristic relevance that, in light of a "critical translation" in different contexts, can guide the researcher to explore and understand key trends arising in other historical moments—in our case, illiberal changes in the state within the crisis of capitalism. More specifically, a discussion of the concept of organic crisis can help to understand some key elements of the contemporary crisis of neoliberal capitalism and its authoritarian manifestations (Bieler et al. 2015, 147–150).

In many newspaper articles during his pre-prison time written in socialist outlets such as *L'Avanti!*, *L'Ordine Nuovo*, and *L'Unità,* Gramsci enquired into the roots of the dissolution of the parliamentary regime and the establishment of the fascist state[1] (see also Martin 2015). To a considerable extent, the *social* conditions that led to fascism and to the transformations in the state occupied a great deal of Gramsci's attention. In 1920, two years before the March on Rome (the key event that allowed the fascist movement to seize the power), Gramsci wrote that "the national apparatus of production and distribution has brought down middle classes to the proletarian condition; parliamentary democracy loses its bases of support, the country cannot be governed by constitutional means, there is no parliamentary majority capable to express a strong and vital government capable to win the consensus of the 'public opinion,' of the 'country,' namely of middle classes" (*L'Ordine Nuovo* [1920] 1975, 81). Gramsci saw in the crisis of the Italian *piccola borghesia* (middle class) a critical factor for the advent of fascism, through which he was able to interpret the reactionary nature of the subversive stance of this social class—that he brilliantly defined as "*sovversivismo reazionario*" (reactionary subversivism), in turn well represented by the "subversive past of the very new reactionary" Benito Mussolini (*L'Ordine Nuovo* [1921] 1975, 117). The crisis of capitalist relations after World War I is therefore at the forefront of Gramsci's analysis. This crisis, he noted, was an international phenomenon. "Capital becomes reactionary"—Gramsci wrote—"when it can no longer dominate the productive forces of a country," adding that "this 'reaction' is not just Italian: it is an international phenomenon" (*Avanti!* [1920] 1975, 89–90). In historical terms, Gramsci observed how, within the crisis of capitalism, new reactionary forms of political agency and discourse were able to exploit the hegemonic crisis of the liberal order and root themselves into a specific national class fraction, the already mentioned *piccola borghesia*.

Crucially, Gramsci did not see the transition from the liberal state to fascism as a total break in societal or political structures. Rather he conceived fascism as a sort of *authoritarian sublimation* of the previous liberal order which aimed to secure continuity within the existing social class structure, yet through a different hegemonic project (Martin 2015, 41). Once again, the state is a key perspective from which to understand the continuities and changes between two orders. Since Gramsci conceived fascism as a form of passive revolution for the twentieth century (1975, 1089; Q8§236; Burgio 2014, ch. 16), he importantly noted that the Fascist Party "cannot create its own State because it is already confused with the State, and already finds its own *centralization* in the current government" (*L'Avanti!* [1920] 1975, 94; emphasis added). Thus, the substantive continuity between the "liberal" state and the fascist regime was secured with a new hegemonic project through which ruling classes continued to hold together the state and society (see Antonini 2016, 173).

In the *Prison Notebooks*, Gramsci returned to the dissolution of one order into another, namely the liberal into the fascist, and developed further reflections on the question of organic crisis (see 1975, 1603–1613; Q13§23). An organic crisis concerns the *structure* of a historical bloc, affecting its political system and then the entire apparatus of the state. It is a crisis of political authority of ruling classes and existing institutions. Broadly speaking, an organic crisis occurs when parties and the party system increasingly detach themselves from their social bases, and thus a decisive break in the mechanisms of political representation—and therefore legitimation—emerges. In other words, the nexus between political society and civil society is set on a path of increasing deterioration and a crisis of authority and hegemony emerges. Thus, this crisis "from the terrain of parties is reflected into the entire body of the state" (1975, 1603; Q13§23). On the other hand and importantly, the solutions to the organic crisis are always left to political agency given the existing power relations and historical context. For instance, a response to such a crisis/stalemate, noted Gramsci, can be that of the charismatic leader. This eventuality occurs when two conflicting forces (progressive and reactionary) are equally balanced and a particularly charismatic individual (his examples were people such as Caesar, Napoleon, Napoleon III, Bismarck) can resolve the stalemate either in a progressive or in a reactionary direction, a political occurrence that Gramsci defines as "Caesarism." In regard to this, Mussolini's fascist movement acted historically as a form of "reactionary Cesarism" which, on the one hand, managed to represent the impoverished and radicalized middle classes while, on the other, renewed capitalist hegemony in a new authoritarian form in the state (Antonini 2016, 174; see also Antonini 2020 for a fuller statement). In the dialectics between revolution and restoration, restoration prevailed.

Gramsci's analysis of the transition from the liberal order to fascism against the background of the capitalist crisis after World War I is enlightening for understanding some contemporary dynamics, as well as for the period he was writing in. A caveat, though, needs to be put forth: notwithstanding the organic crisis of the contemporary international liberal order, it would be misleading (and naive) to theorize, for the present times and near future, a sort of "automatic" return of new fascist-style reactionary forms as seen in Italy one hundred years ago. On the other hand, Gramsci's analytical method of socio-historical enquiry remains relevant for exploring the *political* dynamics of capitalist crises and coercive state transformations. The core of this method is the attention paid to the dialectical relation between social dynamics and political agency. Politics and political crises, the latter for instance emerging as a fundamental crisis in the mechanism of political representation, are always dialectically rooted in the evolution of social relations. In this regard, the "structuring conditions of global capitalism" (Bieler and Morton 2018, 38) in the neoliberal epoch have produced serious, widespread, and structural imbalances. Inequalities have skyrocketed in the West and beyond, within and between states (Milanovic 2016). The global class structure is increasingly assuming a pyramid form between those at the top who own wealth and resources and the masses of those who struggle at the bottom. The crisis of middle and working classes in the West, the stagnation of wages, mass unemployment (for instance in Southern Europe) have deeply affected the stability of many political systems and undermined the authority of state institutions. In many cases, the authority of traditional parties and political classes of the left and the right—the "greater neoliberal centre" (Cozzolino and Giannone 2019)—has been seriously put in question, while more radical forms of politics seem to be emerging all over the political spectrum.

Echoing Nancy Fraser (2017), the current political juncture in many capitalist states is increasingly characterized by the conflict between a progressive form of neoliberalism, which in Europe takes the form of what I called "neoliberal-progressive Europeanism" and is characterized by a liberal-meritocratic politics and entrepreneurial culture (ultimately benefiting the wealthy elites), and a reactionary form of neoliberalism embodied by individuals such as Donald Trump or, in the Italian case, The League led by Matteo Salvini. In this last case, such individuals are able to exploit the resentment of those who have been impoverished and marginalized after many years of crisis, and could not find adequate representation in the political mainstream (especially on the centre-left/progressive field). Yet, it is worth stressing that this form of "nationalist neoliberalism" (Cozzolino 2018a) is neoliberal business as usual, and as such it continues to shift the costs of capitalist crises and restructuring onto the working population—as I documented in the case of Trumpism (ibid.). It is worth noting, however, that it also fosters a *cultural* authoritarian turn in society.

The question of the novel forms and figures linked to the current wave of political (neo)authoritarianism, in and beyond the state, needs to be addressed further by rethinking the relation between (neo)liberalism and coercive forms of capitalist restructuring by means of executivized and authoritarian state powers. Gramsci aptly noted that the Fascist Party already found in the process of power centralization in the liberal state, for instance through the massive abuse of decrees, a critical precondition for its seizure of political power, so that it actually constituted a particular evolution, rather than a break, compared to the previous regime. In chapter 6, I demonstrated that the imposition of neoliberal policy in Italy occurred through a centralization of power in the state and also by resorting on a regular basis to emergency measures and procedures. This happened, as noted by Ian Bruff, through the "reconfiguring of state and institutional power in an attempt to insulate certain policies and institutional practices from social and political dissent" (2014, 115; see also Bieler, Bruff and Morton 2015; Clua-Losada and Ribera-Almandoz 2017; Sotiris 2017; Koch 2018; Wigger 2019). Especially after the crisis of 2008, the use of increasingly coercive legal and constitutional means to impose neoliberal and austerity policy has strengthened further the coercive dimension of neoliberalism. As a consequence, Bruff adds,

> under authoritarian neoliberalism dominant social groups are less interested in neutralizing resistance and dissent via concessions and forms of compromise that maintain their hegemony, favouring instead the explicit exclusion and marginalization of subordinate social groups through the constitutionally and legally engineered self-disempowerment of nominally democratic institutions, governments, and parliaments. (ibid., 116; see also Tansel 2017; Bruff and Tansel 2019)

Thus, instead of regarding the advent of many reactionary/neoliberal populists as a break with the (neo)liberal order, the continuities between the two forms of politics and political economy must be emphasized along with the changes (chapter 7). In this case and once again, the state as perspective—*and the state as "practical activity"*—is the litmus test of the intrinsically undemocratic tendency of neoliberal capitalism with respect to its real historical and political-institutional forms. In other words, in theory contemporary Western capitalist democracies are still liberal: the constitutions are in place, party competition is free, the press is (mostly) free, the rule of law is mostly secured. Yet if we understand authoritarianism as a *process* rather than an ossified political category, and if we look at the increasingly coercive state practices through which the imperatives of transnational capitalist accumulation are imposed, then the *tendency* towards an authoritarian twist in contemporary democratic states appears more clearly (Bruff 2014; Tansel 2017; Wigger 2019).

Where are we now, then? While this book was being completed in 2019–2020, mass protests were occurring in so many countries that some have spoken of the *global* rebellion against neoliberalism (Ehrenreich 2019; see also Wigger 2019, for concrete examples of alternatives to neoliberalism in Europe). With the impact of the Covid-19 pandemic during 2020, and its effects in terms of economic crisis and mass unemployment, the situation will escalate and likely bring a new wave of mass protests around the world (e.g., in response to the killing of George Floyd in Minneapolis, United States). The interregnum observed by Gramsci during the crisis of the 1920s seems to characterize *this* phase of the political history of the capitalist epoch, too. On the other hand, "capitalist realism," as Mark Fisher remarked (2009), has damaged the power to imagine alternative futures, so that the frustration with the global capitalist system may also take the form of a reactionary resentment. Authoritarian capitalism, however, is neither a historical necessity nor a faith. There are many forms of resistance and political alternatives currently emerging and capable of expressing a counter-hegemonic power (see, among others, Bailey et al. 2017; Wigger 2019). In Italy, such counter-hegemonic power has been expressed in particular by the movement for the defence of public water against privatizations (Bieler 2021), and for the protection of the commons against commodification and ever-new enclosures (Muehlebach 2018). Thus, the collective action related to the commons has proposed not only a better grassroots management of common goods and services (from education to health, from water to transportation) but also a brand new idea of participatory democracy and political relations. Despite being opposed by mainstream parties, the battle for the commons in Italy became a widespread political practice rooted in radical forms of democracy—rather than "only" something to defend—and aimed to envision new institutions for a post-capitalist and more fully democratic future for all (Micciarelli 2017, 2018).

Yet it is also worth remarking that such social power did not find adequate political representation within state institutions and in existing parties, which pursued an even fiercer separation from civil society and grassroots organizations, thus—especially on the left—sawing away the branch upon which they were seated. In the years to come, democratic struggles will be more effective if, first of all, along with the domestic political system they will be able to intersect in creative and flexible ways national struggles with transnational forms of political organization and discourse. Second, a counter-hegemonic power necessarily needs to be autonomous from existing imaginaries and hegemonic forms linked, for example, to progressive or reactionary neoliberalism. As Gramsci remarked, even prior to becoming a form of organized political action, autonomy is a mode of thought conceivable as a critical precondition to avoid the trap of *trasformismo*—a form of political domination and passive revolution—and thus to avoid falling again into existing common sense and dominant conceptions of the world. In other words, there is no alternative if there is no real autonomy in imagining and practising alternative routes from the existing ones.

FROM 1920S TO 2020S: HISTORY, DIALECTICS, POLITICS

This book is being completed at the end of the first twenty years of the twenty-first century. As happened more than one hundred years ago, the liberal order trembles everywhere in the West and beyond within the crisis of the capitalist market economy. As occurred with the collapse of nineteenth-century civilization, the free market utopia has turned into the reality of (permanent) instability. And—again as happened more than one hundred years ago—hybrid forms of nationalism(s) emerge as a possible political outcome to the stalemate of democracy and the authority crisis of established political classes. Yet while new nationalist phenomena seem to be advancing in the battle for hegemony, they cannot resolve the social and environmental crises of capitalism—rather, they can only speed them up.

The crisis of democratic institutions, on the other hand, is deeply rooted in the breakup of the mechanisms of political representation and processes. Generally, political representation is based on the *fictio* of popular sovereignty, which is in fact exercised through the intermediation of the modern prince, the political party, the link between society and the state. This *fictio,* while ideologically covering social divisions and fostering the image of the state as a neutral servant of the national community, actually managed to produce—for some decades after World War II until the neoliberal counterrevolution—a certain degree of correspondence between representatives (in the state) and represented or, in broader terms, between political forces and social classes. This "correspondence," however, was part and parcel of the broader balance between social classes in and outside the terrain of the state (chapter 4). Historically, the redefinition of this compromise occurred through an array of transnational processes of neoliberalization and neoliberal class agency. Neoliberalism, on the other hand, ably mixed a progressive, modern, and dynamic vision of market society with a gradual enclosure of the institutional channels for the political representation of different social class interests. It actually fostered—and naturalized—a new vision of society against its own intrinsic contradictions. The neoliberal turn reflected the broader shifts between social class relations and power asymmetries at national and transnational levels, and helped produce transformations of the state.

But these transformations do not take place in an empty space: they occur within a determined, structured and structuring world form, the capitalist, which gives rise to determined social class power relations that are spatially and institutionally stratified. While the channels of ordinary politics have remained (mainly) a national framework, processes of neoliberalization have occurred through and beyond the boundaries of the state. In other words, a critical aspect of neoliberal restructuring lies in the capacity to conjugate patterns of political change at the domestic level with forms of international elites-level coordination and transnational patterns of capitalist restructuring and competition. Thus, this transformation occurred on the terrain of states but also through/beyond their infrastructures.

Throughout this book, I maintained that the transformations of the state are not a discrete, isolated process of change. Multiform processes of transformation are at the heart of the critical junction between the globalized neoliberal economy and the evolution (involution?) of national institutions. We return, thus, to contemporary organic crisis as a crisis of political representation in a time when grassroots pressures for social and economic change dramatically increase. In fact, the trans/national processes of neoliberalization did not hollow out the state as such: above all, such path-dependent dynamics disarticulated, on structural grounds, the broader sociopolitical representation (especially on the part of national working populations) in state institutions, while also discouraging effective bottom up political participation. At the same time, they disempowered democratic and accountable institutions—as national parliaments—so as these were embedded (clearly not without important contradictions and limitations, as I showed with respect to the Italian case) into the frameworks of the post–World War II social-democratic state. This is why neoliberalism ultimately remains, despite its frequent progressive rhetoric, a reactionary historical movement. The current multiform and heterogeneous outburst of political turmoil, on the other hand, increasingly signals the mismatch between the necessity of social change and the foreclosure of existing political-institutional channels in the state through novel authoritarian forms. Gramsci taught us that this is a situation in which the "old is dying and the new cannot be born" because what he called—having fascism in mind—the "morbid symptoms" obstruct the avenues for societal change. Yet, Gramsci also knew that this is the space for politics and for the power of radical imagination. Thus, after some decades of *apparent* neoliberal pacification and only occasional outbursts of conflict, the dialectics between revolution and restoration seems to have returned full-blown again on the stage of history—a stage that is still in the making.

Appendix

Centre-Left Coalitions during the Second Republic

Year and DPEF issued	*Prime minister and ministries of the economy and finance*	*Party Coalition*
May 1996–October 1998 DPEF 1997–1999 DPEF 1998–2000 DPEF 1999–2001	Romano Prodi (independent) Carlo Azeglio Ciampi (independent), Minister of Treasury, Budget and Economic Planning Vincenzo Visco (independent), Minister of Finance	• Party of the Democratic Left • Italian People's Party • Democratic Union • Federation of the Greens • Italian Socialists • Italian Renovation—Dini's group
October 1998–December 1999 DPEF 2000–2003	Massimo D'Alema (Democratic Left) Giuliano Amato (independent), Minister of Treasury, Budget and Economic Planning Vincenzo Visco (independent), Minister of Finance	• Democratic Left • Italian People's Party • Democratic Union for the Republic • Party of the Italian Communists • Federation of the Greens • Italian Renovation - Dini's group • Italian Social Democrats • La rete
December 1999–April 2000	Massimo D'Alema (Democratic Left) Giuliano Amato (independent), Minister of Treasury, Budget and Economic Planning Vincenzo Visco (independent), Minister of Finance	• Democratic Left • Italian People's Party • The Democrats • Udeur • Party of the Italian Communists • Federation of the Greens • Italian Renovation—Dini's group • Italian Social Democrats

Year and DPEF issued	Prime minister and ministries of the economy and finance	Party Coalition
April 2000–May 2001 DPEF 2001–2004	Giuliano Amato (independent) Vincenzo Visco (independent), Minister of Treasury, Budget and Economic Planning Ottaviano del Turco, Minister of Finance	• Democratic Left • Italian People's Party • The Democrats • Udeur • Party of the Italian Communists • Federation of the Greens • Italian Renovation—Dini's group • Italian Social Democrats
May 2006–January 2008 DPEF 2007–2011 DPEF 2008–2011	Romano Prodi (Democratic Party) Tommaso Padoa-Schioppa (independent), Minister of the Economy and Finance	• Democratic Party • Communist Refoundation • Federation of the Greens • Party of the Italian Communists • Udeur • Italia dei Valori • Socialist Party (Rosa nel Pugno) • Democratic Left • Socialists United
April 2013–February 2014	Enrico Letta (Democratic Party) Fabrizio Saccomanni (independent), Minister of the Economy and Finance	• Democratic Party • Scelta Civica (Monti group) • Union of Christian Democrats/ Centrist Union • New Centre-Right • Forza Italia*
February 2014–December 2016 DEF 2014 DEF 2015 DEF 2016	Matteo Renzi (Democratic Party) Pier Carlo Padoan (independent), Minister of the Economy and Finance	• Democratic Party • New Centre-Right • Scelta Civica (Monti group) • Union of Christian Democrats/ Centrist Union • Italian Socialist Party • Democratic Centre
December 2016–March 2018 DEF 2017	Paolo Gentiloni (Democratic Party) Pier Carlo Padoan (independent), Minister of the Economy and Finance	• Democratic Party • Popular Alternative • Centrists for Europe (former New Centre-Right party) • Civici e Innovatori • Democratic Centre

* Until November 26, 2013.

Notes

CHAPTER 1

1. The title of the Sixth and final chapter of this book is even more eloquent: *Rescued, but Still Free to Harm Itself* (Ferrera and Gualmini 2004, 149–169).

2. The *Economic and Financial Planning Document* [Documento di Programmazione Economico-Finanziaria, heretofore: DPEF]. The Document was introduced for the first time in 1986 and then permanently from 1988, a period in which the foundations of the consolidation of neoliberal macroeconomic policies during the 1990s and 2000s were laid. The DPEF was replaced in 2010 by the Public Finance Decision [*Decisione di Finanza Pubblica*], and from 2011 to present by the Document of Economy and Finance [*Documento di Economia e Finanza*: heretofore, DEF]. When this book—for example, in Chapter 5—refers to DPEFs in general, this (unless otherwise stated) refers to both DPEFs and DEFs, because they have the same function.

3. It is worth noting that it is not the first application of CDA to Italian politics. For example, Daniela Caterina has (2019) explored the hegemonic struggles revolving around the key labour reform of 2012 through the CDA approach.

4. According to the types of law, these are (a) ordinary law; (b) law of conversion; (c) budget law and finanziaria; (d) legislative decrees concerning domestic issues; (e) legislative decrees that enact EU legislation (mainly directives and regulations); (f) constitutional law. With respect to political economy policy domains, these are eleven, plus fifty-eight specific sub-domains. Thus, each law was classified according to the main domain and then to the specific sub-domain. Data were collected through the government database www.normattiva.it, which gathers all the acts passed in Italy from 1948 onwards.

CHAPTER 2

1. According to pluralist theory (see Dahl 1971), power is indeed fragmented and dispersed among different social and political groups, and policymaking results from a process of bargaining and compromises.

2. A "meso-theoretical" approach can be conceived as a third way between "grand" theories – such as Marxism, Liberalism or critical realism – which reflect on the overall features of human society, and the empiricism of positivist and behaviourist approaches.

3. Understood as the power of national institutions to coordinate and govern domestic linkages between public and private actors.

4. Jessop describes post-Fordism as, among other things, a form of knowledge-based economy (especially thanks to information and communication technologies and a general attention towards innovation) characterized by flexible, decentralized, and networked patterns of production and organization, with a greater role for private banks and the proliferation of financial products (2003, 97–103).

5. Rather than speaking of "emerging" economies in cases such as China, India, Brazil, South Korea, Taiwan, and so on, I prefer to define these as *consolidating economies* given the overall characteristics and political-economic processes of such countries.

CHAPTER 3

1. Moreover, some of the notes were also written more than once in different periods, meaning that the conceptual structure of the *Notebooks* emerges and is clarified progressively as a process of ongoing fine-tuning (Francioni 1984).

2. For this kind of analysis of the concept of hegemony, see Francioni (1984), Cospito (2006), Thomas (2009).

3. See Buci-Glucksmann (1980) for an assessment of Gramsci's pre-prison concept of hegemony.

4. To be sure, the word "hegemony" recurs very often in the *Notebooks*. Prima facie, it *seems* to cover a "weak" meaning (Cospito 2006, 76) that can be associated with the capacity of states, social groups, a class, cities (e.g., Florence) or even institutions like the Vatican to exert influence over a broad array of social and political referents (other states, social groups or the entirety of society). Moreover, the term often appears in association with terms such as "political hegemony" (Q1§44; Q6§81; Q7§83; Q19§9), "social hegemony" (Q12§1), "civil hegemony" (Q6§81; Q8§52; Q11§65; Q13§7), "cultural, moral intellectual hegemony" (Q19§24), "ethico-political hegemony" (Q13§18), "political-intellectual hegemony" (Q13§18).

5. The translation of this passage is taken from Thomas (2009, 163).

6. The view of hegemony as dialectic/combination of force and consensus is also evident in Gramsci's *Notes on Machiavelli*. Here, resorting to Machiavelli's image of the Centaur, Gramsci talks of "dual perspective" and "two fundamental levels

[*due gradi fondamentali*]" in political life and the state, writing that "[t]he dual perspective—can present itself on various levels, from the most elementary to the most complex; but these can all theoretically be reduced to two fundamental levels, corresponding to the dual nature of Machiavelli's Centaur—half-animal and half-human. They are the levels of force and of consent, authority and hegemony, violence and civilisation" (1975, 1576; Q13§14; cf. Q13§5).

7. The apparatuses of hegemony are all those institutions (public and private) which, in Cox's words, help 'to create in people certain modes of behaviour and expectations consistent with the hegemonic social order' (1993, 51). These can be the church, the educational system, the press, and so on.

8. Usually, the form of state (monarchy, republic) and the type of government (parliamentary, presidential, semi-presidential) is recognized in the constitution (the *Grundnorm*), along with social, political, and civil rights.

CHAPTER 4

1. The title is taken by a book of Nanni Balestrini and Primo Moroni, *L'Orda d'Oro* [*The Golden Horde*], first published in 1988. The book, unfortunately not translated in English, is an impressive collection of essays, newspaper articles, documents, debates, and many other interventions produced during the "long Italian '68" (1968–1977). This book is of particular importance for understanding not only the extent of contestation and everyday struggles but also their creative and ever-changing forms, and how they dramatically overcame the labour question to put in question society as a whole.

2. The wave of struggles, in fact, gradually overcame the "economic" cycle (Franzosi 1989) to demand labour rights and reforms in areas such as health, housing, social services, and transportation (Pizzorno 1977; Accornero 1992), and accompanied the widespread and profound cultural upheavals against the Catholic bigotry of the time (Farneti 1976, 95). The hallmark of the "hot autumn," as the years 1968–1969 were labelled, was the *Statuto dei Lavoratori* (Workers' Charter), promulgated in 1970 and comprising a series of important labour and union rights (concerning in particular layoffs and the working environment).

3. Among others: *Nota Aggiuntiva La Malfa, Saraceno Report, Pieraccini Plan, Giolitti Plan, Progetto 80*. For an overview, see Carabba (1977).

4. For example: Committee for Economic Planning; Inter-ministerial Committee for Economic Planning; Institute for the Study of the Economic Conjuncture.

5. This occurred through a mere exchange of letters between the minister of Treasury Beniamino Andreatta and the then governor of the bank, Carlo A. Ciampi.

6. The PSI formed with the DC the first centre-left government in 1963. In the 1960s, the roots of the party were still anchored in the working class. The major transformation of the PSI occurred under Craxi's leadership and especially during the 1980s, when the party 'espoused many policies favoured by capital, adopting a

"'modern,' managerial image" (Amyot 2004, 102). The PSI was also the main party involved in the corruption scandal of Tangentopoli in 1992.

7. A first tentative attempt to move in this direction occurred in 1978, with the introduction of the law *finanziaria.*

8. In 1993, six of these committees (prices, industrial policy, foreign political economy, emigration, transportations, development, and cooperation) were incorporated into the Interministerial Committee for Economic Planning (CIPE). The CIPE was created in 1967 as the principal committee entrusted with economic planning. While during the 1990s the CIPE played an important role in the process of privatization of public-owned enterprises, in 2006 it was moved from the Ministry for the Economy and Finance to the Prime Minister's headquarters to strengthen the overall economic coordination and direction of the executive.

9. Interestingly, the empowerment of the Treasury and its influence over the domestic political economy (in a period of intense change in the wake of the Maastricht Treaty) occurred when the minister was Guido Carli, already governor of the BI during the 1960s, who strengthened the relation between the BI and the Treasury.

10. In a book of 1980 (*Una Repubblica da Riformare*), Amato had already called for a reform of democracy to improve *governability* through a semi-presidential system to curb the power of parties and their centrality in the political system—he even coined the term *partitocrazia* to connote a system dominated by parties.

11. A "semi-technocratic" government (as the Amato government) denotes a case in which offices are assigned to both politicians and technocrats.

12. Ciampi executive created a specific commission, the *Committee for Privatizations* (1993).

13. Among others: Ente Nazionale Idrocarburi (chemicals, gas, oil); Agenzia Nazionale Petroli (oil); Istituto per la Ricostruzione Industriale (industrial policy and production); Ente Nazionale Energia Elettrica (electricity); Istituto Nazionale Assicurazioni (insurance); Banca Nazionale del Lavoro (bank); Ferrovie (railways); Banca Commercial Italiana and Credito Italiano (banks), Istituto Mobiliare Italiano (credit).

14. As reported by Alvaredo and Pisano, real GDP grew at a rate of 2.3 percent per year between 1983 and 1992, 1.7 percent per year between 1994 and 2003, and 0.3 percent per year between 2004 and 2005 (2010, 627).

15. For an analysis of the falling wage share since the 1980s at the international level, see Bengtsson and Ryner (2015).

16. The word "concertation" denotes a policy alliance between the main unions and the centre-left. This led to the acceptance of wage moderation in particular. Davide Bradanini (2012), through a neo-Gramscian lens, has aptly noted that, while a resistance against neoliberal restructuring would be the expected outcome in the early 1990s, unions accepted the "need" to make "sacrifices" due to the deep introjection of the *weakness* of Italian economy vis-à-vis the global economy.

17. The fortunes (and misfortunes) of parties in Italy would deserve an entire book. Let me just remark here that parties did not disappear as such, but turned into less popular democratic agencies, increasingly "presidentialized" in their own

structures. The works of the political scientists Pietro Ignazi (2013) and Mauro Calise (2015) on the "personalization" of party politics—and on the crisis of parties more broadly—are particularly important for understanding the Italian transition since the 1990s.

18. I will return to this in the next chapter, dovetailing empirically the *discursive* construction of the question of "stability" and its political-economic meanings.

CHAPTER 5

1. See the Introduction for a discussion of this research methodology approach.

2. Introduced for the first time in 1986 and still in force (though since 2011 with another name: Document of Economy and Finance, DEF), the DPEF was conceived, along with the financial law (which was introduced in 1978) as the main policy instrument to tighten the control of the executive and economic ministries on the country's economic policy. The DEPFs (and DEFs) are elaborated by experts in the economic ministries under the political direction of the government, and then presented to the parliament. The documents outline the budgetary, economic, and fiscal policies, and the institutional reforms, to be implemented in the following three-year or four-year period. On occasion, this chapter will refer to DPEFs in general, which—unless otherwise stated—refers to both DPEFs and DEFs, because they have the same function.

3. In the previous chapter, I analysed the fundamental importance of the early 1990s as the moment of change in intrastate relations and branches, and of the quickening of the neoliberalization process.

4. In particular, by the "Yellow-Green" government composed by Five Star Movement and The League. The specific contradictions of this government are analysed in chapter 7.

5. In the previous chapter, I already mentioned two contingent causes that occurred in the early 1990s: *Tangentopoli*, and the fiscal crisis of 1992.

6. DPEF 1988–1992: 5 (govt.: pentapartito).

7. DEPF 1993–1995, 1 (govt.: technocratic).

8. DPEF 1994–1996, 1 (govt.: technocratic).

9. See all the DPEFs from 1988 to 1996, were this set of policies is the only presented in terms of policy solutions.

10. DPEF 1991–1993, 5 (govt.: pentapartito).

11. DPEF 1994–1996, 1 and 2 (govt.: technocratic).

12. Especially by the left, as I show later in this chapter.

13. Meaningfully, the heading of an important study of Maurizio Ferrera and Elisabetta Gualmini (2004) devoted to Italian Europeanization is *Rescued by Europe?*

14. DPEF 1992–1994, 19 (govt.: pentapartito).

15. DPEF 1991–1993, 1 (govt.: pentapartito).

16. DPEF 1993–1995, 17 (govt.: technocratic).

17. DPEF 1993–1995, 1 (govt.: technocratic).

18. DPEF 1995–1997, V (govt.: centre-right).

19. DPEF 1998–2000, VII (govt.: centre-left).

20. DPEF 2007–2011, 33 (govt.: centre-left).
21. DPEF 1997–1998, 25 (govt.: centre-left).
22. DPEF 1998–2000, VII (govt.: centre-left).
23. DPEF 1999–2001, X–XII (govt.: centre-left).
24. See the previous chapter for the analysis of the changes in the state associated with budget procedures.
25. The DPEF 1988–1992 (8, govt.: centre-left) maintains that "the differential between the average cost of debt and GDP growth is rather large. The real cost of debt in our country is higher due to the high deficit and debt [. . .] In order to come closer to writing off the differential, it is necessary to be more incisive on the overall balance net of interests by generating primary surpluses."
26. Out of twenty-nine Documents analysed, all assert the "necessity" of *risanamento* multiple times; the only exception is the 1996–98 DPEF, where the term is mentioned once.
27. See the already mentioned DEPF 1993–1995, 1 (technocratic).
28. DPEF 1991–1993, 6 (govt.: pentapartito).
29. DPEF 1997–1999, V (govt.: centre-left).
30. DPEF 2001–2004, V (govt.: centre-left; emphasis added). See also the DPEF 1994–1996, 1 (govt.: technocratic).
31. DPEF 2010–2013, 2 (govt.: centre-right).
32. DPEF 1998–2000, VII (govt.: centre-left).
33. DPEF 2001–2004, V (govt.: centre-left).
34. DPEF 1995–1997, 1 (govt.: centre-right).
35. DPEF 1993–1995, 1 (govt.: technocratic).
36. DEF 2013, III (govt.: technocratic). As noted in footnote 2 for this chapter, DPEFs and DEFs have the same function (the latter being the new acronym from 2011 onwards).
37. DPEF 2002–2006, V (govt.: centre-right).
38. DPEF 2007–2011, 33 (govt.: centre-left). Also, "[f]rom many years now the Italian economy suffers a series of structural imbalances that determine an unsatisfying growth rate, which is systematically lower than that of other industrialized countries. The potential growth, which was more than 4 percent in the 1970s, fell to 3 percent at the beginning of the 1980s, 1.5 percent in the half of the 1990s, and 1.3 percent today" (DPEF 2006–2009, 2; govt.: centre-left).
39. For an excellent critical reconstruction of the crisis management in the years of the crisis, see Daniela Caterina (2019, 110–121).
40. DEF 2013, 2 (govt.: technocratic).
41. DEF 2013, 2 (govt.: technocratic).
42. In fact, we read that "[r]isanamento of public finance succeeds only if it is accompanied by the exit of the State from direct economic activity, which should be left just to the market [. . .] An essential contribution to economic growth in conditions of stability will come from the redefinition of the relation between the public sector and private initiative, programmes of privatization of public-owned enterprises, "flexibilization" of labour market, promotion of private business, and the

reduction of bureaucracy to make public administration action more effective" (DPEF 1995–1997, 10). See also all the DPEFs from 2001 to 2005.

43. The expression "centre-left" was coined, initially, to indicate the alliance between an array of centrist parties, led by the Christian Democracy, with the Italian Socialist Party. The first centre-left government was led by Aldo Moro in 1961, and saw the alliance between the Christian Democracy (especially its progressive wing), the Italian Socialist Party, the Italian Republican Party, and the Italian Socialist and Democratic Party.

44. All the DPEFs in the period considered present this kind of political economy choice.

45. DPEF 1997–1999, 9–10 (govt.: centre-left).

46. Such reluctance is also due to the fact that centre-right governments were faced by several infringements proceedings, in 2005 and 2009, by the European Commission due to excess budget deficits.

47. DPEF 1998–2000, VII (govt.: centre-left).

48. DPEF 1998–2000: 84 (govt.: centre-left).

49. DPEF 1995–1997: 10 (govt.: centre-right).

50. DPEF 2009–2013: VI (govt.: centre-right).

51. DPEF 1997–1999: 20 (govt.: centre-left).

52. This was eventually amended with Law n. 94/1997.

53. DPEF 1997–1999, 39 (govt.: centre-left).

54. DPEF 1988–1992, 9 (govt.: pentapartito); DPEF 1992–1994: 18 (govt.: pentapartito); DPEF 1996–1998, 26 (govt.: technocratic); DPEF 1998–2000, 69 (govt.: centre-left).

CHAPTER 6

1. Let me here also emphasize that another relevant institutional actor in the transformations—was the President of the Republic. For the changing role of this institution during the Second Republic, see in particular Amoretti and Giannone (2014).

2. See the methodological section in the Introduction for the details concerning the methods of this part of the research and the outline of the PolEcon Dataset.

3. The vote of no-confidence in the government (*mozione di sfiducia,* art. 94 of the Italian constitution) can be raised by the parliament when the relation between the parliamentary majority and the executive (which is expressed by that majority) has deteriorated.

4. Methodologically, this allows me to take into account data concerning just the laws eventually approved.

5. Here, I gather all the measures concerning public finance (especially spending cuts) introduced outside the annual budget law. However, it is worth noting that the ordinary financial bills and budget laws also experienced a quantitative decline over

time, coupled with the drastic limitation of the parliament's powers to amend the set of budget measures (Cozzolino 2018c).

CHAPTER 7

1. The OECD defines the poverty gap as the "ratio by which the mean income of the poor falls below the poverty line. The poverty line is defined as half the median household income of the total population" (OECD 2019d).

CHAPTER 8

1. The articles are gathered in the volume *Sul Fascismo*, edited by Enzo Santarelli (1975).

References

Abrams, Philip. [1977] 1988. 'Notes on the Difficulty of Studying the State'. *Journal of Historical Sociology* 1(1): 58–89.

Accornero, Aris. 1992. *La Parabola del Sindacato: Ascesa e Declino di una Cultura*. Bologna: Il Mulino.

Albertazzi, Daniele, Arianna Giovannini, and Antonella Seddone. 2018. '"No Regionalism Please, We Are *Leghisti!*" The Transformation of the Italian Lega Nord Under the Leadership of Matteo Salvini'. *Regional and Federal Studies* 28(5): 645–671.

Albertini, Marco. 2013. 'The Relation Between Social Class and Economic Inequality: A Strengthening Or Weakening Nexus? Evidence From the Last Three Decades of Inequality in Italy'. *Research in Social Stratification and Mobility* 33(September issue): 27–39.

Albrow, Martin. 1996. *The Global Age: State and Society Beyond Modernity*. Cambridge: Polity Press.

Almagisti, Marco, Luca Lanzalaco, and Luca Verzichelli. Eds. 2016. *La Transizione Politica Italiana: Da Tangentopoli a oggi*. Roma: Carocci.

Almond, Gabriel, and Brigham G. Powell. 1966. *Comparative Politics: A Developmental Approach*. Boston: Little, Brown.

Alvaredo, Facundo, and Elena Pisano. 2010. 'Top Incomes in Italy 1974–2004'. In *Top Incomes: A Global Perspective*, edited by Anthony B. Atkinson and Thomas Piketty, 625–658. Oxford: Oxford University Press.

Amato, Giuliano. 1980. *Una Repubblica da Riformare*. Bologna: Il Mulino.

Amoretti, Francesco, and Diego Giannone. 2014. 'The Power of Words. The Changing Role of the Italian Head of State During the Second Republic'. *Modern Italy* 19(4): 439–455.

Amyot, Grant. 2004. *Business, the State and Economic Policy: The Case of Italy*. London: Routledge.

Anderson, Benedict. [1983] 2006. *Imagined Communities: Reflections on the Origins and Spread of Nationalism*. London: Verso.

Anderson, Perry. 1974. *Lineages of the Absolutist State*. London: NLB.

Anderson, Perry. 1976. 'The Antinomies of Antonio Gramsci'. *New Left Review* 100: 5–78.

Antonini, Francesca. 2016. 'Il vecchio muore e il nuovo non può nascere'. *International Gramsci Journal* 2(1): 167–184.

Antonini, Francesca. 2020. *Caesarism and Bonapartism in Gramsci: Hegemony and the Crisis of Modernity*. Leiden: Brill.

Arrighi, Giovanni. 1994. *The Long Twentieth Century: Money, Power and the Origins of Our Time*. London: Verso.

Associazione per lo sviluppo dell'industria nel Mezzogiorno (SVIMEZ). 2019. *Report on the Economy and Society of Mezzogiorno*. Available at: http://lnx.svimez.info/svimez/rapporto-2019-tutti-i-materiali/.

Bailey, David J., Monica Clua-Losada, Niko Huke, and Olatz Ribera-Almandoz. 2017. *Beyond Defeat and Austerity: Disrupting (The Critical Political Economy Of) Neoliberal Europe*. London: Routledge.

Baldini, Gianfranco. 2013. 'Don't Count Your Chickens Before They're Hatched: The 2013 Italian Parliamentary and Presidential Elections'. *Southern European Society and Politics* 18(4): 473–497.

Balducci, Renato, and Mauro Marconi. 1981. 'L'Accumulazione di Capitale nella Visione del Governo, della Banca d'Italia e della Confederazione Generale dell'Industria'. In *Scelte Politiche e Teorie Economiche in Italia, 1945–1978*, edited by Giorgio Lunghini, 71–107. Torino: Einaudi.

Balestrini, Nanni, and Primo Moroni. Eds. 1997. *L'Orda d'Oro: 1968–1977: la Grande Ondata Rivoluzionaria e Creativa, Politica ed Esistenziale*. Milano: Feltrinelli.

Bank of Italy. 2018. *Survey on Italian Household Income and Wealth*. March 18, 2018. Available at: https://www.bancaditalia.it/pubblicazioni/indagine-famiglie/index.html?com.dotmarketing.htmlpage.language=1.

Barba, Aldo. 2011. 'La Redistribuzione del Reddito nell'Italia di Maastricht'. In *Un'Altra Italia in un'Altra Europa: Mercato e Interesse Nazionale*, edited by Leonardo Paggi, 60–81. Roma: Carocci.

Barbagallo, Francesco. 2002. *L'Italia Contemporanea*. Roma: Carocci.

Barbieri, Cristina. 2003. 'L'Europeizzazione del Gabinetto e il Ruolo del Presidente del Consiglio'. In *L'Europeizzazione dell'Italia: L'Impatto dell'Unione Europea sulle Istituzioni e le Politiche Italiane*, edited by Sergio Fabbrini, 55–79. Roma-Bari: Laterza.

Barrow, Clyde W. 2008. 'The Intellectual Origins of New Political Science'. *New Political Science* 30(2): 215–244.

Beck, Ulrich. 2002. 'The Cosmopolitan Society and its Enemies'. *Theory, Culture & Society* 19(1–2): 17–44.

Bellofiore, Riccardo. 2001. 'I lunghi anni Settanta. Crisi Sociale e Integrazione Economica Internazionale'. In *Le radici della crisi. L'Italia tra gli anni Sessanta e Settanta*, edited by Luca Baldissara, 57–102. Rome: Carocci.

Bengtsson, Erik, and Magnus Ryner. 2015. 'The (International) Political Economy of Falling Wage Shares: Situating Working-Class Agency'. *New Political Economy* 20(3): 406–430.

Berger, Peter L., and Thomas Luckmann. [1966] 1991. *The Social Construction of Reality: A Treatise in the Sociology of Knowledge*. London: Penguin.

Bieler, Andreas. 2021. *Fighting for Water: Resisting Privatisation in Europe*. London: Zed Books.

Bieler, Andreas, and Adam D. Morton. 2003. 'Globalisation, the State and Class Struggle: A "Critical Economy" Engagement with Open Marxism'. *British Journal of Politics and International Relations* 5(4): 467–499.

Bieler, Andreas, and Adam D. Morton. 2006a. 'A Critical Theory Route to Hegemony, World Order and Historical Change: Neo-Gramscian Perspectives in International Relations'. In *Global Restructuring, State, Capital and Labour: Contesting Neo-Gramscian Perspectives*, edited by Andreas Bieler, Werner Bonefeld, Peter Burnham, and Adam D. Morton, 9–27. London: Palgrave Macmillan.

Bieler, Andreas, and Adam D. Morton. 2006b. 'Globalization, the State and Class Struggle: A 'Critical Economy' Engagement with Open Marxism'. In *Global Restructuring, State, Capital and Labour: Contesting Neo-Gramscian Perspectives*, edited by Andreas Bieler, Werner Bonefeld, Peter Burnham, and Adam D. Morton, 155–175. London: Palgrave Macmillan.

Bieler, Andreas, and Adam D. Morton. 2006c. 'Class Formation, Resistance and the Transnational: Beyond Unthinking Materialism'. In *Global Restructuring, State, Capital and Labour: Contesting Neo-Gramscian Perspectives*, edited by Andreas Bieler, Werner Bonefeld, Peter Burnham, and Adam D. Morton, 196–206. London: Palgrave Macmillan.

Bieler, Andreas, and Adam D. Morton. 2008. 'The Deficits of Discourse in IPE: Turning Base Metal into Gold?'. *International Studies Quarterly* 52(1): 103–128.

Bieler, Andreas, and Adam D. Morton. 2018. *Global Capitalism, Global War, Global Crisis*. Cambridge: Cambridge University Press.

Bieler, Andreas, Bruff Ian, and Adam D. Morton. 2015. 'Gramsci and 'the International': Past, Present and Future'. In *Antonio Gramsci*, edited by Mark McNally, 137–155. London: Palgrave Macmillan.

Bieler, Andreas, Werner Bonefeld, Peter Burnham, and Adam D. Morton. 2006. *Global Restructuring, State, Capital and Labour: Contesting Neo-Gramscian Perspectives*. London: Palgrave Macmillan.

Biorcio, Roberto. 1999. 'La Lega Nord e la Transizione Italiana'. *Italian Political Science Review/Rivista Italiana di Scienza Politica* 29(1): 55–87.

Biorcio, Roberto. 2014. 'The Reasons for the Success and Transformations of the 5 Star Movement'. *Contemporary Italian Politics* 6(1): 37–53.

Biraschi, Paolo, and Antonella Crescenzi. 2007. 'L'Italia verso l'Unione Monetaria Europea: la Svolta e le Riforme negli anni '90'. In *I Documenti di Programmazione: Una Lettura della Politica Economica dell'Italia dal Piano Marshall al DPEF 2008–2011*, edited by Antonella Crescenzi, 263–396. Roma: Luiss University Press.

Boltanski, Luc, and Eve Chiapello. 2005. *The New Spirit of Capitalism*, translated by Gregory Elliot. London: Verso.

Bonefeld, Werner. 2015. 'European Economic Constitution and the Transformation of Democracy: On Class and the State of Law'. *European Journal of International Relations* 21(4): 867–886.

Bonefeld, Werner. 2017. *The Strong State and the Free Economy*. London: Rowman & Littlefield.

Borghetto Enrico, Giuliani Marco, and Francesco Zucchini. 2012. 'Leading Governments and Unwilling Legislators: The European Union and the Italian Law Making (1987–2006)'. In *The Europeanization of Domestic Legislatures: The Empirical Implications of the Delors' Myth in Nine Countries*, edited by Sylvain Brouard, Oliver Costa, and Thomas Köning, 109–131. New York: Springer.

Börzel, Tanja A., and Thomas Risse. 2016. 'Dysfunctional State Institutions, Trust, and Governance in Areas of Limited Statehood'. *Regulation & Governance* 10(2): 149–160.

Bourdieu, Pierre. 2015. *On the State: Lectures at the Collége de France, 1989–1992*, edited byPatrick Champagne, Remi Lenoir, Franck Poupeau, and Marie-Christine Riviere, translated by David Fernbach. Malden, MA: Polity.

Boyer, Robert. 1990. *The Regulation School: A Critical Introduction*. New York: Columbia University Press.

Bradanini, Davide. 2012. *Common Sense and 'National Emergency': Neoliberal Hegemony in 1990s Italy*. PhD diss.

Bremmer, Ian. 2011. *The End of the Free Market: Who Wins the War Between Corporations and States*. New York: Portfolio.

Brenner, Niels, Peck Jamie, and Niels Theodore. 2010. 'After Neoliberalization?'. *Globalizations* 7(3): 327–345.

Brouard, Sylvain, Olivier Costa, and Thomas Köning. Eds. 2012. *The Europeanization of Domestic Legislatures: The Empirical Implications of the Delors' Myth in Nine Countries*. New York: Springer.

Brown, Wendy. 2019. *In the Ruins of Neoliberalism: The Rise of Antidemocratic Politics in the West*. New York: Columbia University Press.

Bruff, Ian. 2005. 'Making Sense of the Globalisation Debate When Engaging in Political Economy Analysis'. *British Journal of Politics and International Relations* 7(2): 261–80.

Bruff, Ian. 2008. *Culture and Consensus in European Varieties of Capitalism: A "Common Sense" Analysis*. London: Palgrave Macmillan.

Bruff, Ian. 2011a. 'What About the Elephant in the Room? Varieties of Capitalism, Varieties in Capitalism'. *New Political Economy* 16(3): 481–500.

Bruff, Ian. 2011b. 'Overcoming the State/Market Dichotomy'. In *Critical International Political Economy: Dialogue, Debate and Dissensus*, edited by Stuart Shields, Ian Bruff, and Huw Macartney, 80–98. Basingstoke: Palgrave Macmillan.

Bruff, Ian. 2014. 'The Rise of Authoritarian Neoliberalism'. *Rethinking Marxism* 26(1): 113–129.

Bruff, Ian, and Cemal Burak Tansel. 2019. 'Authoritarian Neoliberalism: Trajectories of Knowledge Production and Praxis'. *Globalizations* 16(3): 233–244.

Bruff, Ian, and Kathryn Starnes. 2019. 'Framing the Neoliberal Canon: Resisting the market myth via Literary Enquiry'. *Globalizations* 16(3): 245–259.

Bruff, Ian, and Laura Horn. 2012. 'Varieties of Capitalism in Crisis?' *Competition & Change* 16(3): 161–168.

Brunazzo, Marco, and Mark Gilbert. 2017. 'Insurgents Against Brussels: Euroscepticism and the Right-Wing Populist Turn of the Lega Nord Since 2013'. *Journal of Modern Italian Studies* 22(5): 624–641.

Buch-Hansen, Hubert, and Angela Wigger. 2011. *The Politics of European Competition Regulation: A Critical Political Economy Perspective*. New York: Routledge.

Buci-Glucksmann, Christine. 1980. *Gramsci and the State*, translated by David Fernbach. London: Lawrence and Wishart.

Bull, Martin J., and Gianfranco Pasquino. 2018. 'Italian Politics in an Era of Recession: The End of Bipolarism?' *South European Society and Politics* 23(1): 1–12.

Burgio, Alberto. 2014. *Gramsci: Il Sistema in Movimento*. Roma: Derive Approdi.

Burnham, Peter. 2001. 'New Labour and the Politics of Depoliticisation'. *British Journal of Politics and International Relations* 3(2): 127–149.

Cable, Vincent. 1995. 'The Diminished Nation-State: A Study in the Loss of Economic Power'. *Daedalus* 124(2): 23–53.

Cahill, Damien. 2014. *The End of Laissez-Faire? On the Durability of Embedded Neoliberalism*. Cheatham, UK: Edward Elgar.

Caiani, Emanuela. 2019. 'The Populist Parties and Their Electoral Success: Different Causes Behind Different Populisms? The Case of The Five-Star Movement and The League'. *Contemporary Italian Politics*, online first version. DOI: 10.1080/23248823.2019.1647681.

Calise, Mauro. 2005. 'Presidentialization, Italian Style'. In *The Presidentialization of Politics: A Comparative Study of Modern Democracies*, edited by Thomas Poguntke and Paul D. Webb, 88–106. Oxford: Oxford University Press.

Calise, Mauro. 2010. *Il Partito Personale: I Due Corpi del Leader*. Roma-Bari: Laterza.

Calise, Mauro. 2015. 'The Personal Party: An Analytical Framework'. *Italian Political Science Review* 45(3): 301–315.

Calise, Mauro. 2016. *La Democrazia del Leader*. Roma-Bari: Laterza.

Calise, Mauro, and Renato Mannheimer. 1982. *Governanti in Italia: Un Trentennio Repubblicano 1946–1976*. Bologna: Il Mulino.

Calvano, Roberta. 2014. 'La Decretazione d'Urgenza Nella Stagione delle Larghe Intese'. *Associazione Italiana dei Costituzionalisti* 2: 1–23.

Capano, Giliberto. 2003. 'Administrative Traditions and Policy Change: When Policy Paradigms Matter. The Case of Italian Administrative Reform During the 1990s'. *Public Administration* 81(4): 781–801.

Capano, Giliberto, and Marco Giuliani. Eds. 2001. *Parlamento e Processo Legislativo in Italia: Continuità e Mutamento*. Bologna: Il Mulino.

Carabba, Manin. 1977. *Un Ventennio di Programmazione*. Roma-Bari: Laterza

Carney, Richard W. 2015. 'The Stabilizing State: State Capitalism as a Response to Financial Globalization in One-Party Regimes'. *Review of International Political Economy* 22(4): 838–873.

Cassese, Sabino. 2016. 'La decretazione d'urgenza: le colpe dello Stato liberale'. In *Parlamentoe Storia d'Italia II: Procedure e Politiche*, edited by Vincenzo Casamassima and Andrea Frangioni, 209–213. Pisa: Edizioni della Normale.

Castells, Manuel. 1996. *The Rise of the Network Society: Volume I: The Information Age: Economy, Society and Culture*. Oxford: Blackwell.

Castronovo, Valerio. 1976. 'Economia e Classi Sociali'. In *L'Italia Contemporanea, 1945–1975*, edited by Valerio Castronovo, 3–60. Torino: Einaudi.

Castronovo, Valerio. [1995] 2013. *Storia Economica d'Italia: Dall'Ottocento ai Giorni Nostri*. Torino: Einaudi.

Caterina, Daniela. 2019. *Struggles for Hegemony in Italy's Crisis Management: A Case Study on the 2012 Labour Market Reform*. Cham, CH: Springer.

Ceccanti, Stefano, and Salvatore Vassallo. Eds. 2004. *Come Chiudere la Transizione: Cambiamento, Apprendimento e Adattamento nel Sistema Politico Italiano*. Bologna: Il Mulino.

Ceccarini, Luigi, and Fabio Bordignon. 2016. 'The Five Stars Continue to Shine: The Consolidation of Grillo's 'Movement Party' In Italy'. *Contemporary Italian Politics* 8(2): 131–159.

Censis. 2019. *Fifty-Third Report on the Social Situation of the Country*. Available at: http://www.censis.it/rapporto-annuale/53%C2%B0-rapporto-sulla-situazione-sociale-del-paese2019-0.

Cento Bull, Anna, and Mark Gilbert. 2001. *The Lega Nord and the Northern Question in Italian Politics*. London: Palgrave.

Cerny, Philip. 1997. 'Paradoxes of the Competition State: The Dynamics of Political Globalization'. *Government and Opposition* 32(2): 251–274.

Cerny, Philip G. 2010. 'The Competition State Today: From Raison d'État to Raison du Monde'. *Policy Studies* 31(1): 5–21.

Chabod, Federico. 1967. *Scritti sul Rinascimento*. Torino: Einaudi.

Chimenti, Andrea. 1992. *Un Parlamentarismo Agli Sgoccioli: Lineamenti della Forma di Governo Italiana nell'Esperienza di Dieci Legislature*. Torino: Giappichelli.

Ciccarone, Giuseppe, and Enrico Saltari. 2015. 'Cyclical Downturn or Structural Disease? The Decline of the Italian Economy in the Last Twenty Years'. *Journal of Modern Italian Studies* 20(2): 228–244.

Clua-Losada, Monica, and Olatz Ribera-Almandoz. 2017. 'Authoritarian Neoliberalism and the Disciplining of Labour'. In *States of Discipline: Authoritarian Neoliberalism and the Contested Reproduction of Capitalist Order*, edited by Cemal Burak Tansel, 29–45. London: Rowman & Littlefield International.

Conti, Nicolò, and Vincenzo Memoli. 2015. 'The Emergence of a New Party in the Italian Party System: Rise and Fortunes of the Five Star Movement'. *West European Politics* 38(3): 516–534.

Corrigan, Philip, and Derek Sayer. 1985. *The Great Arch: English State Formation as Cultural Revolution*. Oxford: Basil Blackwell.

Corte Costituzionale, Servizio Studi. 2017. *La Decretazione d'Urgenza nella Giurisprudenza Costituzionale*. September 2017. Edited by Riccardo Nevola. Available at: https://www.cortecostituzionale.it/studiRicerche.do.

Cospito, Giuseppe. 2005. 'Egemonia'. In *Le Parole di Gramsci: Per un Lessico dei Quaderni del Carcee*, edited by Guido Liguori and Fabio Frosini, 74–92. Roma: Carocci.

Cox, Robert W. 1981. 'Social Forces, States and World Orders: Beyond International Relations'. *Millennium* 10(2): 126–155.

Cox, Robert W. 1987. *Production, Power and World Order: Social Forces in the Making of History*. New York: Columbia University Press.

Cox, Robert W. 1989. 'Production, the State and Change in World Order'. In *Global Changes and Theoretical Challenges: Approaches to World Politics for the 1990s*, edited by Ernest-Otto Czepiel and Jamiee N. Rosenau, 37–50. Lexington, MA: Lexington.

Cox, Robert W. 1993. 'Gramsci, Hegemony and International Relations: An Essay in Method'. In *Gramsci, Historical Materialism and International Relations*, edited by Stephen Gill, 49–66. Cambridge: Cambridge University Press.

Cozzolino, Adriano. 2018a. 'Trumpism as Nationalist Neoliberalism: A Critical Enquiry Into Donald Trump's Political Economy'. *Interdisciplinary Political Studies* 4(1): 47–73.

Cozzolino, Adriano. 2018b. 'L'onda neo-nazionalista e l'Unione Europea come frattura politica'. In *Europa: che fare? L'Unione Europea tra Crisi, Populismi e Prospettive di Rilancio Federale*, edited by Adriano Cozzolino, Flavia Palazzi, and Francesco Y. Forte, 47–58. Guida: Napoli.

Cozzolino, Adriano. 2018c. *The Political Economy of State Transformation in Italy from the Crisis of the Keynesian Welfare State to the Crisis of the Neoliberal Paradigm*. PhD diss.

Cozzolino, Adriano. 2019a. 'Reconfiguring the State: Executive Powers, Emergency Legislation, and Neoliberalization in Italy'. *Globalizations* 16(3): 336–352.

Cozzolino, Adriano. 2019b. 'Rating Agencies, Symbolic Capital and the Evaluation of Nation-States: A Preliminary Exploration'. *Cartografie Sociali: Rivista di Sociologia e Scienze Umane* 8(4): 139–158.

Cozzolino, Adriano. 2020. 'The Discursive Construction of Europe in Italy in the Age of Permanent Austerity'. *Journal of Common Market Studies* 58(3): 580–593.

Cozzolino, Adriano, and Diego Giannone. 2019. 'State Transformations and Neoliberalization in Italy: A Critical Discourse Analysis of Governments' Political Economy, 1988–2009'. *New Political Science* 41(3): 443–458.

Crescenzi, Antonella. Ed. 2007. *I Documenti di Programmazione: Una Lettura della Politica Economica in Italia dal Piano Marshall al DPEF 2008–2011*. Rome: LUISS University Press.

Crescenzi, Antonella, and Gianluca Dente. 2007. 'L'Avvio della Ricostruzione e i Primi Interventi Programmatici negli Anni '50'. In *I Documenti di Programmazione: Una Lettura della Politica Economica dell'Italia dal Piano Marshall al DPEF 2008–2011*, edited by Antonella Crescenzi, 1–60. Roma: Luiss University Press.

Crespy, Amandine, and Pierre Vanheuverzwijn. 2019. 'What "Brussels" Means by Structural Reforms: Empty Signifier or Constructive Ambiguity?' *Comparative European Politics* 17(1): 92–111.

Criscitiello, Annalisa. 2004. *Il Cuore dei Governi: Le Politiche di Riforma degli Esecutivi in Prospettiva Comparata*. Napoli: Edizioni Scientifiche Italiane.

Criscitiello, Annalisa. 2019. 'La Macchina dell'Esecutivo e la sua Difficile Evoluzione'. In *Il Governo in Italia: Profili Costituzionali e Dinamiche Politiche*, edited by Fortunato Musella, 123–149. Bologna: Il Mulino.

Culpepper, Pepper D. 2014. 'The Political Economy of Unmediated Democracy: Italian Austerity Under Mario Monti'. *West European Politics* 37(6): 1264–1281.

Dagnes, Joselle, Marianna Filandri, and Luca Storti. 2018. 'Social Class and Wealth Inequality in Italy Over 20 Years, 1993–2014'. *Journal of Modern Italian Studies* 23(2): 176–198.

Dahl, Robert A. 1971. *Polyarchy: Participation and Opposition*. New Haven, CT: Yale University Press.

Davanzati Forges, Guglielmo, Andrea Pacella, and Angelo Salento. 2019. 'Financialisation in Context: The Case of Italy'. *Cambridge Journal of Economics* 43(4): 917–936.

Della Sala, Vincent. 1997. 'Hollowing Out and Hardening the State: European Integration and the Italian Economy'. *West European Politics* 20(1): 14–33.

De Micheli, Chiara. 2016. 'Il ruolo delle commissioni parlamentari nella primaesperienza repubblicana (1948–1992)'. In *Parlamentoe Storia d'Italia II: Procedure e Politiche*, edited by Vincenzo Casamassima and Andrea Frangioni, 129–145. Pisa: Edizioni della Normale.

De Micheli, Chiara, and Luca Verzichelli. 2004. *Il Parlamento*. Bologna: Il Mulino.

De Nardis, Fabio. 2017. 'The Concept of Depolicitisation and its Consequences'. *Participation and Conflict* 10(2): 340–356.

De Sio, Lorenzo. 2018. *Il Ritorno del Voto di Classe, Ma al Contrario (Ovvero: Se il PD è il Partito delle élite)*. March 18. Available at: https://cise.luiss.it/cise/2018/03/06/il-ritorno-del-voto-di-classe-ma-al-contrario-ovvero-se-il-pd-e-il-partito-delle-elite/.

Diamanti, Ilvo. 2014. 'The 5 Star Movement: A Political Laboratory'. *Contemporary Italian Politics* 6(1): 4–15.

Di Nolfo, Ennio. 2016. *Storia delle Relazioni Internazionali: Dalla Fine della Guerra Fredda ad Oggi, Volume III*. Roma-Bari: Laterza.

Diodato, Emidio. 2014. *Il Vincolo Esterno: Le Ragioni della Debolezza Italiana*. Milano: Mimesis.

Di Palma, Giuseppe, Sergio Fabbrini, and Giorgio Freddi. Eds. 2000. *Condannata al Successo? L'Italia nell'Europa Integrata*. Bologna: Il Mulino.

Draghi, Mario. 2011. 'Una Scelta Coraggiosa che Guarda Avanti'. In *L'Autonomia della Politica Monetaria: Il Divorzio Tesoro–Banca d'Italia Trent'Anni Dopo*, edited by Maria Teresa Salvemini, 32–45. Bologna: Il Mulino.

Dunleavy, Peter, and Duncan O'Leary. 1987. *Theories of the State: The Politics of Liberal Democracy*. London: Macmillan Education.

Dyson, Kenneth, and Kevin Featherstone. 1996. 'Italy and EMU as a "Vincolo Esterno": Empowering the Technocrats, Transforming the State'. *South European Society and Politics* 1(2): 272–299.

Eagleton, Terry. 1991. *Ideology: An Introduction*. London: Verso.

Easton, David. 1953. *The Political System: An Inquiry into the State of Political Science*. New York: Knopf.

Easton, David. 1981. 'The Political System Besieged by the State'. *Political Theory* 9(3): 303–325.

Ehrenreich, Ben. 2019. 'Welcome to the Global Rebellion Against Neoliberalism'. *The Nation*, November 25, 2019. Available at: https://www.thenation.com/article/archive/global-rebellions-inequality/.

Evans, Peter. 1997. 'The Eclipse of the State? Reflections on Stateness in an Era of Globalization'. *World Politics* 50(1): 62–87.

Evans, Peter B., Rueschemeyer Dieter, and Theda Skocpol. Eds. 1985. *Bringing the State Back In*. New York: Cambridge University Press.

Fabbrini, Sergio. Ed. 2003. *L'Europeizzazione dell'Italia: L'Impatto dell'Unione Europea sulle Istituzioni e le Politiche Italiane*. Roma-Bari: Laterza.

Fabbrini, Sergio. 2006. 'The Italian Case of a Transition Within Democracy'. *Journal of Southern Europe and the Balkans* 8(2): 145–161.

Fabbrini, Sergio, and Alessia Donà. 2003. 'Europeanisation as Strengthening of Domestic Executive Power? The Italian Experience and the Case of the "Legge Comunitaria"', *Journal of European Integration* 25(1): 31–50.

Fabbrini, Sergio, and Simona Piattoni. Eds. 2007. *Italy in the European Union: Redefining National Interest in a Compound Polity*. London: Rowman & Littlefield.

Fairclough, Norman. [1989] 2001. *Language and Power*. Harlow: Pearsons Education.

Fairclough, Norman. 1992. *Discourse and Social Change*. Cambridge: Polity Press.

Fairclough, Norman, and Ruth Wodak. 1997. 'Critical Discourse Analysis'. In *Discourse as Social Interaction: Volume II*, edited by Teun Van Dijk, 258–284. London: Sage.

Farneti, Paolo. 1976. 'I Partiti Politici e il Sistema di Potere'. In *L'Italia Contemporanea, 1945–1975*, edited by Valerio Castronovo, 61–104. Torino: Einaudi.

Ferrera, Maurizio, and Elisabetta Gualmini. 2004. *Rescued by Europe? Social and Labour Market Reforms in Italy from Maastricht to Berlusconi*. Amsterdam: Amsterdam University Press.

Flinders, Matthew, and Matt Wood. 2014. 'Depoliticisation, Governance and the State'. *Policy & Politics* 42(2): 135–149.

Foa, Vittorio. 1976. 'Sindacati e Classe Operaia'. In *L'Italia Contemporanea, 1945–1975*, edited by Valerio Castronovo, 253–227. Torino: Einaudi.

Francioni, Gianni. 1984. *L'officina Gramsciana: Ipotesi Sulla Struttura dei 'Quaderni del carcere'*. Napoli: Bibliopolis.

Franzini Maurizio, Granaglia Elena, and Michele Raitano. 2016. *Extreme Inequalities in Contemporary Capitalism: Should We Be Concerned About the Rich?* Chatam, CH: Springer.

Franzosi, Paolo, Marone Francesco, and Eugenio Salvati. 2015. 'Populism and Euroscepticism in the Italian Five Star Movement'. *The International Spectator: Italian Journal of International Affairs* 50(2): 109–124.

Fraser, Nancy. 2017. 'From Progressive Neoliberalism to Trump—And Beyond'. *American Affairs* 1(4): 46–64.

Fratianni, Nicola, and Ferruccio Spinelli. 2005. *A Monetary History of Italy*. Cambridge: Cambridge University Press.

Garzia, Diego. 2019. 'The Italian Election of 2018 and the First Populist Government of Western Europe'. *West European Politics* 42(3): 670–680.

Genschel, Philipp, and Bernhard Zangl. 2014. 'State Transformations in OECD Countries'. *Annual Review of Political Science* 17: 337–354.

Genschel, Philipp, and Laura Seelkopf. 2015. 'The Competition State: The Modern State in a Global Economy'. In *The Oxford Handbook of Transformations of the State*, edited by Stephan Leibfried, Evelyn Huber, Matthew Lange, Jonah D. Levy, Frank Nullmeier, and John D. Stephens, 237–252. Oxford: Oxford University Press.

Giannetti, Daniela, Andrea Pedrazzani, and Luca Pinto. 2017. 'Party System Change in Italy: Politicising the EU and the Rise of Eccentric Parties'. *Southern European Society and Politics* 22(1): 21–42.

Giannone, Diego. 2010. *La Democrazia Neoliberista: Concetto, Misure, Trasformazioni*. Roma: Franco Angeli.

Giannone, Diego. 2015. 'Suspending Democracy? The Governance of the EU's Political and Economic Crisis as a Process of Neoliberal Restructuring'. In *The European Union in Crisis: Explorations in Representation and Democratic Legitimacy*, edited by Kyriakos N. Demetriou, 101–119. Cham, CH: Springer.

Giannone, Diego. 2019. *In Perfetto Stato. Indicatori Globali e Politiche di Valutazione dello Stato Neoliberale*. Milano: Mimesis.

Giardina, Andrea. 1997. *L'Italia Romana: Storie di un'Identità Incompiuta*. Roma-Bari: Laterza.

Gill, Stephen. Ed. 1993. *Gramsci, Historical Materialism and International Relations*. Cambridge: Cambridge University Press.

Gill, Stephen. 1998. 'European Governance and New Constitutionalism: Economic and Monetary Union and Alternatives to Disciplinary Neoliberalism in Europe'. *New Political Economy* 3(1): 5–26.

Gill, Stephen, and David Law. 1993. 'Global Hegemony and the Structural Power of Capital'. In *Gramsci, Historical Materialism and International Relations*, edited by Stephen Gill, 93–124. Cambridge: Cambridge University Press.

Ginsborg, Paul. 1990. *A History of Contemporary Italy: Society and Politics, 1945–1988*. London: Penguin.

Giovagnoli, Agostino. 2019. *La Repubblica degli Italiani, 1945–2016*. Roma-Bari: Laterza.

Glyn, Andrew. 2006. *Capitalism Unleashed: Finance, Globalization, and Welfare*. Oxford: Oxford University Press.

Gramsci, Antonio. 1971. *Selections from the Prison Notebooks*, edited and translated by Quintin Hoare and Geoffrey Nowell Smith. London: Lawrence and Wishart.

Gramsci, Antonio. 1975a. *Quaderni Del Carcere*, edited by Valentino Gerratana, 4 Vol. Torino: Einaudi.

Gramsci, Antonio. 1975b. *Sul Fascismo*, edited by E. Santarelli. Roma: Editori Riuniti.

Graziani, Augusto. 1976. 'Mercato Interno e Relazioni Internazionali'. In *L'Italia Contemporanea, 1945–1975*, edited by Valerio Castronovo, 307–336. Torino: Einaudi.

Graziani, Augusto. 1998. *Lo Sviluppo dell'Economia Italiana: Dalla Ricostruzione alla Moneta Unica*. Torino: Bollati Boringheri.

Gritsch, Maria. 2005. 'The Nation-State and Economic Globalization: Soft Geo-Politics and Increased State Autonomy?'. *Review of International Political Economy* 12(1): 1–25.

Habermas, Jurgen. 1999. 'The European Nation-State and the Pressures of Globalization', *New Left Review* 235(May–June): 46–59.

Hanau-Santini, Ruth. 2018. *Limited Statehood in Post-Revolutionary Tunisia: Citizenship, Economy, Security*. London: Palgrave.

Hardt, Michael, and Antonio Negri. 2001. *Impero*. Milano: RCS Libri.

Harvey, David. 2005. *A Brief History of Neoliberalism*. Oxford: Oxford University Press.

Hay, Colin. 2004. 'Re-Stating Politics, Re-Politicising the State: Neo-Liberalism, Economic Imperatives and the Rise of the Competition State'. *The Political Quarterly* 75(s1): 38–50.

Hay, Colin. 2014. 'Neither Real Nor Fictitious But "As If Real"? A Political Ontology of the State'. *The British Journal of Sociology* 65(3): 459–480.

Held, David. 1995. *Democracy and the Global Order: From the Modern State to Cosmopolitan Governance*. Stanford, CA: Stanford University Press.

Held, David, and Andrew McGrew. Eds. 2003. *The Global Transformations Reader*. Cambridge: Polity Press.

Hobson, John M., and M. Ramesh. 2002. 'Globalisation Makes of States What States Make of It: Between Agency and Structure in the State/Globalisation Debate'. *New Political Economy* 7(1): 5–22.

Huntington, Samuel P., Crozier Michel, and Joji Watanuki. 1975. *The Crisis of Democracy: Report on the Governability of Democracies to the Trilateral Commission*. New York: New York University Press.

Hurrelman, Achim, Stephan Leibfried, Kerstin Martens, and Peter Mayer. Eds. 2007. *Transforming the Golden-Age Nation State*. London: Palgrave Macmillan.

Hutter, Swen, Edward Grande, and Hanspeter Kriesi. 2016. *Politicising Europe: Integration and Mass Politics*. Cambridge: Cambridge University Press.

Ignazi, Pietro. 2013. *Forza Senza Legittimità: Il Vicolo Cieco dei Partiti*. Roma-Bari: Laterza.

Istituto Nazionale di Statistica (ISTAT). 2016. *Annual Report on the Situation of the Country*. Available at: https://www.istat.it/it/archivio/185497.

Istituto Nazionale di Statistica (ISTAT). 2019. *Annual Report on the Situation of the Country*. Available at: https://www.istat.it/it/archivio/230897.

Jäger, Johannes, Horn Laura, and Joachim Becker. 2010. 'Critical International Political Economy and Method'. In *The Palgrave Handbook of Critical International Political Economy*, edited by Alan Cafruny, Simona L. Talani, and Gonzalo Pozo-Martin, 101–118. London: Palgrave.

Jessop, Bob. 1990. *State Theory: Putting the Capitalist State in its Place*. Cambridge: Polity Press.

Jessop, Bob. 2002. *The Future of the Capitalist State*. Cambridge: Polity Press.

Jessop, Bob. 2010. 'Critical Political Economy and Critical Policy Studies'. *Critical Policy Studies* 3(3–4): 336–356.

Jessop, Bob. 2016. *The State: Past, Present and Futures*. Cambridge: Polity Press.

Kalecki, Michał. 1990. *Political Aspects of Full Employment*. In *Selected Works. Volume I: Capital. Business Cycles and Full Employment,* edited by Jerzy Osiatynski, translated by Chester Adam Kisiel, 347–356. Oxford: Oxford University Press.

Koch, Insa Lee. 2018. *Personalizing the State: An Anthropology of Law, Politics, and Welfare in Austerity Britain.* Oxford: Oxford University Press.

Krasner, Stephen D. 1976. 'State Power and the Structure of International Trade'. *World Politics* 28(3): 317–347.

Krasner, Stephen D. 1978. *Defending the National Interest: Raw Materials Investments and U.S. Foreign Policy*. Princeton, NJ: Princeton University Press.

Krasner, Stephen D., and Thomas Risse. 2014. 'External Actors, State-Building, and Service Provision in Areas of Limited Statehood: Introduction'. *Governance* 27(4): 545–567.

Kreppel, Amie. 2009. 'Executive-Legislative Relations and Legislative Agenda Setting in Italy: From Leggine to Decreti and Deleghe'. *Bulletin of Italian Politics* 1(2): 183–209.

Kreuder-Sonnen, Christian. 2016. 'Beyond Integration Theory: The (Anti-) Constitutional Dimension of European Crisis Governance'. *Journal of Common Market Studies* 54(6): 1350–1366.

Kurlantzick, Joshua. 2016. *State Capitalism: How the Return of Statism Is Transforming the World*. Oxford: Oxford University Press.

Lacher, Hannes. 2006. *Beyond Globalization: Capitalism, Territoriality and the International Relations of Modernity*. London: Routledge.

Lake, David. 2008. 'The State in International Relations'. In *The Oxford Handbook of International Relations*, edited by Chris Reus-Smit and David Snidal, 41–61. Oxford: Oxford University Press.

La Palombara, Joseph. 1987. *Democracy, Italian Style*. New Haven, CT: Yale University Press.

Leibfried, Stephan, Evelyn Huber, Matthew Lange, Jonah D. Levy, Frank Nullmeier, and John D. Stephens. 2015a. 'Conclusion: States Transforming'. In *The Oxford Handbook of the Transformations of the State*, edited by Stephan Leibfried, Evelyn Huber, Matthew Lange, Jonah D. Levy, Frank Nullmeier, and John D. Stephens, 815–839. Oxford: Oxford University Press.

Leibfried, Stephan, Evelyn Huber, Matthew Lange, Jonah D. Levy, Frank Nullmeier, and John D. Stephens. Eds. 2015b. *The Oxford Handbook of Transformations of the State*. Oxford: Oxford University Press.

Leibfried, Stephan, and Michael Zürn. Eds. 2005. *Transformations of the State?* Cambridge: Cambridge University Press.

Liguori, Guido. 'Stato-Società Civile'. In *Le Parole di Gramsci: Per un Lessico dei Quaderni del Carcee*, edited by Guido Liguori and Fabio Frosini, 208–226. Roma: Carocci.

Liguori, Guido, and Fabio Frosini. Eds. 2005. *Le Parole di Gramsci: Per un Lessico dei Quaderni del Carcere*. Roma: Carocci.

Lijphart, Arendt. 1999. *Patterns of Democracy: Government Forms and Performance in Thirty-Six Countries*. New Haven, CT: Yale University Press.

Mair, Peter. 2013. *Ruling the Void: The Hollowing of Western Democracy*. London: Verso.

Majone, Giandomenico. 1994. 'The Rise of the Regulatory State in Europe'. *West European Politics* 17(3): 77–101.

Mann, Michael. 1984. 'The Autonomous Power of the State: Its Origins, Mechanisms and Results'. *European Journal of Sociology* 25(2): 185–213.

Mann, Michael. 1993. *The Rise of Classes and Nation-States, 1760–1914. Volume II, The Sources of Social Power*. New York: Cambridge University Press.

Mann, Michael. 1997. 'Has Globalization Ended the Rise and Rise of the Nation-State?'. *Review of International Political Economy* 4(3): 472–496.

Marotta, Sergio. 2019. *Le forme dell'acqua: Economia e Politiche del Diritto nella Gestione delle Risorse Idriche*. Napoli: Editroriale Scientifica.

Martin, James. 2015. 'Morbid Symptoms: Gramsci and the Crisis of Liberalism'. In *Antonio Gramsci*, edited by Mark McNally, 34–51. London: Palgrave Macmillan.

Martin, Shaw. 1997. 'The State of Globalization: Towards a Theory of State Transformation'. *Review of International Political Economy* 4(3): 497–513.

Marx, Karl. [1858] 1993. *Grundrisse: Foundations of the Critique of Political Economy*. New York: Penguin.

Marx, Karl. 2017. *Antologia*. Milano: Feltrinelli.

Marx, Karl, and Frederich Engels. [1846] 1974. *The German Ideology. Part One*, edited and introduced by Christofer J. Arthur. London: Lawrence & Wishart.

McNally, Christofer A. 2013a. 'Refurbishing State Capitalism: A Policy Analysis of Efforts to Rebalance China's Political Economy'. *Journal of Current Chinese Affairs* 42(4): 45–71.

McNally, Christofer A. 2013b. 'The Challenge of Refurbished State Capitalism: Implications for the Global Political Economic Order'. *der moderne staat-dms: Zeitschrift für Public Policy, Recht und Management* 6(1): 33–48.

Micciarelli, Giuseppe. 2017. 'Introduzione All'uso Civico E Collettivo Urbano: La Gestione Diretta Dei Beni Comuni Urbani'. *Munus* 1: 135–162.

Micciarelli, Giuseppe. 2018. *Commoning: Beni comuni urbani come nuove istituzioni, Materiale per una teoria dell'autorganizzazione*. Napoli: Editoriale Scientifica.

Milanovic, Branko. 2016. *Global Inequality: A New Approach for the Age of Globalization*. Cambridge, MA: Harvard University Press.

Mitchell, Timothy. 1991. 'The Limits of the State: Beyond Statist Approaches and Their Critics'. *American Political Science Review* 85(1): 77–96.

Mitchell, Timothy. 2006. 'Society, Economy, and the State Effect'. In *The Anthropology of the State: A reader*, edited by Aradhana Sharma and Akhil Gupta, 169–186. Malden, MA: Blackwell.

Monti, Mario. 2012. *Le parole e i fatti*, edited by Federico Fubini. Milano: Rizzoli.

Moore, Jason W. 2015. *Capitalism in the Web of Life: Ecology and the Accumulation of Capital*. London: Verso.

Morton, Adam D. 2007. *Unravelling Gramsci: Hegemony and Passive Revolution in the Global Political Economy*. London: Pluto Press.

Moschella, Manuela. 2017. 'Italy and the Fiscal Compact: Why Does a Country Commit to Permanent Austerity?' *Italian Political Science Review/ Rivista Italiana di Scienza Politica* 47(2): 205–225.

Moschella, Manuela, and Martin Rhodes. 2020. 'A Tale of Two Populisms. The League and the Five Star Movement in Power'. *Contemporary Italian Politics*, online first version. DOI: 10.1080/23248823.2020.1743472.

Mouffe, Chantal. 2005. *On the Political*. Abingdon: Routledge Press.

Muehlebach, Andrea. 2012. *The Moral Neoliberal. Welfare and Citizenship in Italy*. Chicago and London: The University of Chicago Press.

Muehlebach, Andrea. 2018. 'Commonwealth: On Democracy and Dispossession in Italy'. *History and Anthropology* (29)3: 342–358.

Musacchio, Aldo, and Sergio G. Lazzarini. 2014. *Reinventing State Capitalism: Leviathan in Business: Brazil and Beyond*. Cambridge, MA: Harvard University Press.

Musella, Fortunato. 2012. 'Governare Senza il Parlamento? L'uso dei Decreti Legge nella Lunga Transizione Italiana (1996–2012)'. *Rivista italiana di scienza politica* 42(3): 459–480.

Musella, Fortunato. 2014. 'A Premier Without Parliament: The Legislative Process in the Italian Second Republic'. *Journal of Comparative Politics* 7(1): 4–17.

Musella, Fortunato. 2019a. 'Introduzione: Il Governo in Italia tra Partiti e Presidenti'. In *Il Governo in Italia: Profili Costituzionali e Dinamiche Politiche*, edited by Fortunato Musella, 11–26. Bologna: Il Mulino.

Musella, Fortunato. Ed. 2019b. *Il Governo in Italia: Profili Costituzionali e Dinamiche Politiche*. Bologna: Il Mulino.

Naisbitt, John. 1994. *The Global Paradox*. New York: Avon.

Nardozzi, Giacomo. 1981. 'Accumulazione di Capitale e Politica Monetare: Il Punto di Vista della Banca d'Italia'. In *Scelte Politiche e Teorie Economiche in Italia, 1945–1978*, edited by Giorgio Lunghini, 109–123. Torino: Einaudi.

Natale, Paolo. 2014. 'The Birth, Early History and Explosive Growth of the Five Star Movement'. *Contemporary Italian Politics* 6(1): 16–36.

Nettl, John P. 1968. 'The State as a Conceptual Variable'. *World Politics* 20(4): 559–592.

Nölke, Andreas. 2014a. 'Introduction. Toward State Capitalism 3.0'. In *Multinational Corporations from Emerging Markets: State Capitalism 3.0*, edited by Andreas Nölke, 1–13. London: Macmillan.

Nölke, Andreas. Ed. 2014b. *Multinational Corporations from Emerging Markets: State Capitalism 3.0*. London: Palgrave.

Nordlinger, Eric. 1981. *On the Autonomy of the Democratic State*. Cambridge, MA: Harvard University Press.

Nordlinger, Eric. 1988. 'The Return to the State: Critiques'. *American Political Science Review* 82(3): 875–885.

Oberndorfer, Lukas. 2015. 'A New Economic Governance Through Secondary Legislation? Analysis and Constitutional Assessment: From New Constitutionalism, Via Authoritarian Constitutionalism to Progressive Constitutionalism'. In *The*

Economic and Financial Crisis and Collective Labour Law in Europe, edited by Niklas Bruun, Klaus Lorcher, and Isabelle Schomann, 25–54. London: Bloomsbury Publishing.

O'Connor, James. 2002. *The Fiscal Crisis of the State [1973]*. New Brunswick, NJ: Transaction Publishers.

OECD. 2019a. *General Government Debt (Indicator)*. DOI: 10.1787/a0528cc2-en.

OECD. 2019b. *Unemployment Rate (Indicator)*. DOI: 10.1787/997c8750-en.

OECD. 2019c. *Youth Unemployment Rate (Indicator)*. DOI: 10.1787/c3634df7-en.

OECD. 2019d. *Poverty Gap (Indicator)*. DOI: 10.1787/349eb41b-en.

OECD. 2020. *Hospital Beds (Indicator)*. DOI: 10.1787/0191328e-en.

Offe, Claus. 1984. *Contradictions of the Welfare State*, edited by John Keane. London: Hutchinson.

Ohmae, Kenichi. 1996. *The End of the Nation State: The Rise of Regional Economics*. London: HarperCollins.

Paggi, Leonardo, and Massimo D'Angelillo. 1986. *I Comunisti Italiani e il Riformismo: Un confronto con le Socialdemocrazie Europee*. Torino: Einaudi.

Pasquino, Gianfranco. 1994. 'Italy: The Twilight of the Parties'. *Journal of Democracy* 5(1): 18–29.

Pasquino, Gianfranco. 2018. 'Introduction: Not a Normal Election: Roots and Consequences'. *Journal of Modern Italian Studies* 23(4): 347–361.

Pianta, Mario. 2020. 'Italy's Political Upheaval and the Consequences of Inequality'. *Intereconomics* 55(1): 13–17.

Piketty, Thomas. 2014. *Capital in the Twenty-First Century*. Cambridge, MA: Harvard University Press.

Poggi, Gianfranco. 1978. *The Development of the Modern State: A Sociological Introduction*. Stanford, CA: Stanford University Press.

Poguntke, Thomas, and Paul D. Webb. Eds. 2005. *The Presidentialization of Politics: A Comparative Study of Modern Democracies*. Oxford: Oxford University Press.

Poulantzas, Nicos. 1974. 'Internationalisation of Capitalist Relations and the Nation-State'. In *The Poulantzas Reader: Marxism, Law, and the State*, edited by James Martine, 220–257. London: Verso.

Poulantzas, Nicos. 1978. *State, Power, Socialism*, translated by Patrick Camiller. London: Verso.

Pradella, Lucia. 2015. 'The Working Poor in Western Europe: Labour, Poverty and Global Capitalism'. *Comparative European Politics*, online first version. DOI: 10.1057/cep.2015.17.

Quaglia, Lucia. 2005. 'Civil Servants, Economic Ideas, and Economic Policies: Lessons from Italy'. *Governance* 18(4): 545–566.

Radaelli, Claudio. 2002. 'The Italian State and the Euro: Institutions, Discourse, and Policy Regimes'. In *European States and the Euro: Europeanization, Variation and Convergence*, edited by Kenneth Dyson, 212–237. Oxford: Oxford University Press.

Radaelli, Claudio, and Fabio Franchino. 2004. 'Analysing Political Change in Italy'. *Journal of European Public Policy* 11(6): 941–953.

Revelli, Marco. 1994. *Le Due Destre: Le Derive Politiche del Postfordismo*. Torino: Bollati Boringheri.

Risse, Thomas. 2011a. 'Governance in Areas of Limited Statehood: Introduction and Overview'. In *Governance Without a State? Policies and Politics in Areas of Limited Statehood*, edited by Thomas Risse, 1–38. New York: Columbia University Press.

Risse, Thomas. Ed. 2011b. *Governance Without a State? Policies and Politics in Areas of Limited Statehood*. New York: Columbia University Press.

Robinson, William I. 2004. *A Theory of Global Capitalism: Production, Class, and State in a Transnational World*. Baltimore, MD: John Hopkins University Press.

Romanelli, Raffaele. 1976. 'Apparati Statali, Ceti Burocratici e Modo di Governo'. In *L'Italia Contemporanea, 1945–1975*, edited by Valerio Castronovo, 145–190. Torino: Einaudi.

Rosenau, Jamiee N., and Ernest-Otto Czempiel. Eds. 1993. *Governance Without Government: Order and Change in World Politics*. Cambridge: Cambridge University Press.

Rossi, Ugo. 2012. 'There's No Hope: The Global Economic Crisis and the Politics of Resistance in Southern Europe'. *Belgeo: Revue Belge de Gepgraphy*, Inaugual Issue (1–2): 1–18.

Rossi, Ugo. 2013. *Ascesa e crisi dell'Europa meridionale nell'era neoliberale*, edited by Orizzonti Meridiani collective. Verona: Ombre Corte.

Rossi, Ugo. 2017. *Cities in Global Capitalism*. Cambridge: Polity.

Rothgang, Heinz, and Steffen Schneider. Eds. 2015. *State Transformations in OECD Countries: Dimensions, Driving Forces and Trajectories*. London: Palgrave Macmillan.

Rupert, Mark. 1993. 'Alienation, Capitalism and Interstate System: Toward a Marxian/Gramscian Critique'. In *Gramsci, Historical Materialism and International Relations*, edited by Stephen Gill, 67–92. Cambridge: Cambridge University Press.

Saad-Filho, Alfredo, and Deborah Johnston. Eds. 2005. *Neoliberalism: A Critical Reader*. London: Pluto Press.

Sandbeck, Sune, and Etienne Schneider. 2014. 'From the Sovereign Debt Crisis to Authoritarian Statism: Contradictions of the European State Project'. *New Political Economy* 19(6): 847–871.

Sartori, Giovanni. 1963. *Il Parlamento Italiano, 1945–1963*. Napoli: Edizioni Scientifiche Italiane.

Sartori, Giovanni. 1982. *Teoria dei Partiti e Caso Italiano*. Milano: Sugarco.

Sassen, Saskia. 1997. *Losing Control? Sovereignty in an Age of Globalization*. New York: Columbia University Press.

Sassen, Saskia. 1999. 'Making the Global Economy Run: The Role of National States and Private Agents'. *International Social Science Journal* 51(161): 409–416.

Sassen, Saskia. 2008. *Territory, Authority, Rights: From Medieval to Global Assemblages*. Princeton, NJ: Princeton University Press.

Sayer, Andrew. 2010. *Method in Social Science: A Realist Approach*. New York: Routledge.

Schadee, Hans, Paolo Segatti, and Cristiano Vezzoni. 2019. *L'Apocalisse della Deocrazia Italiana: Alle Origini di Due Terremoti Elettorali*. Bologna: Il Mulino.

Shaikh, Anwar. 2005. 'The Economic Mythology of Neoliberalism'. In *Neoliberalism: A Critical Reader*, edited by Alfredo Saad-Filho and Deborah Johnston, 41–50. London: Pluto Press.

Sharma, Aradhana, and Akhil Gupta. 2006. 'Introduction: Rethinking Theories of the State in an Age of Globalization'. In *The Anthropology of the State: A Reader*, edited by Aradhana Sharma and Akhil Gupta, 1–41. Malden, MA: Blackwell.

Simonazzi, Annamaria. 1999. 'I Processi Economici: Produzione, Consumi e Imprenditorialità'. In *L'Italia dopo la Grande Trasformazione: Trent'Anni di Analisi Censis, 1966–1996*, edited by Carlo Felice Casula, 71–85. Roma: Carocci.

Skocpol, Theda. 1985. 'Bringing the State Back In: Strategies of Analysis in Current Research'. In *Bringing the State Back In*, edited by Peter B. Evans, Dieter Rueschemeyer, and Theda Skocpol, 3–37. New York: Cambridge University Press.

Soederberg, Susanne, Georg Menz, and Philip G. Cerny. Eds. 2005. *Internalizing Globalization: The Rise of Neoliberalism and the Decline of National Varieties of Capitalism*. London: Palgrave Macmillan.

Sørensen, Georg. 2004. *The Transformation of the State: Beyond the Myth of Retreat*. London: Palgrave Macmillan.

Sotiris, Panagiotis. 2017. 'The Authoritarian and Disciplinary Mechanism of Reduced Sovereignty in the EU: The Case of Greece'. In *States of Discipline: Authoritarian Neoliberalism and the Contested Reproduction of Capitalist Order*, edited by Cemal Burak Tansel, 171–187. London: Rowman & Littlefield.

Spruyt, Hendrick. 1994. *The Sovereign State and Its Competitors*. Princeton, NJ: Princeton University Press.

Stamati, Furio. 2020. '"Sovereignism" and the Challenge of Welfare Reform: Pensions and Social Assistance Between innovation, Continuity and Reversions to the Past'. *Contemporary Italian Politics*, online first version. DOI: 10.1080/23248823.2020.1744891.

Stefano, Sacchi. 2015. 'Conditionality by Other Means: EU Involvement in Italy's Structural Reforms in the Sovereign Debt Crisis'. *Comparative European Politics* 13(1): 77–92.

Steinmetz, George. 1999. 'Introduction: Culture and The State'. In *State/Culture: State-Formation After the Cultural Turn*, edited by George Steinmetz, 1–75. Ithaca, NY: Cornell University Press.

Storm, Servaas. 2019. 'How to Ruin a Country in Three Decades'. Institute of New Economic Thinking. Available at: https://www.ineteconomics.org/perspectives/blog/how-to-ruin-a-country-in-three-decades.

Strange, Susan. 1996. *The Retreat of the State: The Diffusion of Power in the World Economy*. Cambridge: Cambridge University Press.

Streeck, Wolfgang. 2014. *Buying Time: The Delayed Crisis of Democratic Capitalism*, translated by Patrick Camiller. London: Verso.

Sylos Labini, Paolo. 1974. *Saggio Sulle Classi Sociali*. Roma-Bari: Laterza.

Talani, Leila Simona. 2017. *The Political Economy of Italy in the Euro: Between Credibility and Competitiveness*. London: Palgrave.

Talani, Leila Simona. 2019. 'Assessing the Relation Between the Underground Economy and Irregular Migration in Italy'. *The International Spectator: Italian Journal of International Affairs* 54(2): 102–122.

Tansel, Cemal Burak. 2017a. 'Authoritarian Neoliberalism: Towards a New Research Agenda'. In *States of Discipline: Authoritarian Neoliberalism and the Contested Reproduction of Capitalist Order*, edited by Cemal Burak Tansel, 1–28. Boulder, CO: Rowman & Littlefield.

Tansel, Cemal Burak. Ed. 2017b. *States of Discipline: Authoritarian Neoliberalism and the Contested Reproduction of Capitalist Order*. Boulder, CO: Rowman & Littlefield.

Tebaldi, Mauro. 2014. 'From Notary to Ruler: The Role of the President of the Republic During the Italian Crisis (2010–14)'. *South European Society and Politics* 19(4): 561–581.

Thomas, Peter D. 2009. *The Gramscian Moment: Philosophy, Hegemony and Marxism*. Leiden: Brill.

Tilly, Charles. Ed. 1975. *The Formation of National States in Western Europe*. Princeton, NJ: Princeton University Press.

Trentin, Bruno. 1999. *Autunno Caldo: Il Secondo Biennio Rosso, 1968–1969*, interview by Guido Liguori. Roma: Editori Riuniti.

Tronconi, Filippo. 2018. 'The Italian Five Star Movement During the Crisis: Towards Normalisation?' *South European Society and Politics* 23(1): 163–180.

van Apeldoorn, Bastiaan, Jan Drahokoupil, and Laura Horn. Eds. 2009. *Contradictions and Limits of Neoliberal European Governance: From Lisbon to Lisbon*. London: Palgrave Macmillan.

van Apeldoorn, Bastiaan, Nana de Graaff, and Henk Overbeek. 2012. 'The Reconfiguration of the Global State-Capital Nexus'. *Globalizations* 9(4): 471–486.

van der Pijl, Kees. [1985] 2012. *The Making of an Atlantic Ruling Class*. London: Verso.

Verba, Sydney, and Gabriel Almond. 1963. *The Civic Culture: Political Attitudes and Democracy in Five Nations*. Princeton, NJ: Princeton University Press.

Vercesi, Michelangelo. 2019. 'Il Decision-Making dell'Esecutivo'. In *Il Governo in Italia: Profili Costituzionali e Dinamiche Politiche*, edited by Fortunato Musella, 219–241. Bologna: Il Mulino.

Verney, Susannah, and Anna Bosco. 2013. 'Living Parallel Lives: Italy and Greece in an Age of Austerity'. *South European Society and Politics* 18(4): 397–426.

Vicarelli, Fausto. 1981. 'Note in Tema di Accumulazione di Capitale in Italia (1947–63)'. In *Scelte Politiche e Teorie Economiche in Italia, 1945–1978*, edited by Giorgio Lunghini, 13–69. Torino: Einaudi.

Volpi, Virginia. 2018. 'Eurobarometro: Alto il Sostegno all'UE, Italia la Più Euroscettica'. Istituto Affari Internazionali. Available at: http://www.affarinternazionali.it/2018/10/eurobarometro-italia-euroscettica/.

Wallerstein, Immanuel. 1979. *The Capitalist World-Economy*. Cambridge: Cambridge University Press.

Waltz, Kenneth N. 1979. *Theory of International Politics*. Reading, MA: Addison-Wesley.

Weber, Max. 1978. *Economy and Society: An Outline of Interpretive Sociology*. Berkeley: University of California Press.

Weiss, Linda. 1998. *The Myth of the Powerless State*. Ithaca, NY: Cornell University Press.

Weiss, Linda. Ed. 2003. *States in the Global Economy: Brining Domestic Institutions Back In*. Cambridge: Cambridge University Press.

Wendt, Alexander. 1992. 'Anarchy Is What States Make of It: The Social Construction of Power Politics'. *International Organization* 46(2): 391–425.

Wigger, A. 2019. 'The New EU Industrial Policy: Authoritarian Neoliberal Structural Adjustment and the Case for Alternatives'. *Globalizations* 16(3): 353–369.

Wood, Ellen Meiksins. 2002. *The Origin of Capitalism: A Longer View*. London: Verso.

World Bank. 1997. *World Development Report. The State in a Changing World*. Oxford: Oxford University Press.

Zamagni, Vera. 1997. *The Economic History of Italy, 1860–1990*. Oxford: Clarendon Press.

Index

www.ingramcontent.com/pod-product-compliance
Lightning Source LLC
LaVergne TN
LVHW102005210926
848483LV00009B/77

* 9 7 8 1 7 8 6 6 1 4 7 3 5 *